Principles of Good Clinica

Introduction to the Pharmacy Business Administration Series

Books in the Pharmacy Business Administration Series have been prepared for use in university-level graduate and professional-level courses, as well as for continuing education and self-study uses. The series includes books covering the major subject areas taught in Social and Administrative Pharmacy, Pharmacy Administration, and Pharmacy MBA programs.

World class authors with well-regarded expertise in the various respective areas have been selected and the book outlines, as well as the books themselves, have been reviewed by a number of other experts in the field. The result of this effort is a new integrated and coordinated series of books that is up to date in methodology, research findings, terminology, and contemporary trends and practices.

This is one book in that series of about 10 subjects in total. It is intended that each of the books will be revised at least every five years. While the books were intended for the North American market, they are just as relevant in other areas.

Titles in the series currently include:
Health Economics
Health Policy and Ethics
Principles of Good Clinical Practice
Research Methods for Pharmaceutical Practice and Policy
Pharmaceutical Marketing: A Practical Guide
Financial Analysis in Pharmacy Practice

The series editor-in-chief is Professor Albert Wertheimer, PhD, MBA, of Temple University School of Pharmacy, Philadelphia.

Suggestions and comments from readers are most welcome and should be sent to Commissioning Editor, Pharmaceutical Press, 1 Lambeth High Street, London SE1 7JN, U.K.

Principles of Good Clinical Practice

Edited by
Michael J. McGraw
Senior Manager, Regulatory Affairs, Teva Neuroscience, Inc.
Adjunct Associate Professor, Temple University

Adam N. George
Medical Information Manager, Cephalon, Inc.
Adjunct Associate Professor, Temple University

Shawn P. Shearn
Clinical Research Scientist, GlaxoSmithKline

Rigel L. Hall
Home Care Clinical Pharmacist, Children's Hospital of Philadelphia

Thomas F. Haws, Jr
Principal Clinical Research Scientist, GlaxoSmithKline

London • Chicago **Pharmaceutical Press**

Published by Pharmaceutical Press

1 Lambeth High Street, London SE1 7JN, UK
1559 St. Paul Avenue, Gurnee, IL 60031, USA

© Pharmaceutical Press 2010

(**PP**) is a trade mark of Pharmaceutical Press

Pharmaceutical Press is the publishing division of the Royal Pharmaceutical Society of
Great Britain

First published 2010

Typeset by Thomson Digital, Noida, India
Printed in Great Britain by TJ International, Padstow, Cornwall

ISBN 978 0 85369 790 9

A catalogue record for this book is available from the British Library.

FSC
Mixed Sources
Product group from well-managed
forests and other controlled sources

Cert no. SGS-COC-2482
www.fsc.org
© 1996 Forest Stewardship Council

All views and opinions expressed in this publication are solely those of the
individual authors. They are not representative of those held by their
employers or academic institutions.

Contents

Preface

Clinical research involving human subjects is conducted in order to establish generalizable knowledge for the understanding and promotion of human health and wellness. It has produced many advances in medicine over the years, but continues to present ethical questions that must be considered. Clinical research has fallen under intense scrutiny due to serious transgressions that have occurred over the years. This text describes the ethical principles and guidelines that influence the current and future conduct of clinical research and provides a historical perspective of the clinical research landscape.

Michael J. McGraw
February 2010

About the editors

Michael J. McGraw is a registered pharmacist and a Senior Manager of Regulatory Affairs at Teva Pharmaceuticals, Inc. in Horsham, PA, USA, where he serves as a Global Regulatory Strategy Lead for investigational products. He completed his post-doctoral training at Temple University School of Pharmacy specializing in the ethics and conduct of clinical research. He has also worked in the pharmaceutical industry managing early phase clinical trials in the cardiovascular therapeutic area at GlaxoSmithKline Pharmaceuticals, USA and as a Senior Regulatory Affairs Associate at Shire Pharmaceuticals, Inc. Dr. McGraw has taught for the Quality Assurance and Regulatory Affairs and Doctor of Pharmacy programs of the Temple University School of Pharmacy, where he received his MS in QA/RA and PharmD degrees.

Adam N. George received his Doctor of Pharmacy degree from Temple University and is a registered pharmacist. He completed his post-doctoral training at Temple University School of Pharmacy specializing in the ethics and conduct of clinical research. Since that time he has worked in the pharmaceutical industry managing early phase clinical trials in oncology at Bristol Myers-Squibb. More recently Dr. George is a Medical Information Manager at Cephalon, Inc. supporting the company's marketed CNS products. Additionally, he is adjunct faculty at Temple University School of Pharmacy teaching and coordinating an elective clinical research track for pharmacy students.

Rigel L. Hall, PharmD earned her Bachelor of Science in Medical Technology from The University of the Sciences in Philadelphia and continued there to complete her Doctor of Pharmacy degree. She began her career in the pharmaceutical industry as a Clinical Research Scientist focused on Phase I and Phase II studies. Currently, Dr. Hall is a Home Care Clinical Pharmacist for the Children's Hospital of Philadelphia.

Shawn P. Shearn is a Clinical Research Scientist at GlaxoSmithKline Pharmaceuticals, USA and has 10 years' experience in drug development ranging from target validation through Phase II clinical trials. He has a background in biochemistry and clinical pharmacology and holds an MS in

Quality Assurance and Regulatory Affairs from Temple University. His experience in GCP includes clinical trial management, site selection and clinical trial monitoring.

Thomas F. Haws, Jr is a Principal Clinical Research Scientist at GlaxoSmithKline Pharmaceuticals, USA and has 13 years' experience in pharmaceutical drug development ranging from target validation through Phase II clinical trials. He has a background in molecular biology and clinical pharmacology and holds a BS in biology from Ursinus College. His experience in GCP includes clinical trial management, site selection, and clinical trial monitoring.

Contributors

Elizabeth Bodi, Instructor, Boston College, School of Nursing and Senior Consultant, Halloran Consulting Group Inc.

Catherine Burgess, PhD, Associate Director of Regulatory Oncology at Bristol-Myers Squibb

Barbara S. Davis, Assistant Professor, The George Washington University, Department of Clinical Research and Leadership, and Director of Clinical Development, The Clinical Research Center of Northwest, Florida

Sean W. Develin, MA, Falcon Consulting Group, Senior Quality Engineer at Olympus America, Inc. and Adjunct Associate Professor at Temple University School of Pharmacy

Donna W. Dorozinsky, RN, MSN, CCRC, Managing Partner at Interactive Consulting and President at DWD & Associates

Steven Gelone, PharmD, Vice President, Clinical Development at ViroPharma, Inc. Incorporated

Barbara Godlew, RN, President and Principal Analyst at The FAIRE Company

Jesse Goldman, MD, Professor of Medicine at Temple University Hospital

Michael R. Jacobs, PharmD, Professor at Temple University School of Pharmacy and Chair of Temple University Institutional Review Board

Thomas Jacobsen, PharmD, MS, Associate Director of Medical Affairs at ViroPharma Incorporated

Stephen Klincewicz, MD, MPH, JD, Vice-President Safety Sciences, Benefit–Risk Management at Johnson & Johnson

Guy Nys, Director, Worldwide Regulatoy Compliance-Europe at Bristol-Myers Squibb

Marie-Laure Papi, Associate Director, Regulatory Science at Bristol-Myers Squibb

Vickie T. Payne, BSN, RN, CCRA, Protocol Team Lead at Quintiles, Inc.

Shawn Pelletier, Associate Director at Bristol Myers Squibb

Patrick Scoble, PharmD, Manager, Medical Affairs at ViroPharma Inc.

Peter E. Smith, PhD, President at Research Quality Assurance, Inc.

Steven P. Steinbrueck, Assistant Professor, The George Washington University, Department of Clinical Research and Leadership, and President, Stonebridge GCP Consulting Inc.

Maureen Strange, Medical Business Operations Consultant, Clinical Trial Registry at Eli Lilly and Company

Adrian Thomas, MD, FRACP, Worldwide Vice-President Health Economics & Pricing and Chief Safety Officer for the Pharmaceutical sector of Johnson & Johnson

Kristel van de Voorde, Director, Worldwide Regulatory Compliance-Europe at Bristol-Myers Squibb

Yuung Yuung Yap, PhD, Legal Counsel at Johnson & Johnson

Abbreviations

AAHRPP	Association for the Accreditation of Human Research Protection Programs
AAMC	American Association of Medical Colleges
ACE	Aid to Capacity Evaluation
ACTIS	AIDS Clinical Trials Information Service
ADR	Adverse Drug Reaction
AE	Adverse Event
AIDS	acquired immune deficiency syndrome
AMA	American Medical Association
BLA	Biologics License Application
CBER	Center for Biologics Evaluation and Research
CDA	Confidentiality and Disclosure Agreement
CDC	Centers for Disease Control and Prevention
CDER	Center for Drug Evaluation and Research
CDRH	Center for Devices and Radiological Health
CFR	Code of Federal Regulations
CHMP	Committee for Medicinal Products for Human Use
CIOMS	Council for International Organizations of Medical Sciences
CISCRP	Center for Information and Study on Clinical Research Participation
CFR	Code of Federal Regulations
COMP	Committee for Orphan Medicinal Products
CQA	Clinical Quality Assurance
CRA	clinical research associate
CRF	Case Report Form
CRO	Contract Research Organization
CSR	clinical study report
CTA	Clinical Trial Application
CVMP	Committee for Medicinal Products for Veterinary Use
DSMB	Data Safety Monitoring Board
DSMP	Data and Safety Monitoring Plan

DTC	direct to consumer
EDC	electronic data capture
EFPIA	European Federation of Pharmaceutical Industries and Associations
EFTA	European Free Trade Association
EMA	European Medicines Agency
FD&C Act	US Food, Drug and Cosmetic Act
FDA	US Food and Drug Administration
FDAAA	Food and Drug Administration Amendments Act of 2007
FDAMA	Food and Drug Administration Modernization Act of 1997
GCP	Good Clinical Practice
GMP	Good Manufacturing Practice
GPRD	General Practice Research Database
HDE	humanitarian use device
hESCs	human embryonic stem cells
HIPAA	Health Insurance Portability and Accountability Act of 1996
HMPC	Committee on Herbal Medicinal Products
HOPE Act	Health Omnibus Programs Extension Act
HRPP	Human Research Protection Program
IB	Investigator's Brochure
ICF	Informed Consent Form
ICH	International Conference on Harmonisation
IEC	Independent Ethics Committee
IFPMA	International Federation of Pharmaceutical Manufacturers & Associations
IIT	investigator-initiated trial
IMP	investigational medicinal product
IMPD	Investigational Medicinal Product Dossier
IND	Investigational New Drug Application
IP	investigational product
IRB	Institutional Review Board
IVRS	interactive voice response system
JPMA	Japan Pharmaceutical Manufacturers Association
MAA	Marketing Authorization Application
MACCAT-CR	MacArthur Competency Assessment Tool for Clinical Research
MHLW	Ministry of Health, Labor and Welfare, Japan
MTD	maximum tolerated dose
NDA	New Drug Application
NIH	National Institutes of Health
NIMP	non-investigational medicinal products
NLM	National Library of Medicine

NME	New Molecular Entity
PDCO	Paediatric Committee (EMA)
PDUFA	Prescription Drug User Fee Act
PhRMA	Pharmaceutical Research and Manufacturers of America
PI	principal investigator
PSUR	Periodic Safety Update Reports
PWG	Pharmacogenetics Working Group
QA	quality assurance
QC	quality control
RAC	Recombinant DNA Advisory Committee
SAE	Serious Adverse Event
SAWP	Scientific Advice Working Party
SMMSE	Standardized Mini-Mental Status Examination
SOPs	Standard Operating Procedures
SUSAR	Serious Unexpected Adverse Drug Reaction
USDA	United States Department of Agriculture
USPHS	United States Public Health Service
WHO	World Health Organization
WMA	World Medical Association

1

Introduction to Good Clinical Practice

Sean W. Develin

At its core, Good Clinical Practice (GCP), in all its major variants, is an attempt to administer and enforce a code of medical ethics.

The twentieth century saw the development of three landmark 'ethical pillars' of GCP: the Nuremberg Code, the Declaration of Helsinki, and the Belmont Report. These 'pillars' came about largely as the result of crimes committed against racial and ethnic groups and vulnerable populations, often in the name of some allegedly greater cause. The Nuremberg Code sprang from the Holocaust and the famed 'Doctors' Trial' held in the city of the same name. The Tuskegee Syphilis Experiment, notorious as the longest non-therapeutic trial on humans in history, yielded the Belmont Report. In between, the first version of the Declaration of Helsinki appeared. The importance of these documents is without question, but, their authority is questioned every day, with potentially dire consequences.

The Nuremberg Code, the Declaration of Helsinki, and the Belmont Report all tell sponsors and clinical researchers what they should do, not what they must do. In themselves, the ethical pillars have no force, no authority, and no ability to prevent transgressions against basic human rights.

On the surface, the intent and importance of GCP may not be immediately recognized. To simply read the regulatory requirements outside of their historical context can leave one with the impression that they are dry and mundane in nature. Yet that could not be further from the truth. GCP provides an established and measurable framework for implementing and enforcing key principles of the ethical pillars, and in doing so, it protects human lives in a very complex and dangerous arena where the full extent of the risk is only learned through individual sacrifice.

Clinical research is fraught with tensions owing to an inconvenient fact: in order to study the progression of a disease or the effects of a drug in humans, one must ultimately conduct research on humans. No amount of academic or professional literature, animal models, and computer simulations can get around this obstacle. In the end, the data must come from the bodies of human subjects. This guarantees some level of risk to the subjects without necessarily providing them any benefit in return. It also logically identifies physicians as the individuals most suited to conduct the research. This can lead to moral conflict as historically the physician's role is to protect the life, well-being, and dignity of the patient.

These protections are accomplished through a thorough knowledge of the human body coupled with personal and professional ethics. This knowledge, however, can be turned to other purposes. Therapy can be combined with research or experimentation.

The Declaration of Helsinki recognizes that the physician must also be, to some extent, an innovator as he or she must have sufficient freedom to pursue novel therapies when it is believed to be in the best interest of the patient. When any element of broader research is introduced to the treatment of a patient, the potential for conflict arises. What is in the best interest of the patient may not be what is best for gathering knowledge. That knowledge may benefit thousands or millions, while the patient is only a single person. Thus begins a pull away from the commitment to patients, and a focus on the pursuit of knowledge and benefit to society as a whole. The patient is no longer the first priority, but rather a means to an end. This conflict can test even the most ethical doctor.

Tensions also exist around distribution of risks and benefits and selection of study subjects. What of research in which the patient does not stand to receive direct benefits? This is commonly true of Phase I studies in which healthy volunteers are used to assess toxicity. Whereas a patient enrolled in a study can potentially benefit if a drug is found to be effective, a healthy volunteer is yielding information for the benefit of society and the risk of toxicity is assumed by the subject participating in such a study.

The ever-present conflict between individual and society is kept in check only when the value of the individual is recognized and protected by society. Notions of the 'greater good' are simply a numbers game in which the individual is on the losing end. There are legitimate health crises in which the Public Health will trump personal rights out of necessity, such as a pandemic. But these are passing events, not normal operating conditions. When society forces itself on the individual, human rights become subjugated. Science may not be questioned by those who allegedly cannot grasp its importance. Ends are used to justify the means.

History has demonstrated time and again what happens when racism and prejudice are allowed to subvert or deny the worth of individuals based on membership of a particular group. Whites are declared superior to blacks; Aryans are superior to Jews; men are valued over women; the young take precedence over the elderly; and so on.

Once such a claim is made, it need only be backed by sufficient force, not reason. With less worth come fewer rights, other than the 'right' to serve those in a position of power. As a specific example, to the Nazis, Jews and gypsies were *untermenschen* – subhumans – a form of 'life unworthy of life.'[1] This prejudice translated into extermination and torture at the hands of corrupt physicians who turned medical knowledge into a weapon, and murdered by whim. Similarly, in the United States, the Tuskegee Syphilis Study used rural, impoverished blacks to study a disease that was also prevalent in whites. Saul Krugman's hepatitis studies at the Willowbrook State School made use of mentally retarded children.

In the clinical arena, it is only the implementation of GCP that prevents the individual from being subordinated to science, society, and prejudice. GCP does this with particular emphasis on the value and autonomy of each and every individual. Voluntary legal consent (addressed in Chapter 3) that contains information both appropriate in content and understood by the subject must be obtained. Before a study may even recruit patients, the study must first be approved by the Independent Ethics Committee (IEC) or Institutional Review Board (IRB) providing independent oversight of the research. Doctors and study sponsors carry explicit obligations to the subject. Through a series of checks and balances, of which these are just a few, GCP implements the goals of the ethical pillars. The first of the three pillars is the Nuremberg Code.

The Nuremberg Code is a feat of reverse engineering, a distillation of the horrors of Auschwitz-Birkenau, Dachau, Buchenwald, Ravensbrück, and a host of other infamous facilities. Men, women, and children were brought to these camps to die. Whether or not they would serve the Reich beforehand, and in what capacity, would be determined during 'selections.'[1]

Arriving prisoners, disoriented, lice-ridden, and terrified, had their immediate fates determined by camp officers. Many would suffer beatings as they were separated from loved ones for the final time. Others would be shot on the spot. For the majority it was assignment to varying forms of slave labor or immediate transportation to firing squad or gas chamber.

There was also a third choice for the camp doctors: hold the prisoner for inclusion in experimentation. Concentration camps and death camps offered a continuous, seemingly unlimited supply of potential subjects, replenished on a daily basis. This availability of 'material' is in part why Josef Mengele, a decorated Waffen SS officer, specifically requested to be assigned to Auschwitz-Birkenau.[1]

The full extent of what Nazi doctors did to living human beings will never be known. The world's knowledge of the crimes was gained following the liberation of the camps, using survivors' testimony, extant protocols, notes and medical records, and documentation maintained by German universities that assisted in the experimentation. In the case of Mengele, who escaped to South America prior to the end of the war and was never brought to justice, the vast majority of his records were destroyed so that they could not be discovered.[1]

In December 1946 began the most well known of the proceedings at Nuremberg: the Doctors' Trial. The prosecution was led by Brigadier General Telford Taylor and defendants were drawn from those individuals who were known to have participated in the experimentation and were also in Allied custody. The proceedings focused on crimes committed while attempting to gather valid data for military uses. The trial did not address random and whim-driven experimentation, which was commonplace and rampant in the camps. The Doctors' Trial was not the only such trial, with the US Army presiding over a separate military court concerning crimes committed at Dachau.

The Nuremberg Code would emerge in part from testimony and evidence given during the proceedings; it was not, however, the standard used to judge the defendants in the Doctors' Trial. The defendants were charged on four counts: (1) Common Design or Conspiracy, (2) War Crimes, (3) Crimes against Humanity, and (4) Membership in a Criminal Organization.[2]

During the course of the trial, Dr. Leo Alexander, a medical advisor to the prosecution, drafted a set of six principles for the ethical conduct of research.[3] These principles were based on Alexander's knowledge of Nazi experimentation and focused on protection of the subject. He submitted them to the United States Counsel for War Crimes, who later added four additional points and incorporated them into their 1947 verdict, under the title 'Permissible Medical Experiments.'[3] These ten points became known as the Nuremberg Code.

The central theme of Nuremberg is clear from the outset: informed consent. Academically, the question is not 'Why is informed consent necessary?' but rather 'Is informed consent necessary?' The former question is predicated on an assumption. But the Nuremberg Code is not an academic exercise, nor did it have to begin with an assumption. The Code's very being emerged from the direct knowledge of what is possible in the absence of informed consent:

- high-altitude experiments in which victims were placed into a low-pressure chamber
- freezing experiments during which victims were submerged in ice water, often until death
- malaria experiments in which deliberate infections led to pain, permanent disability, and death
- mustard gas experiments involving deliberately inflicted wounds that were subsequently infected with toxic gas
- sulfanilamide experiments involving deliberately inflicted wounds that were infected with gangrene or tetanus, then filled with wood shavings or ground glass

- transplantation experiments, involving vivisection and grafting
- sea water experiments in which victims were forced to drink saltwater, resulting in pain, madness, and death
- jaundice experiments in which the victims were deliberately infected, causing pain and death
- sterilization experiments conducted via X-ray, surgical procedures, and drugs
- typhus experiments in which victims were deliberated infected with the disease, normally resulting in death
- poison experiments in which toxins were administered by food or poison-tipped bullets, after which autopsies were performed
- incendiary bomb experiments involving the deliberate infliction of phosphorus burns.[2]

This list is by no means all inclusive; it constitutes only the crimes evaluated at the Doctors' Trial.

The fact that various branches of the German military, including the Luftwaffe and Kriegsmarine, intended to use the data derived from these experiments[2] raises interesting and disturbing questions. For starters, if one buys into the Aryan mythos, and the Jews, gypsies, and other victims are in fact believed to be subhuman or of an altogether different race, then what good is the data? At best, it is a form of animal model, yet it was not being treated as such. The intent of the experiments in most cases was to yield data directly applicable to what German soldiers experienced. In doing so, there is an unacknowledged, staggering hypocrisy. This was tacitly understood to be data gathered from humans, for use with humans.

Another question, commonly asked: If some of the data was scientifically valid, is it ethical to use it despite the manner in which it was obtained? This question is almost never answered, but rather evaded, often through claims that none of the data could possibly be valid. Instead of coming to terms with an answer, yes or no, the question itself is assailed.

Enforcement of GCP would tackle this question head on without flinching – data obtained without proper informed consent may never be used to support regulatory applications. Many researchers and clinical practitioners fail to understand this concept, arguing that the data is scientifically valid and should therefore be used. The exclusion of the data from the application has nothing to do with science, however. The manner in which the data was obtained was unethical and its exclusion is a punishment.

In Germany in 1948, seven men would hang by the neck until dead for their crimes. In the USA, the existence of the Nuremberg Code and its content was known but at the same time could be considered irrelevant as the Nuremberg Code was never entered into US or German law.[3] To US researchers, adherence to the code was, at best, optional. The code applied to something that happened on the other side of the world and something that was already over. This attitude is exemplified by the Tuskegee Syphilis Study.

In Macon County, Alabama, the United States Public Health Service (USPHS) in conjunction with the Tuskegee Institute and others were some 16 years into what would become infamous as the longest non-therapeutic study on humans in history: The Tuskegee Syphilis Study. Unlike Nazi experimentation, the initial concept and intent of the research was good, stemming from USPHS's efforts to determine the prevalence of syphilis in the local black populace. During this initial survey, patients often received some level of drug therapy, in the form of Salvarsan, the pre-penicillin standard of care.

Following the initial surveys, Taliaferro Clark, head of the USPHS Venereal Disease Section, was running a series of six syphilis control programs throughout the American South, including one in Macon County. These programs were intended to improve the health of the local black populace and to demonstrate the efficacy and value of such efforts. Financing for these 'demonstrations' came not from the US government, but primarily from the Rosenwald Fund, who provided money for the treatment arm.[4] The control programs were a primary initiative for Clark who considered them successful and looked forward to expanding their scope and size.

During a November 1931 trustees' meeting, the Rosenwald Fund notified Dr. Clark that there were no longer sufficient funds to support the program.[4]

Clark's immediate reaction was the correct one – the syphilis control demonstrations would have to be cancelled. In consultation with doctors Raymond Vonderlehr and Oliver Wenger, both of the USPHS and veterans of the control programs, he found another option. The US government had largely cut off funding for syphilis treatment following World War I, when the need for healthy male citizens to serve as soldiers came to an end.[4] By continuing to run the Macon County program and documenting the untreated progress of the disease, Clark and his staff could make a case for reinstatement of funding based on the severity of the problem. The men used in the program might not benefit, but hypothetically the black community, and US society as a whole, would benefit.

There would also be scientific prestige. A study in Oslo, Norway, published in 1929, had documented the ravages of syphilis upon autopsy.[4] The USPHS had an opportunity to complement that data by recording and publishing data on the advancement of the disease in blacks. The Oslo study had used only whites.

Clark, Vonderlehr, and Wenger convinced themselves they would gather anywhere from 6 to 12 months of data[4] then take their findings to make their case.

But who would want to participate in such a study? How could you expect a man to learn he has syphilis and not try to do something about it, even if he was of limited means? First, Clark, Vonderlehr, and Wenger had deceived themselves; next they would do it to their future study subjects. There was a term used by much, but not all, of the black populace in and about Macon County: 'Bad Blood.'

That term, unscientific and imprecise, was used by the community to describe a number of ailments ranging in severity. One of these was syphilis.[4] It would be possible to recruit and retain subjects for 'treatment' of 'Bad Blood.' In 1932, Clark converted the Macon County syphilis control program into an experimental study using 399 syphilitic black males and 201 controls. He retired the following year, leaving Vonderlehr at the helm.[4]

The case for reinstating government funding was never made. While the exact progression of the disease, especially with regard to neurological and cardiovascular damage in blacks was not known, what was clearly known was that nothing good was happening to the men in the study. But this would not matter as the decision was made to track the men to autopsy.[4]

In order to retain their subjects, many of whom lived miles from the Tuskegee Institute where the majority of the study was conducted, a battery of incentives was put in place to keep the men coming back. The institute provided meals and a bed when they came in for 'treatments.' They were provided burial insurance,[4] which was something they could never afford on their own. They received medical examinations, something many of them had never had. Their government was paying attention to them.

Nurse Eunice Rivers, who worked on the study for its entire 40-year duration, was a friend of many of the families, and she engendered trust in the men. Provided with a government car, she would drive into the field to pick up the study subjects. The study was often referred to as 'Miss Rivers' Lodge.'[4] Men uninvolved in the study routinely inquired as to how they might enroll, without the knowledge that the actual 'members' were dying.

In the event some of the men might seek medical attention elsewhere, an effort was made to convince all known physicians within Macon to withhold treatment for syphilis from these men. The men were to be treated for anything other than syphilis and not to be told that they had syphilis. While the study team routinely deceived the study subjects, they made no effort to hide what they were doing from the rest of the world. They published papers, enlisted support of other government entities, and continuously rotated government and Tuskegee staff through the study. The American Heart Association was contacted with data from the study, which it promptly dismissed as scientifically invalid because of Vonderlehr's subjective methods. In addition, many of the 399 syphilitic subjects had received some amount of Salvarsan. These men did not have untreated syphilis; they had under-treated syphilis.[4]

In 1947, two particularly damning things happened: the Nuremberg Code was documented and penicillin became widely available. Penicillin had been discovered several years previously, but was in limited distribution. This new standard of care was highly effective against syphilis in all its stages. It would be the USPHS who ran the Rapid Treatment Centers delivering penicillin to the US public. This made it possible for the Tuskegee Study to continue its 'do not treat' initiatives with study subjects being turned away from even the Rapid Treatment Centers.[4] The study was scientifically invalid and now, as a result of penicillin, the knowledge was useless. There was no possible reason for the study to continue, yet it did.

The Tuskegee Study is incompatible with the Nuremberg Code. The two are mutually exclusive. But the Nuremberg Code, with no legal authority, had no impact of any kind on Tuskegee. In 1964, while Tuskegee continued unhindered, the second of the three pillars was published: The Declaration of Helsinki.

The Declaration of Helsinki was written by the World Medical Association (WMA), an international organization of physicians organized following the Second World War. Its First General Assembly was held in September 1947[5] one month after the verdict from the Nuremberg Doctors' Trial was read. The WMA describes its mission as follows:

> The purpose of the WMA is to serve humanity by endeavoring to achieve the highest international standards in Medical Education, Medical Science, Medical Art and Medical Ethics, and Health Care for all people in the world.[5]

The Declaration of Helsinki first appeared in draft form, published for comment in the British Medical Journal in October 1962.[6] The Declaration built on Nuremberg's requirements for informed consent as well as emphasizing physicians' responsibilities. Helsinki introduced considerations for the ethical conduct of research combined with therapy, emphasizing that the research component is ethical only so long as it is in the best interests of the patient. It also established a set of rules for Non-therapeutic Clinical Research:

1. In the purely scientific application of clinical research carried out on a human being it is the duty of the doctor to remain the protector of the life and health of that person on whom clinical research is being carried out.
2. The nature, the purpose, and the risk of clinical research must be explained to the subject by the doctor.
3a. Clinical research on a human being cannot be undertaken without his free consent, after he has been fully informed; if he is legally incompetent the consent of the legal guardian should be procured.
3b. The subject of clinical research should be in such a mental, physical, and legal state as to be able to exercise fully his power of choice.
3c. Consent should as a rule be obtained in writing. However, the responsibility for clinical research always remains with the research worker; it never falls on the subject, even after consent is obtained.

4a. The investigator must respect the right of each individual to safeguard his personal integrity, especially if the subject is in a dependent relationship to the investigator.

4b. At any time during the course of clinical research the subject or his guardian should be free to withdraw permission for research to be continued. The investigator or the investigating team should discontinue the research if in his or their judgment it may, if continued, be harmful to the individual.[7]

As with the Nuremberg Code, these principles are in direct opposition to the Tuskegee Syphilis Study, yet do nothing to stop it. The beginning of the end for the Tuskegee study arrived when Peter Buxton, a USPHS employee based in San Francisco, learned of the study and was appalled that it was continuing. Buxton began internal efforts to halt the study but was not surprised when he was first ignored then subjected to threats and hostility when he refused to drop the matter. Buxton left the USPHS of his own doing in 1967 and a year later resumed pursuit of the matter as a private citizen. As his ethical objections failed to achieve the desired goal, Buxton put a pragmatic spin on his next letter, addressed not to the USPHS but to the Centers for Disease Control (CDC). He argued that given the state of racial tensions in the USA, the discovery of the existence of this study, using all black citizens, was a veritable powder keg.[4]

Buxton's letter was forwarded to the director of the CDC, resulting in a 'blue-ribbon' panel charged with determining whether the study should continue or be terminated. The panel, however, had no intention of terminating the study. There was brief discussion of changing its emphasis, but to give up the human material at CDC's disposal was out of the question. The panel was solely interested in discussing science and would not hear ethical considerations. In 1969, with no possible use for the study's data, the CDC concluded that the study must continue through autopsy of the remaining subjects.[4]

In July 1972, Peter Buxton went to the Associated Press. On July 25, 1972 the American public first learned of the study in the Washington Star. Public outrage, legal action, and government inquiry (into its own actions) followed. Over 100 US citizens were dead either directly from syphilis or from complications related to syphilis. Numerous wives had been infected and babies born with congenital syphilis.[4]

The Tuskegee Study caused deep, long-term damage to the African American community. Trust in government has been undermined to the point where many believe HIV is a government sponsored attempt at genocide of the black race.[4] Black participation in clinical research has dropped dramatically.

Telling the subjects that they had 'Bad Blood' was not a lie – but it was substantially less than the truth. Had the subjects understood that their 'Bad Blood' was specifically syphilis, they most likely would have sought treatment. That treatment might have been unavailable for financial reasons or might have been ineffective, as Salvarsan, the pre-penicillin standard of care, often was, but they could have tried nonetheless. This is why arguments that the study was not unethical until 1947, when penicillin became widely available through USPHS Rapid Treatment Centers, are not legitimate. A white male with syphilis would have been told exactly what he was suffering from, regardless of whether or not he could afford treatment.

In the wake of Tuskegee came the National Research Act.[4] While it did not directly create GCP, it required informed consent for all study subjects and use of independent IRBs in any study on humans that is using government funds. In addition to these controls, it also created the National Commission for the Protection of Human Subjects of Biomedical and Behavioral Research.[8] The commission summarized its mandate as follows:

> One of the charges to the Commission was to identify the basic ethical principles that should underlie the conduct of biomedical and behavioral research involving human subjects and to develop guidelines which should be followed to assure that such research is conducted in accordance with those principles. In carrying out the above, the Commission was directed to consider: (i) the boundaries between biomedical and behavioral research and the accepted and routine practice of medicine, (ii) the role of assessment of risk–benefit criteria in the determination of the appropriateness of research involving human subjects, (iii) appropriate guidelines for the selection of human subjects for participation in such research and (iv) the nature and definition of informed consent in various research settings.[8]

The commission was comprised of doctors, lawyers, and university professors including, most notably, Albert Jonsen as a representative of the fledgling academic field of Bioethics. They published the results of their work in 1979 as the Belmont Report, named for the Smithsonian Institution's Belmont Conference Center where early deliberations of commission were conducted.[8] And so the third ethical pillar, the Belmont Report, is the direct result of the Tuskegee Syphilis Study.

The Belmont Report is more philosophical in nature than Nuremberg and Helsinki and returns the focus of protections solely to humans (as tasked by the commission's name). While Helsinki's primary focus is certainly human subjects, it does acknowledge responsibility to both animals and the environment and in so doing incorporates the 'biosphere' aspect of bioethics. Belmont does, however, broaden the focus to include a framework for assessing psychology experiments, which also pose risk to experimental subjects, as Stanley Milgram's Obedience to Authority experiment and the Stanford Prison Experiment both demonstrated.

Belmont does an admirable job of differentiating between research and the accepted practice of medicine. The combination of the two could result in a murky, gray area; however, Belmont refuses to be led down this path. If any aspect is research, it is all deemed research and special protections apply for subjects.

The body of the report consists of the commission's Basic Ethical Principles, of which there are three: Respect for Persons, Beneficence, and Justice.

Respect for Persons is ultimately recognition of autonomy, and this is to be implemented through informed consent. The Belmont Report follows Nuremberg's lead and will not engage in debate on the matter. It is a given; a requirement from the outset. In order for informed consent to be possible, it must be voluntary in nature, the proper quality and quantity of information must be present, and there must be comprehension on the part of the subject.

Beneficence is commonly phrased as 'do no harm' and its implementation can only be achieved through proper risk–benefit analysis. Belmont concedes that to do no harm one must first know what is harmful, which is a learning process. While the risk is always to the subject, the benefit ultimately may be to society. In these cases, additional scrutiny is required.

Justice, for Belmont, means the equitable distribution of benefit and burden through ethical subject selection. In exploring this principle, Belmont acknowledges its own origins:

> In this country, in the 1940's, the Tuskegee syphilis study used disadvantaged, rural black men to study the untreated course of a disease that is by no means confined to that population.[8]

For all the power of that statement, it is somewhat idiosyncratic that they single out the 1940s, when it also applied to the 1930s, the 1950s, the 1960s, and the 1970s. It is hard to say when the Tuskegee study would have ended had it been allowed to continue to deaths of all subjects, as the CDC had wished.

History has made it clear that ethical principles cannot be optional. Nazi experimentation and Tuskegee are two of the best-known examples, and are those with direct ties to genesis of the Ethical Pillars and GCP. But they are only two examples. It is absolutely terrifying to realize that they are not aberrations, not one-time events, and that while they are unquestionably unique and significant, variants on their themes are occurring somewhere in the world to this day.

The passage of the National Research Act into US Law in 1974 is recognition that research cannot be self-policing. In the United States, increasing vigilance has lead to the creation of Title 45 CFR (Code of Federal Regulations) Part 46, better known as 'The Common Rule.' This regulation covers the ethical conduct of clinical trials on humans where the focus of the study is a disease state. The study of investigational new drugs in humans is the jurisdiction of the Food and Drug Administration (FDA) and as such GCP appears under Title 21.

Within Title 21, Good Clinical Practice consists of Parts 50, 54, 56, and 312 with Part 812 replacing 312 when the study focuses on a device rather than a drug. One often sees Part 11 included in this list, although to do so is misleading, as Part 11 does not belong to any 'GxP' (Good Manufacturing Practice; Good Laboratory Practice, and Good Clinical Practice, collectively); rather they all belong to it, serving as 'Predicate Rules.' Further discussion of these regulations can be found in Chapter 2.

Through the efforts of the International Conference on Harmonisation (ICH), GCP is documented in an internationally accepted manner in ICH E6. While the FDA and ICH versions are not identical (nor are they the only implementations of GCP; numerous countries have their own requirements) they diligently address the same major topics, including but not limited to:

- informed consent
- financial disclosure (to identify conflicts of interest)
- ethics committees/institutional review board
- investigator's qualifications
- responsibilities and obligations.

In establishing requirements for the ethical conduct of clinical trials, require-ments that are directly extracted in many cases from the ethical pillars, GCP aims to make participation in research as safe as possible for the human subject. In turn, society benefits through the approval of new therapies. Without GCP Nuremberg, Helsinki, and Belmont – all landmarks – are merely exercises in preaching to the converted. GCP is actionable, measurable, and enforceable. Violation of GCP requirements, for any reason, opens the door to a variety of repercussions, all of which have monetary impact, direct or indirect. Financial loss is one thing that the pharmaceutical and medical device industries clearly understand, even if there are individuals in those arenas who struggle with ethics.

Enforcement by regulatory authorities is always necessary. However, GCP will only be as effective as those who implement it. While focus is often on the negatives that led to the inception of the regulations, there exist unsung heroes:

- the doctors who are studying drugs, devices, and disease states for the betterment of the world, who never lose sight of the fact that their first concern is the well-being of the patients in their care
- the IRB members who take time from their hectic schedules to thoroughly read and analyze every protocol they receive, then ask the necessary questions and demand answers
- the Clinical Research Associates who travel relentlessly, work in sometimes hostile environments, and write reports whenever and

wherever they can, all the while wondering if there isn't a better line of work for them.

History is rife with violations of human rights in the name of science and, unfortunately, more will occur. Just not on their watch.

References

1. Lifton RJ. *The Nazi Doctors*. New York: Basic Books, 2000.
2. Spitz V. *Doctors from Hell*. Boulder, CO: Sentient Publications, 2005.
3. United States Holocaust Memorial Museum (2008). Available from: http://www.ushmm.org (accessed August 29, 2008).
4. Jones JH. *Bad Blood*. New York: The Free Press, 1981.
5. World Medical Association (2008). Available from: http://www.wma.net (accessed August 29, 2008).
6. Human, D, Fluss SS. *The World Medical Association's Declaration of Helsinki: Historical and Contemporary Perspectives*. Available from: URL: http://www.wma.net/e/ethicsunit/helsinki.htm (accessed August 29, 2008).
7. Ethical Committee of the World Medical Association. Draft Code of Ethics on Experimentation. *BMJ* 1964; 2: 177–180.
8. Office of Human Subjects Research (2008). Available from: http://ohsr.od.nih.gov/guidelines/ (accessed August 29, 2008).

2

Regulatory requirements

Catherine Burgess, Marie-Laure Papi, Kristel Van de Voorde,

and Guy Nys

Introduction

Extensive legislation related to the conduct of clinical studies and the requirements to register a drug were initially developed in response to fraudulent practices on the part of researchers, such as the generation of data on non-existent patients or data that were not properly represented. While these regulations result in a significant burden for both the researchers and health authorities, they have proven to be valuable. Well-conducted research in the scientific and clinical community can help establish the most optimal treatment strategy. In addition, the data from this research, when conducted according to international standards, may be used for registrational purposes in many countries, resulting in an economic benefit to the medical community as well as the sponsor of the research. Inspections associated with this regulatory framework demonstrate that deficiencies still occur in the collection of data. Therefore, oversight of the regulatory process internally, by the sponsor of registrational research, as well as externally, by a health authority, is essential for generating reliable drug research that benefits both the patient and the community.

This chapter provides an overview of the regulatory framework critical for the initiation of clinical trials and subsequent availability of new drugs with an emphasis on the United States and European Union regulatory systems with regard to the requirements for study start, protection of subjects, and approval of new medicines in the leading markets.

International Conference on Harmonisation requirements

In order to achieve greater global harmonization in the interpretation and application of technical guidelines and requirements for medicinal product registration, the International Conference on Harmonisation of Technical

Requirements for Registration of Pharmaceuticals for Human Use (ICH) was established in April 1990. This joint initiative brought together the regulatory authorities of Europe, Japan, and the United States, in collaboration with experts from the pharmaceutical industry of the three regions, to discuss scientific and technical aspects of product registration with the goal of improving international harmonization for medicinal product registration. The objective of the harmonization initiative is to facilitate a more global development by eliminating duplicate testing (clinical, non-clinical, and manufacturing) while maintaining safeguards on quality, safety, and efficacy.

Structure of ICH

The International Conference on Harmonisation is comprised of six parties that are directly involved in the harmonization process, as well as three Observers and representatives from the International Federation of Pharmaceutical Manufacturers & Associations (IFPMA). The six parties are the founding members of ICH, which represents the regulatory bodies and the research-based industry in the European Union, Japan, and the USA. These parties include the European Medicines Agency (EMA), the European Federation of Pharmaceutical Industries and Associations (EFPIA), the Ministry of Health, Labor and Welfare, Japan (MHLW), the Japan Pharmaceutical Manufacturers Association (JPMA), the US Food and Drug Administration (FDA) and the Pharmaceutical Research and Manufacturers of America (PhRMA).[1]

The Observers are representatives of the World Health Organization (WHO), the European Free Trade Association (EFTA), and Health Canada. This group of non-voting members acts as a link between the ICH and non-ICH countries and regions.[1]

Relevant ICH documents related to clinical trials

The ICH topics are divided into Safety, Quality, and Efficacy to reflect the three criteria that are the basis for approving and authorizing new medicinal products in all participating countries of the ICH. Guidelines are categorized on the ICH website by the first letter associated with the relevant criteria. The Quality (Q) topics are those relating to chemical and pharmaceutical quality assurance associated with the manufacturing process. The Safety (S) topics are related to *in vitro* and *in vivo* pre-clinical studies. The issues involving clinical trials in human subjects and are included in the Efficacy (E) topics. Guidelines that cover topics not mentioned above (e.g., terminology, standards for submission) are termed Multidisciplinary (M).[2]

ICH efficacy guidelines cover numerous aspects of clinical trial design, conduct, and analysis. There are several ICH guidelines related to clinical trials and which cover topics such as:

- good clinical practice (E6)
- trials in specific populations such as geriatrics (E7) and pediatrics (E11)
- general considerations with regard to trial design and the different phases of development (E8)
- choice of control group and the impact and implications of this selection (E10)
- statistical principles associated with the analysis of patient data collected from a clinical trial (E9)
- clinical trial design, conduct, and analysis pertaining to specific therapeutic classes of drugs (various guidelines).

The key ICH guideline related to Good Clinical Practice (GCP) is the consolidated E6 Guideline on Good Clinical Practice, which was finalized in May 1996. This guideline was developed over a period of 5 years and describes the responsibilities and expectations of all participants in the conduct of clinical trials including investigators, monitors, sponsors, and ethics committees. It covers aspects of monitoring, reporting, and archiving of clinical trials and incorporates addenda on essential documents including the Investigator's Brochure. While formulating this guidance, clinical approaches considered novel during the development of the E6 (remote data entry and the use of data safety monitoring boards) were taken into consideration, making this guidance broadly applicable to all aspects of trial conduct.[3] A complete list of all topics can be found on the ICH website: http://www.ich.org.

The United States (US) regulatory framework

Food and Drug Administration: roles and responsibilities

The FDA is the agency of the United States Department of Health and Human Services (HHS) that regulates foods, dietary supplements, drugs, vaccines, biological medical products, blood products, medical devices, radiation-emitting devices, veterinary products, and cosmetics amounting to over 1 trillion dollars' worth of US products every year.[4]

The original Federal Food and Drugs Act (also known as the Wiley Act) was passed by Congress in 1906. This Act prohibited the interstate marketing of misbranded and adulterated foods, drinks, and drugs and empowered the US Department of Agriculture (USDA) Division of Chemistry to examine all products and seize or prosecute violators.[5] The FDA was officially organized with these powers in 1931. However, the extent of these powers was strictly limited to misbranding and adulteration. No true regulation of therapeutic efficacy was given to the FDA until the 1962 Drug and Amendments Act (also known as the Kefauver–Harris Amendment). This amendment expanded FDA's oversight of drug approval and required drug manufacturers to demonstrate 'substantial evidence' of their drugs' efficacy for a specific indication as well as to demonstrate pre-marketing safety prior to drug approval. This new FDA oversight of efficacy was extended retroactively to those drugs approved between 1938 and 1962, allowing FDA to fully align the drug approval process. The FDA requirement for 'adequate and well-controlled clinical studies,' as well as the requirement for informed consent, is an essential element of this amendment.[6]

In 1992, the Prescription Drug User Fee Act (PDUFA) was passed and authorized FDA to collect fees from companies that produce certain drugs and biological products for the US market. Accordingly, when a sponsor company submits a product for FDA review and approval, an application and user fees must also be submitted to support the process. Annual fees are also paid for each marketed product and manufacturing facility. In exchange for this funding, FDA agrees to meet specified drug-review performance goals.[7]

In 2007, PDUFA was reauthorized and the powers of FDA were significantly extended when Congress passed the FDA Amendments Act (FDAAA). Under FDAAA, the agency can require additional safety studies as post-marketing commitments, oversee risk communication strategies, force manufacturers to rapidly update labels with new safety information, and levy fines for failure to comply with these or any post-marketing commitments. Additionally, the FDAAA established a clinical trials registry that requires public disclosure of all trial results on marketed products in the near term and will require disclosure of all trial results, regardless of market status, in the future.[8] See Chapter 10 for additional discussion of clinical trials registration and results reporting.

Most federal laws administered through the FDA are codified into the Food, Drug and Cosmetic Act, Title 21, Chapter 9 of the United States Code (21 USC 9). The implementation of these laws, as published by the Federal Register, can be found in Title 21 of the Code of Federal Regulations (21 CFR, Parts 1–1299). Additional but non-binding clarifications can be found in the FDA guidances available for review on the FDA website (www.fda.gov/cder/guidance/index.htm). Under these regulations, the FDA oversees almost every facet of prescription drugs including testing, manufacturing, labeling, advertising, marketing, efficacy, and safety. In addition, FDA regulates other products with a set of published standards enforced through facilities inspections. The FDA is organized into a number of major subdivisions focusing on specific areas of regulatory responsibility. For the purposes of discussing Good Clinical Practice (GCP), the centers of primary importance are Center for Drug Evaluation and Research (CDER), Center for Biologics Evaluation and Research (CBER), and Center for Devices and Radiological Health (CDRH).

CDER is responsible for the assessment of all prescription and over-the-counter drugs in order to assure that they are safe and effective. CDER evaluates all new drugs before they are sold and oversees the more than 10 000 drugs on the market in order to maintain that they continue to meet the highest standards of safety and efficacy. CDER also routinely monitors television, radio, and print direct to consumer (DTC) advertising to ensure all advertisements are accurate and balanced.

CBER is responsible for assuring the safety, purity, potency, and effectiveness of biological and related products (blood and blood products, vaccines and allergenic extracts, human cells and tissue products) including their use in xenotransplantation, gene therapy, and human cloning for disease prevention and treatment.

CDRH assures that new medical devices are safe and effective before they are marketed. Many of these devices are the first of a kind (e.g., a robotic arm for surgery) designed to prevent, diagnose or treat cancer, heart disease, and other health problems. The CDRH also oversees the safety performance of non-medical devices that emit certain types of electromagnetic radiation (i.e., cellular phones, televisions, and screening devices). The center monitors devices throughout the product life cycle, including oversight of a nationwide post-market surveillance system.

In the USA, FDA oversight of the development, approval, and commercialization of a drug is facilitated by two types of dossier submissions:

- The Investigational New Drug Application (IND): required prior to initiation of a clinical investigation.
- The New Drug Application/Biologic License Application (NDA/BLA): required prior to commercialization of a new drug.

The US regulations and FDA organization allow for a continuous interaction between FDA and the sponsor. These interactions begin at the time of the IND submission and can continue throughout the life of the drug, as long as the Marketing Authorization is valid.

Title 21 CFR 312: The Investigational New Drug Application

What is an IND?

An IND is legally required under the US Food, Drug and Cosmetic Act (FD&C Act) to allow the shipment of drugs across states, preventing initiation of clinical research with a non-approved investigational product intended for therapeutic use in the US without FDA oversight. All phases of a clinical investigation are covered by an IND (i.e., Phase I to Phase IV studies).

Exemptions to the submission of an IND are listed under 21 CFR 312.1(a) (e.g., clinical research with an already approved drug and for which the clinical investigation does not involve an increase in risk of the drug use such as a dosage level or patient population). Waivers can also be granted in emergency situations. The FDA guidance, IND Exemptions for Studies of Lawfully Marketed Drug or Biological Products for the Treatment of Cancer provides additional information regarding situations where an IND submission may be waived.[9]

The FDA's intent with the review of the first IND submission is to ensure the safety of the subjects and the quality of the investigative material.

IND content and format

As previously mentioned, an IND is submitted prior to the conduct of the first clinical research investigation of a new molecule in the United States. Specific regulations and guidances provide detailed explanations of the content and format of an IND.[10,11] At the time of the first submission, the IND must contain the following information:

- **The cover sheet (FDA Form 1571).** The cover sheet contains the chemical name of the compound and all legal information regarding the sponsor (name, address, telephone), as well as information such as the date of the application, the commitment from the sponsor not to initiate the study prior to the IND being in effect, and the names of the sponsor's representatives for the safety review and clinical conduct oversee of the studies.
- **A table of contents.**
- **An introductory statement and a general investigational plan.** The introduction and the general investigational plan are brief sections with limited detail. These sections provide a high-level overview of the proposed clinical program for at least the following 12 months.
- **The Investigator's Brochure (IB).** The IB is intended to provide a summary of all available information on the investigational product to investigators involved in the various clinical studies. It contains information such as a description of the drug product, a summary of all available safety and efficacy information, and a description of the potential risks and side-effects of the investigational product. FDA requires that the IB be updated annually or more frequently if significant new information that would affect the use of the investigational product becomes available.
- **The protocol(s).** The first IND submission can contain one or more protocols; however, in general, the first IND submission is intended to support the initiation of a Phase I study. In circumstances where the clinical development of a drug was initiated outside of the USA, it is possible for the sponsor to submit an IND to support initiation of a Phase II

or Phase III study. In such cases, the clinical data from previous clinical trials must be included in the IND submission. Once an IND is in effect, all protocols must be submitted to the IND prior to study initiation. New protocols are no longer subject to a 30-day review by FDA.

- **Chemistry, Manufacturing and Control (CMC) information.** The CMC component of the IND is divided into subsections that include all manufacturing data on the drug substance and product, the product label, and an environmental risk assessment. Multiple guidances are available on the FDA website.[12]

- **Pharmacology and toxicology information.** The amount of information included in the first IND submission will depend on the phase and the duration of the proposed study. Pharmacology and toxicology information from non-clinical studies is essential for initiation of the Phase I studies when there is little or no data in humans. The non-clinical safety studies are important for an estimation of the initial safe starting dose for human trials and should characterize the toxic effects of a range of potential starting doses relative to target organs, dose dependence, relationship to exposure, and potential reversibility. In addition, animal toxicity studies should equal or exceed the duration of the planned human clinical trial duration prior to initiation of a human clinical study. The animal data are reviewed to assure the potential risk is acceptable for subjects intended to be enrolled in the trial.

- **Previous human experience data.** In instances where the clinical development of a drug was initiated outside of the USA, all available clinical information from the previous or ongoing clinical trials must be included in the IND submission for FDA review. Supportive information can be found in the FDA guidance, *Acceptance of Foreign Clinical Studies*.[13] In addition, FDA has published a final rule, *Human Subject Protection; Foreign Clinical Studies Not Conducted Under an Investigational New Drug Application*,[14] which replaces the requirement that studies be conducted under the ethical principles defined in the Declaration of Helsinki with the requirement that studies be conducted in accordance with GCP.

- **Additional and relevant information.** Additional information may include data such as dependence and abuse potential information or pediatric plans. In addition, any relevant information needed to support the IND review can be included (e.g., reference to previously submitted information, English translation of foreign documents included in the IND).

The IND review

As stated above, an IND is a legal requirement in order to initiate human clinical studies in the USA. Accordingly, the primary intent of the review of the first IND submission is to ensure the safety of the subjects to be enrolled in the proposed studies and to certify the quality of the investigative material.

The IND review process starts with the IND submission and continues throughout the clinical development of the investigational product/drug. The initial IND submission is followed by a 30-day FDA review period. At the end of the review:

- The FDA can provide a list of deficiencies to be addressed by the sponsor.
  - If the deficiencies are major, FDA will request that they are addressed prior to initiation of the clinical investigation. The IND will not be in effect until these deficiencies are resolved.
  - If there are questions or requests for information that can be addressed during the clinical investigation, the IND can be activated and the trial initiated. If the deficiencies cannot be resolved in a timely manner by the sponsor, the IND will be placed on clinical hold until they are resolved.
  - In either case, the sponsor has the right to withdraw the IND before it is placed on hold.

Or:
- The FDA has no questions or objections and either provides no comments or notifies the sponsor that the trial can be initiated.

A clinical hold is an FDA order to delay the start of a new trial (e.g., trial submitted for approval at the time of the IND submission or new protocol submitted to an IND already in effect) or to suspend an ongoing investigation. The order is issued if the FDA has reason to believe the investigation places subjects at significant risks. The FDA can notify the sponsor of the clinical hold at the end of the initial 30-day review of a new IND. When a trial is on clinical hold, subjects cannot be treated with the investigational product or enrolled within the study. The sponsor must address FDA's concerns in order for the clinical trial to start or resume.

Once an IND is in effect, subsequent protocols are submitted to the same IND prior to each trial initiation along with all the necessary administrative documentation (Forms FDA 1571, FDA 1572, and any other related documentation). For these subsequent submissions, there is no 30-day review and the trials can be initiated without further FDA notification. However, FDA is mandated to review all submitted protocols and, at any time during a clinical investigation, can request a discussion with the sponsor or clarification on any protocol. FDA has the right to put a trial on hold if it is deemed that the safety of the subjects is not guaranteed.

The reporting requirements

It is the responsibility of the sponsor to report any new information related to the study drug. This information is submitted to the IND as an amendment.

Examples of such information include new chemistry or toxicology data, a revised IB, or a change in investigator information. In addition, the sponsor is required to notify FDA and all clinical trial investigators of any adverse experience associated with the drug that is 'both serious and unexpected' and any finding from non-clinical studies suggesting a 'significant risk for human subjects' (e.g., mutagenicity, teratogenicity data).[10] Further discussion of adverse event reporting requirements can be found in Chapter 9.

Finally, the IND sponsor is mandated to submit an IND annual report intended to provide an overview and update of the ongoing investigations. The report is to be submitted in a prespecified format within 60 days of the anniversary date that the IND went into effect. The annual report should also include a general investigational plan for the coming year and an updated IB.

It is the sponsor's responsibility to provide FDA and investigators with up-to-date information on the investigational product (e.g., any new safety information that may impact the conduct of studies or the use of the investigational product) and to ensure proper monitoring of the investigation, in accordance with the investigational plan and US regulations.[10]

21 CFR 50: Protection of Human Subjects

Prior to 1906, when the Federal Food and Drugs Act was passed, there were no regulations regarding the ethical use of human subjects in research. Today, FDA regulations confer protections on human subjects in research when a drug, device, biologic, food additive, color additive, electronic product, or other test article subject to FDA regulation is involved. No investigator may involve a human subject in research covered by these regulations unless the investigator has obtained the subject's (or the subject's legal representative's) legally effective informed consent.[15] See Chapter 3 for a complete discussion of the informed consent process.

21 CFR 54: Financial Disclosure

FDA reviews and evaluates all clinical study data submitted in a marketing application to ensure that appropriate steps have been taken in the design, conduct, reporting, and analysis of the studies in order to minimize bias. Bias may result not only from actions taken on the part of the sponsor of the study, but also by clinical investigators who might benefit financially from the outcome of the study. This benefit, as detailed in 21 CFR Part 54.2, may result from direct compensation to the investigator or from the proprietary interest of the investigator in the product or in the company sponsoring the study. Therefore, FDA mandates that the sponsor and all clinical investigators on 'covered studies' submitted as part of a marketing application disclose any direct or indirect financial relationship.[16]

By definition, only studies used to support the effectiveness of a product or device or studies where a single investigator made a significant contribution to the demonstration of safety are considered 'covered studies.' However, in practice, all studies submitted in the marketing application may arguably be considered supportive of the investigational product or device. Therefore, it is recommended that an applicant consult with FDA as to which studies constitute 'covered studies' for the purposes of complying with financial disclosure requirements.[16]

The certification and disclosure requirements detailed in 21 CFR Part 54 state that a list of all clinical investigators participating in covered clinical studies must be provided to the FDA. The sponsor must also disclose or certify that none of the financial interests of participating clinical investigators meet the financial arrangements described in Part 54 or that, if an arrangement does exist, the sponsor fully disclose the nature of that arrangement to FDA. All disclosures must be retained by the sponsor for a period of two years following the initial NDA approval.[16] Additional information, including FDA actions regarding cases of potential bias, can be found in the guidance *Financial Disclosure by Clinical Investigators*.[17]

21 CFR 56: Institutional Review Boards

According to federal regulations, an Institutional Review Board (IRB) is an administrative body established to protect the rights and welfare of human research participants recruited to participate in research activities subject to FDA oversight and conducted under the auspices of the institution with which it is affiliated.[18]

Although no general guidance is available, FDA maintains a website with updated information sheets designed to provide guidance to IRBs, investigators, and sponsors (www.fda.gov/oc/ohrt/irbs/). A complete discussion of IRB and Independent Ethics Committee (IEC) responsibilities can be found in Chapter 8.

Meetings with the FDA

There are many opportunities to meet with FDA, formally and informally, throughout the development of a new drug and after its commercialization. Informal interactions include e-mail, facsimile, and telephone contacts. Formal interactions follow the IND regulations.[10] A guidance for industry entitled *Formal Meetings with Sponsors and Applicants for PDUFA Products* is also available.[19]

Development meetings

The development meetings are intended to address questions related to the drug development of a specific compound and are scheduled within a defined period of days from the initial meeting request. The sponsor should request a meeting in writing to the appropriate division at FDA. The meeting request should include a cover letter, an agenda and list of questions, a list of sponsor participants and requested FDA participants, and any supporting documentation (e.g., data summary, protocol). A summary of relevant data to support the discussion is to be sent to FDA in advance of the meeting. Following the discussion with the sponsor, FDA is required to issue formal meeting minutes within 30 days.

There are three types of meetings with the FDA: Type A, Type B, and Type C.[10,19]

Type A meeting

Type A meetings are intended to address questions that are impeding the development of the investigational drug. Type A meeting topics include discussion of clinical holds imposed by the FDA, pharmocovigilance issues, discussion of FDA comments to a special protocol assessment submission, or FDA concerns over study design issues that may impact study initiation. The FDA should schedule the meeting within 30 days of the sponsor request. Documentation to support the meeting discussion should be sent to FDA two weeks prior to the meeting date.

Type B meeting

Type B meetings include pre-IND, End-of-Phase I, End-of-Phase II, and Pre-NDA meetings. The FDA should schedule the meeting within 60 days of the sponsor request. Documentation to support the meeting discussion should be sent to the FDA four weeks prior to the meeting date. In general, the sponsor can request only one meeting for each phase of development (e.g., FDA grants one End-of-Phase II meeting for a specific indication). Topics for discussion include clinical plan, study design, and content of a registrational application. CMC discussions are usually handled in separate meetings from clinical or non-clinical discussions. The Type B meetings are described below.

Pre-IND meeting

The pre-IND meeting is the first interaction with the FDA for an investigational product and usually occurs a few months prior to the IND submission. This meeting serves as a forum to obtain FDA feedback on the non-clinical plan, the first clinical studies to be conducted in the USA, and to agree on details related to IND format. The focus of the discussion is on any issues that could affect the safety of subjects that will be enrolled in the first US clinical studies.

End-of-Phase II meeting

The End-of-Phase II (EOP2) meeting is highly recommended prior to moving into registrational Phase III trials. The consultation should focus on:

- the review of the Phase II data in support of the Phase III indication
- an assessment of the Phase III development plan (registrational plan)
- an agreement on the studies needed to support approval in the chosen indication.

The EOP2 meeting should be scheduled such that it does not result in a delay in the initiation of the Phase III trial(s).

The sponsor should submit the following information four weeks prior to the meeting date:

- summary of the Phase I and Phase II data
- the Phase III protocol(s)
- the pediatric plan
- the plan for any other non-clinical studies.

An EOP2 meeting on CMC topics can occur within this meeting or can be scheduled separately. The CMC meeting should address all manufacturing questions and plans for production of the marketed product to be included in the NDA submission.

Pre-NDA meeting
The pre-NDA meeting with FDA occurs prior to NDA submission. The focus of this meeting is to identify any remaining issue(s) or concerns of FDA prior to NDA submission.

This meeting will typically discuss and review:

- the results from pivotal studies
- the proposed statistical analysis plan
- the pediatric plans
- the NDA format
- any remaining issues.

In support of the above agenda, the sponsor should submit the following information four weeks prior to the meeting:

- a clinical data summary
- information on the NDA format (e.g., table of contents, sample tables, electronic format)
- pediatric studies status
- any other relevant information
- questions to be discussed prior to NDA submission.

The pre-NDA meeting is designed to be a technical meeting favoring discussion around sponsor questions regarding format, data presentation, or submission date and to verify the adequacy of the data in preparation for the NDA submission. Scientific issues related to the application (study design, end points, etc.) should have been discussed and addressed with FDA prior to this meeting.

Type C meeting

All other meetings (i.e., non-A, non-B) will be classified as a Type C meeting. FDA should schedule the meeting within 75 days of the sponsor request. Documentation to support the meeting discussion should be sent to FDA two weeks prior to the meeting date. Topics for discussion can be varied and may include protocol design or general scientific discussions.

Advisory Committee meetings

Advisory Committee meetings are public consultation meetings organized by FDA and designed to provide FDA with a scientific and medical opinion on the adequacy of the data for the specified indication. Advisory committees consist of a panel of medical and statistical experts from the relevant discipline. The topics for discussion usually focus on a specific NDA under review but can also include broader or more general scientific discussions. For Advisory Committee meetings intended to discuss an NDA under review, both the sponsor and FDA are invited to present a summary of the data. An open forum discussion among the expert panelists and FDA follows the presentations and the meeting concludes with the vote of the expert panel on specific questions raised by FDA. FDA usually follows the advisory committee advice but is not obligated to rule in alignment with the recommendation.

21 CFR 314: New Drug Application/Biologics License Application

What is an NDA/BLA?

An NDA/BLA is a dossier containing the compilation of all non-clinical, clinical, and pharmaceutical data that were produced for a given investigational product. This dossier is intended to support the commercialization of a specific dosage form (or forms) of the indicated investigational product for a specific indication. The relevant data are compiled by the sponsor according to the regulations defined in 21 CFR 314 and submitted to the FDA for review and approval. An NDA/BLA approval is required prior to the commercialization of a drug in the USA.[20]

The European Union regulatory framework

Regulatory bodies in the European Union

The European Medicines Agency (EMA), established in 1995, coordinates the scientific resources in the European Union (EU) for the evaluation, supervision, and pharmacovigilance of medicinal products. The EMA operates as a decentralized scientific agency of the EU and is responsible for the protection and promotion of human and animal health. The EMA plays no role in the evaluation of Clinical Trial Applications; however, it may give scientific advice to companies for the development of new medicinal products. The EMA also advises the European Commission (EC) and the individual member states. The EMA is comprised of five committees responsible for human medicinal product use (CHMP), veterinary medicinal product use (CVMP), orphan medicinal products (COMP), herbal medicinal products (HMPC), and pediatrics (PDCO).[21]

In addition to the European competent bodies, there are the national health authorities based in each country, commonly termed the Ministries of Health (MoHs), and the associated bodies or agencies (Afssaps in France, BfArm in Germany, MHRA in the UK, etc.). These national competent authorities are the main regulatory bodies that evaluate clinical trial applications in Europe and monitor the conduct of clinical trials through inspections.

Types of legislative/regulatory texts in the EU

For all the EU Member States, regulations exist at the level of the EU, and at the level of the individual Member States. A discussion of the regulations in each of the 27 Member States would be beyond the scope of this text, and we will therefore focus on the regulatory framework of the EU.

All EU regulatory texts on pharmaceuticals are compiled in the *Rules Governing Medicinal Products in the European Union*, which currently consists of 10 volumes. These volumes are sometimes also referred to as the 'EudraLex' collection and can be consulted on the web-site at http://ec.europa.eu/enterprise/pharmaceuticals/eudralex/eudralex_en.htm. This is the most comprehensive source of legislative and guidance documents for the EU. The main types of legislative texts are the Regulation, the Directive, and the Decision. In addition to these there are also the guidelines, which have no legal force.

A Regulation is a legal instrument that has a general application and is binding in its entirety. It is directly applicable in all Member States. As 'Community laws,' regulations must be complied with fully by those to whom they are addressed (individuals, Member States, Community Institutions). Regulations apply directly in all the Member States without requiring a transposition into national law or administrative provisions.

A Directive is a legal instrument that is binding relative to the specified objectives upon each Member State to whom it is addressed. However, unlike the Regulation, each national authority is permitted to define the specific methods needed to achieve the objective. Directives must be transposed into national law in order to become binding to individual citizens or organizations.

The third legal instrument is the Decision, which is directly binding but only to those to whom it is addressed (Member States, companies, individuals).

A Guideline is a Community document that, from a legislative framework, is intended to fulfill a legal obligation or provides advice on the most appropriate way to fulfill a legal obligation. Most guidelines do not have legal force but are to be considered as a harmonized Community position which, if followed, facilitates the assessment, approval, and control of medicinal products in the EU. However, with proper justification, alternative approaches may used.

Directives pertaining to clinical trials

Directive 2001/83/EC on 'the Community code relating to medicinal products for human use,' the associated *Annex I: analytical, pharmaco-toxicological and clinical standards and protocols in respect of the testing of medicinal products*, and Regulation (EC) 726/2004 (establishing the EMA), require that clinical trials in the EU be conducted in accordance with the Directive 2001/20/EC and that all clinical trials outside the EU meet the ethical requirements of this Directive. For trials conducted outside the EU and used to support a registrational application, the Marketing Authorization Application (MAA) should contain a statement to this effect. The Directive and its Annex, which are the cornerstones of the pharmaceutical legislation in the EU, also form the legal basis of further legislation and guidance with regard to clinical trials.

Three additional directives form the framework of the clinical trials legislation in Europe:

- *Directive 2001/20/EC* of the European Parliament and of the Council of April 4, 2001 on the approximation of the laws, regulations and administrative provisions of the Member States relating to the implementation of GCP in the conduct of clinical trials on medicinal products for human use, commonly referred to as the 'Clinical Trial Directive.'[22]
- *Commission Directive 2005/28/EC* of April 8, 2005 establishes the principles and detailed guidelines for GCP relative to investigational medicinal products for human use, as well as the requirements for authorization of the manufacturing or importation of such products, commonly referred to as the 'GCP Directive.'[23]
- *Commission Directive 2003/94/EC* establishes the principles and guidelines of Good Manufacturing Practice (GMP) with respect to medicinal products for human use and investigational medicinal products for human use.[24]

The Clinical Trial Directive requires that all trials be conducted in accordance with the principles of GCP. The Directive refers to GCP as 'a set of internationally recognized ethical and scientific quality requirements which must be observed for designing, conducting, recording, and reporting clinical trials that involve the participation of human subjects';[22] however, there is no reference to a specific set of GCP rules, such as ICH E6 guideline, and, in fact, subtle differences exist between the Directive and the E6 guideline including the definition of 'investigator,' 'adverse events,' and 'adverse reactions.' The Directive does not apply to non-interventional trials where the drug is given according to the terms of the Marketing Authorization and the patient is not subjected to study specific procedures (e.g., no randomization). The Directive covers a broad range of topics including:

- protection of trial subjects, with special attention to minors and incapacitated adults
- ethics committees: one single opinion per country
- notification of Competent Authorities, and notifications to Competent Authorities and Ethics Committees during the trial
- exchange of information between Authorities
- manufacturing and importation of investigational products
- adverse event reporting
- inspections (GCP and GMP).

The Directive refers to a number of specific guidance documents that are compiled in volume 10 of the EudraLex collection.

The GCP Directive is one of the guidance documents issued to implement the Clinical Trial Directive. It contains only very general guidance concerning GCP, while more specific and detailed subsections or articles address manufacturing/import authorizations, the trial master file and archiving requirements, and inspections. Further detailed guidance related to documentation and record-keeping requirements for clinical trials can be found in Annex I to Directive 2001/83/EC.[22]

The GMP Directive requires compliance with GMP for both marketed and investigational medicinal products (IMPs), and establishes specific requirements for IMPs (e.g., the manufacture of IMPs in the EU is subject to authorization by the competent authority; imported IMPs must be in compliance with standards equivalent to EU-GMP; the manufacturer must be accepted by the competent authority). This Directive also refers to further detailed guidance on GMP which is compiled in volume 4 of the EudraLex collection.[24]

Guidance documents pertaining to clinical trials

EudraLex volume 3 is *Scientific Guidelines for Human Medicinal Products* adopted by the CHMP. The guidelines that concern clinical trials are compiled in the section 'Clinical Efficacy and Safety Guidelines,' and consist of general and disease-specific guidelines. Some ICH guidelines have been adopted by the CHMP, including the E6 guideline adopted in July 96.

Other relevant guidelines cover topics such as structure and content of clinical study reports, clinical safety data management, investigator signature on clinical study reports, and so on.

Applications for a clinical trial

Application for the authorization of a clinical trial must be processed through the national authorities for each Member State. The EU provides three guidelines implementing the Clinical Trial Directive with regard to Clinical Trial Applications (CTAs). These can be accessed in EudraLex volume 10, chapter 1:

- *Detailed guidance on the **request to the competent authorities for authorization** of a clinical trial on a medicinal product for human use, notification of substantial amendments and declaration of the end of the trial.*[25]
- *Detailed guidance on the application format and documentation to be submitted in an **application for an Ethics Committee opinion** on a* clinical trial on medicinal products for human use.[26]
- The third document implements articles 11 and 17 of the Clinical Trial Directive, and provides *Detailed guidance on the **European clinical trials database*** (EUDRACT database).[27]

The purpose of the EUDRACT database is to provide the competent authorities with an overview of ongoing EU clinical trials and to facilitate communication across Member States in order to improve the protection of trial subjects.

Safety monitoring and pharmacovigilance

Two guidelines specific to clinical safety are located in EudraLex volume 10, chapter 2:

- *Detailed guidance on the collection, verification and presentation of adverse reaction reports arising from clinical trials on medicinal products for human use*. For the definitions of adverse event, serious adverse event, etc., this guideline refers to the Clinical Trial Directive. Responsibilities of the sponsor and investigator, the evaluation of adverse events (seriousness, causality, and expectedness), standards for expedited reporting, annual safety reports, and the reporting of safety issues after trial completion are outlined within this guidance.[28]
- *Detailed guidance on the European database of Suspected Unexpected Serious Adverse Reactions (SUSAR) (Eudravigilance – Clinical Trial Module)*, implements articles 11, 17 and 18 of the Clinical Trial Directive 2001/20/EC. This guidance is mainly addressed to the competent authorities (EU and Member States) but it also discusses the electronic reporting of SUSARs by sponsors, database entry, and distribution.[29]

This guidance should be viewed in conjunction with the EUDRACT guidance found in volume 10, chapter 1.

Information on the quality of the investigational medicinal product

The rules related to GMP are captured in volume 4 of EudraLex. Investigational medicinal products should also comply with the rules for marketed drugs but additional guidance specifically related to investigational medicinal products is outlined in Annex 13. As the manufacturing of investigational products involves a greater complexity due to incomplete validation of the manufacturing process, the variability in clinical trial designs, the randomization process, and blinding of study personnel, specific attention to the production documentation, and packaging and labeling is given. The annex also contains guidance on the ordering, shipments, returns, and recalls of investigational medicinal products.[30]

Two other guidance documents of relevance in this area are:

- *Guideline on the requirements to the chemical and pharmaceutical quality documentation concerning investigational medicinal products in clinical trials* (October 2006). This guideline addresses the documentation regarding the chemical and pharmaceutical quality of the investigational products (including comparator and placebo) that are submitted as part of the Investigational Medicinal Product Dossier (IMPD) to the competent authorities in order to seek approval to conduct clinical trials.[31]
- *Guidance on Investigational Medicinal Products (IMPs) and other products used in clinical trials.* This guidance document explains the difference between the investigational products and non-investigational medicinal products (NIMP) used in clinical trials. NIMPs include rescue medication, challenge agents, products used to assess end points, and concomitant medicinal products systematically prescribed to study subjects as part of standard care and background treatment. There are specific requirements for NIMPs for the purposes of traceability, compliance, and adverse events assessment.[32]

Recommendations on inspections

GCP inspections conducted in the context of a centralized procedure are adopted by the CHMP and usually requested during the internal review of an MAA, but could also arise post-authorization. EudraLex, volume 10, chapter 4 contains *Recommendations on the qualifications on inspectors verifying compliance in clinical trials with the provisions of Good Clinical Practice.*[33] In addition, it contains several guidance documents on the preparation, conduct and reporting of the different types of inspections, such as investigator site, clinical laboratories, computer systems, sponsor, and Contract Research Organization (CRO). There is also a guidance document about the coordination of inspections and exchange of inspection reports between the Competent Authorities of the Member States of the EU, Ethics Committees, and the EMA. Essential information about inspections and the associated findings are entered in the EUDRACT database. More details on the inspection procedures can be found on the website of the EMA: http://www.ema. europa.eu/Inspections/GCPproc.html

Trial master file and archiving and EudraCT

The content of the trial master files and requirements for archiving are outlined in the related guideline found in EudraLex volume 10, chapter 5. This guideline describes the documents to be retained in the Trial Master File before, during and after completion of the clinical trial. Additionally, the suggested media and the storage conditions to ensure appropriate long-term archiving are discussed.[34] The requirements for document retention are briefly addressed but further information can be found in Annex I to the *Directive on the Community Code for Medicinal products (2001/83/EC)*.[35]

Other

In order to give more and detailed information on the requirements for clinical trials, a 'Questions and answers' link is available on the EudraLex website to a *Frequently asked questions* page. This document provides a legal definition of 'sponsor' and 'legal representative of the sponsor' and provides further advice concerning clinical trial applications.

EU Health Authority meetings

Similarly to the case with the FDA, a sponsor has the opportunity to obtain advice from the EU or national health authorities. Such meetings can include the following:

- Meetings to receive input in development programs
  - EMA Scientific Advice and protocol assistance
  - National Health Authority meetings.
- Meetings related to the MAAs and subsequent submissions
  - MAA pre-submission meetings
  - Oral explanations.
- EMA regulatory advice (1–2 years before anticipated MAA submission).

Meetings to receive input in development programs and life-cycle management programs

EMA Scientific Advice

Scientific Advice (SA), limited to scientific issues, may be requested for all medicinal products for use in human beings, as defined in Directive 2001/83/EC.[35]

Regulatory and administrative questions will be answered by the EMA Secretariat directly during a SA pre-submission meeting if requested, in writing, or at later meetings with EMA.[36]

The request for SA should contain the following information:

- letter of intent
- table of contents of the request
- briefing document including the questions and company's positions
- Annexes (e.g., background information, information relating to the questions or content of previous SA received).

There are two types of SA meetings: Scientific Advice Working Party (SAWP) Pre-submission Meetings and SAWP Discussion Meeting:

- *SAWP Pre-submission Meeting*. This meeting is on a voluntary basis (decision by the applicant) and is an opportunity to receive input in order to refine the questions to be addressed by the SAWP, identify additional issues, establish initial contact with the coordinators reviewing the request, and address regulatory questions with the EMA personnel.
- *SAWP Discussion Meeting*. Thirty days after the initial meeting request, the SAWP determines the necessity of a discussion based on the coordinators' initial reports. This meeting, if required, is scheduled approximately 60 days after the initial request. A detailed list of issues together with a meeting agenda is sent to the company in advance of the meeting. The issues are divided into those to be addressed in writing prior to the discussion meeting and issues to be addressed at the discussion meeting. The company may also propose additional points strictly related to the topics initially raised in the request for discussion.

Meetings with National Health Authorities

Input into development programs can also be requested from national agencies. Requirements for the necessary supportive information and timelines differ from country to country. In general, all requests should include specific questions with a company position and background information.

Meetings related to the Marketing Authorization Applications and subsequent submissions

MAA pre-submission meetings

The MAA pre-submission meeting is organized to address product-specific legal, regulatory, and scientific issues in order to facilitate subsequent validation and assessment of the application and assist sponsors in the finalization of the upcoming MAA.

The pre-submission meeting request form provides an overview of the most relevant topics (checklist) that applicants are advised to consider and also serves as the agenda for the meeting. All meeting background information should be provided no less than two weeks prior to the agreed meeting date.

The *EMA Guidance on Pre-Submission Meetings for initial Marketing Authorisation Applications for Human Medicinal Products in the Centralised Procedure* provides an overview of the process, timelines, and documents required.[37] Additionally, the EMA has a series of web pages with question and answers, meeting guidance, and relevant forms (www.ema. europa.eu/htms/human/presub/).

Oral explanations

Following an MAA submission, the CHMP will discuss the list of outstanding issues (OI) to be answered by the sponsor and determine whether an oral explanation is needed prior to the finalization of the CHMP scientific opinion on a centralized procedure.[38]

Usually a 30-day clock-stop will apply in order to allow the sponsor to prepare for the oral explanation. At least 10 days prior to the oral explanation, the sponsor must provide a written response to each OI to be addressed at the meeting. In some cases, the appropriate CHMP Working Party (WP) or Ad Hoc Working Group (WG) will need to address specific issues related to the list of questions and an additional oral explanation in front of the WP or WG will be requested by the CHMP.

Meetings within the regulatory advice process

Formal regulatory advice, which requires consultation with the CHMP or the EC, follows a 30- to 60-day procedure and relates to questions with no prior regulatory experience (e.g., emerging therapies, borderline products). Regulatory advice is provided before the sponsor has access to EMA procedures (e.g., scientific advice, orphan medicinal product designation, and marketing authorization procedures).

Regulatory advice should be considered well in advance of a marketing application (1–2 years prior to MAA submission) and at least 3 months before the anticipated date of submission of any EMA procedure. Additional information regarding this type of meeting can be found in the guideline *Regulatory advice to applicants on the eligibility to EMA procedures as medicinal products (according to Directive 2001/83/EC).*[39]

The Marketing Authorization Application

The MAA is a dossier containing the compilation of all non-clinical, clinical, and pharmaceutical data that has been produced for a particular investigational product. This dossier is intended to support the commercialization of a specific form (or forms) of the indicated investigational product for a specific indication.

There are two main marketing authorization procedures in Europe:

1   The centralized procedure
2   The decentralized/mutual recognition procedure.

These procedures are described in detail in the *European Commission Notice to Applicants*, EudraLex volume 2A, *Procedures for Marketing Authorization* (chapters 1, 2, and 4). In addition, approval can be sought at the national level; however, approval is only granted in the one member state.

A Marketing Authorization is required prior to the commercialization of a drug in the European Union and is valid for 5 years. Applications for renewal must be made to the EMA at least 6 months prior to the expiration of the Marketing Authorization. Pricing and reimbursement in Europe remain a national responsibility.

A brief description is provided here for the centralized and mutual recognition/decentralized procedures.

The centralized procedure

Scope
The centralized procedure is coordinated by the EMA. A Marketing Authorization granted under the centralized procedure is valid in all European member states. The centralized procedure is mandatory for the EU marketing authorization of the following medicinal products:

- medicinal products derived from biotechnology
- new active substances not already approved in the Community prior to 20 November 2005 and intended for treatment of acquired immune deficiency syndrome, cancer, neurodegenerative disorders, diabetes, autoimmune diseases, and other immune dysfunctions and viral diseases
- orphan medicinal products.

Other new medicinal products may also, at the request of the applicant, be considered for authorization under the centralized procedure.

The mutual recognition and decentralized procedures

The mutual recognition procedure and decentralized procedures must be used for marketing authorization of a medicinal product in more than one member state. The mutual recognition procedure allows concerned member states to recognize the evaluation and recommendation for authorization of a reference member state that is responsible for the scientific evaluation of a product. A detailed description of the mutual recognition and decentralized procedure can be found in Directive 2001/83/EC[35] and Directive 2004/27/EC,[40] respectively.

Summary

The legislation and guidelines related to the conduct of clinical studies help provide a standard framework for both sponsors and researchers beyond that found in the Nuremberg Code, the Declaration of Helsinki, and the Belmont Report. Legislation has helped to codify many of the principles addressed in these documents and has made the attempt to ensure the protection of human subjects and the quality of clinical trial data to be used for product registration.

References

1. International Conference on Harmonisation. *Structure of ICH* [Online]. Available from: http://www.ich.org/cache/compo/276-254-1.html (accessed January 26, 2009).
2. International Conference on Harmonisation. *ICH Guidelines* [Online]. Available from: http://www.ich.org/cache/compo/276-254-1.html (accessed January 26, 2009).
3. International Conference on Harmonisation. *Guidance for Industry: Good Clinical Practice, Consolidated Guidance*, ICH-E6. Geneva: Switzerland, 1996.
4. Swann JP. *History of FDA* [Online] (1998). Available from: http://www.fda.gov/oc/history/historyoffda/default.htm (accessed January 26, 2009).
5. *Federal Food and Drugs Act of 1906 (The "Wiley Act")* [Online] (1906). Available from: http://www.fda.gov/opacom/laws/wileyact.htm (accessed January 26, 2009).
6. Meadows M. *Promoting Safe and Effective Drugs for 100 years* [Online]. Available from: http://www.fda.gov/fdac/features/2006/106_cder.html (accessed January 26, 2009).
7. *Prescription Drug User Fee Act of 1992* [Online] (1992). Available from: http://www.fda.gov/oc/pdufa/ (accessed January 26, 2009).
8. *Food and Drug Administration Amendments Act of 2007* [Online] (2007). Available from: http://www.fda.gov/oc/initiatives/hr3580.pdf (accessed January 26, 2009).
9. Food and Drug Administration [Online] (January 2004). *Guidance for Industry: IND Exemptions for Studies of Lawfully Marketed Drug or Biological Products for the Treatment of Cancer.* Available from: http://www.fda.gov/Cber/gdlns/indcancer.pdf (accessed January 26, 2009).
10. *United States Code of Federal Regulations.* Title 21 Part 312 [Online]. Available from: https://www.accessdata.fda.gov/scripts/cdrh/cfdocs/cfCFR/CFRSearch.cfm?CFRPart=312 (accessed January 26, 2009).
11. Food and Drug Administration [Online] (November 1995). *Guidance for Industry: Guidance for Industry: Content and Format of Investigational New Drug Applications (INDs) for Phase 1 Studies of Drugs, Including Well-Characterized, Therapeutic, Biotechnology-Derived Products.* Available from: http://www.fda.gov/cder/guidance/clin2.pdf (accessed January 26, 2009).
12. Food and Drug Administration [Online] (July 2008). *Guidance for Industry: CGMP for Phase 1 Investigational Drugs.* Available from: http://www.fda.gov/cder/guidance/GMP%20Phase1IND61608.pdf (accessed January 26, 2009).
13. Food and Drug Administration [Online] (March 2001). *Guidance for Industry: Acceptance of Foreign Clinical Studies.* Available from: http://www.fda.gov/CbER/gdlns/clinical031301.pdf (accessed January 26, 2009).
14. Food and Drug Administration [Online] (April 28, 2008). *Human Subject Protection; Foreign Clinical Studies Not Conducted Under an Investigational New Drug Application.* Available from: http://www.fda.gov/cber/rules/forclinstud.pdf (accessed January 26, 2009).
15. *United States Code of Federal Regulations.* Title 21 Part 50 [Online]. Available from: https://www.accessdata.fda.gov/scripts/cdrh/cfdocs/cfCFR/CFRSearch.cfm?CFRPart=50 (accessed January 26, 2009).

16. *United States Code of Federal Regulations.* Title 21 Part 54 [Online]. Available from: https://www.accessdata.fda.gov/scripts/cdrh/cfdocs/cfCFR/CFRSearch.cfm? CFRPart=54 (accessed January 26, 2009).

17. Food and Drug Administration [Online] (March 2001). *Guidance for Industry: Financial Disclosure by Clinical Investigators.* Available from: http://www.fda.gov/oc/guidance/ financialdis.html (accessed January 26, 2009).

18. *United States Code of Federal Regulations.* Title 21 Part 56 [Online]. Available from: https://www.accessdata.fda.gov/scripts/cdrh/cfdocs/cfCFR/CFRSearch.cfm? CFRPart=56 (accessed January 26, 2009).

19. Food and Drug Administration [Online] (February 2000). *Guidance for Industry: Formal Meetings with Sponsors and Applicants for PDUFA Products.* Available from: http:// www.fda.gov/CBER/gdlns/mtpdufa.pdf (accessed January 26, 2009) (accessed January 26, 2009).

20. *United States Code of Federal Regulations.* Title 21 Part 314 [Online]. Available from: https://www.accessdata.fda.gov/scripts/cdrh/cfdocs/cfCFR/CFRSearch.cfm? CFRPart=314 (accessed January 26, 2009).

21. European Medicines Agency [Online]. *About EMA Structure.* Available from: http:// www.ema.europa.eu/htms/aboutus/emeaoverview.htm (accessed January 26, 2009).

22. European Commission [Online] (2001). *Directive 2001/20/EC.* Available from: http://ec. europa.eu/enterprise/pharmaceuticals/eudralex/vol-1/dir_2001_20/dir_2001_20_en.pdf (accessed January 26, 2009).

23. European Commission [Online] (2005). *Directive 2005/28/EC.* Available from: http://ec. europa.eu/enterprise/pharmaceuticals/eudralex/vol-1/dir_2005_28/dir_2005_28_en.pdf (accessed January 26, 2009).

24. European Commission [Online] (2003). *Directive 2003/94/EC.* Available from: http://ec. europa.eu/enterprise/pharmaceuticals/eudralex/vol-1/dir_2003_94/dir_2003_94_en.pdf (accessed January 26, 2009).

25. European Commission [Online] (October 2005). *Detailed Guidance for the Request for Authorization of a Clinical Trial on a Medicinal Product for Human Use to the Competent Authorities, Notification of Substantial Amendments and Declaration of the End of the Trial.* Available from: http://ec.europa.eu/enterprise/pharmaceuticals/ eudralex/vol-10/11_ca_14-2005.pdf (accessed January 26, 2009).

26. European Commission [Online] (February 2006). *Detailed Guidance on the Application Format and Documentation to Be Submitted in an Application for an Ethics Committee Opinion on the Clinical Trial on Medicinal Products for Human Use.* Available from: http://ec.europa.eu/enterprise/pharmaceuticals/eudralex/vol-10/12_ec_guide-line_20060216.pdf (accessed January 26, 2009).

27. European Commission [Online] (April 2003). *Detailed Guidance on the European Clinical Trials Database (EUDRACT Database).* Available from: http://ec.europa.eu/ enterprise/pharmaceuticals/eudralex/vol-10/13_cp_and_guidance_eudract_april_04.pdf (accessed January 26, 2009).

28. European Commission [Online] (April 2006). *Detailed Guidance on the Collection, Verification and Presentation of Adverse Reaction Reports Arising from Clinical Trials on Medicinal Products for Human Use.* Available from: http://ec.europa.eu/enterprise/pharma-ceuticals/eudralex/vol-10/21_susar_rev2_2006_04_11.pdf (accessed January 26, 2009).

29. European Commission [Online] (April 2004). *Detailed Guidance on the European DataBase of Suspected Unexpected Serious Adverse Reactions (Eudravigilance – Clinical Trial Module).* Available from: http://ec.europa.eu/enterprise/pharmaceuticals/ eudralex/vol-10/22_cp_and_guidance_database_susars16_april_2004.pdf (accessed January 26, 2009).

30. European Commission [Online] (July 2003). *Annex 13: Manufacture of Investigational Medicinal Products.* Available from: http://ec.europa.eu/enterprise/pharmaceuticals/ eudralex/vol-4/pdfs-en/an13final_24-02-05.pdf (accessed January 26, 2009).

31. European Medicines Agency [Online] (October 2006). *Guideline on the Requirements to the Chemical and Pharmaceutical Quality Documentation Concerning Investigational*

Medicinal Products in Clinical Trials. Available from: http://ec.europa.eu/enterprise/pharmaceuticals/eudralex/vol-10/18540104en.pdf (accessed January 26, 2009).

32. European Commission [Online] (2007). *Guidance on Investigational Medicinal Products (IMPs) and Other Medicinal Products Used in Clinical Trials [Online].* Available from: http://ec.europa.eu/enterprise/pharmaceuticals/eudralex/vol-10/guidance-on-imp_nimp_04-2007.pdf (accessed January 26, 2009).
33. European Commission [Online] (July 2006). *Recommendations on the Qualifications on Inspectors Verifying Compliance in Clinical Trials with the Provisions of Good Clinical Practice.* Available from: http://ec.europa.eu/enterprise/pharmaceuticals/eudralex/vol-10/v10_chap4.pdf (accessed January 26, 2009).
34. European Commission [Online] (July 2006). *Recommendation on the Content of the Trial Master File and Archiving.* Available from: http://ec.europa.eu/enterprise/pharmaceuticals/eudralex/vol-10/v10_chap5.pdf (accessed January 26, 2009).
35. European Commission [Online] (November 2001). *Directive 2001/83/EC.* Available from: http://ec.europa.eu/enterprise/pharmaceuticals/eudralex/vol-1/dir_2001_83_cons/dir2001_83_cons_en.pdf (accessed January 26, 2009).
36. European Medicines Agency [Online] (January 2007). *EMA Guidance for Companies Requesting Scientific Advice or Protocol Assistance.* Available from: http://www.ema.europa.eu/pdfs/human/sciadvice/426001en.pdf (accessed January 26, 2009).
37. European Medicines Agency [Online] (January 2007). *EMA Guidance on Pre-submission Meetings for Initial Marketing Authorisation Applications for Human Medicinal Products in the Centralised Procedure.* Available from: http://www.ema.europa.eu/htms/human/presub/38271206en.pdf (accessed January 26, 2009).
38. European Medicines Agency [Online] (February 2002). *Guidance to Applicants on CHMP Oral Explanations in Relation to Centralized Applications.* Available from: http://www.ema.europa.eu/pdfs/human/regaffair/239001en.pdf (accessed January 26, 2009).
39. European Medicines Agency [Online] (Oct 2006). *Regulatory Advice to Applicants on the Eligibility to EMA Procedures as Medicinal Products (According to Directive 2001/83/EC).* Available from: http://www.ema.europa.eu/pdfs/human/sop/3138SOP.pdf (accessed January 26, 2009).
40. European Commission [Online] (March 2004). *Directive 2004/27/EC.* Available from: http://ec.europa.eu/enterprise/pharmaceuticals/eudralex/vol-1/dir_2004_27/dir_2004_27_en.pdf (accessed January 26, 2009).

3

Informed consent

Steven P. Steinbrueck, Barbara S. Davis,

and Elizabeth E. Bodi

Freely given informed consent provides the ethical foundation for clinical research. Without adequate consent, research on humans is at best suspect, and at worst unethical and dangerous.

Informed consent is succinctly defined by the International Conference on Harmonisation (ICH) as: 'a process by which a subject voluntarily confirms his or her willingness to participate in a particular trial, after having been informed of all aspects of the trial that are relevant to the subject's decision to participate. Informed consent is documented by means of a written, signed, and dated informed consent document.'[1]

The Belmont Report describes adequate consent as consisting of three elements – information, comprehension, and voluntariness.[2] Each element has been threatened at various points in history. The following excerpt contributes to our understanding of the critical nature of consent in clinical research.

> Respect for persons requires that subjects, to the degree that they are capable, be given the opportunity to choose what shall or shall not happen to them. This opportunity is provided when adequate standards for informed consent are satisfied.

> While the importance of informed consent is unquestioned, controversy prevails over the nature and possibility of an informed consent. Nonetheless, there is widespread agreement that the consent process can be analyzed as containing three elements: information, comprehension and voluntariness.[2]

> Informed consent also has three goals: the provision of comprehensible information to the potential research subject, risk mitigation, and the documentation of the subject's voluntary consent. These goals, especially the first two, are often in direct conflict.[3]

This chapter will begin with review of the historical and regulatory evolution of informed consent, continue with a discussion of its form and content, and close with a brief overview of several consent-related issues: assent by minors, waivers, exceptions to informed consent requirements and the consent of 'vulnerable subjects,' and a few words about impact of the US Health Insurance Portability and Accountability Act (HIPAA) on the informed consent process.

Background

Historical and ethical perspectives of informed consent

A review of the events and laws that established guidelines for ethical research will help to appreciate how the principles of informed consent were developed.

Upton Sinclair's exposé of the meat packing industry, *The Jungle*, spurred the 1906 passage of the Pure Food and Drug Act. Although this law primarily regulated animal health maintenance and sought to control how meat was processed, packaged, and portioned, it also addressed the strength and purity of pharmaceutical products.

The deaths of 107 individuals following ingestion of sulfanilamide dissolved in diethylene chloride provided the impetus for the 1938 passage of a more comprehensive drug law – the Food, Drug and Cosmetic Act (FD&C Act). This new legislation addressed the safety of foods and cosmetics as well as medicines. It required that drugs be labeled with adequate directions for safe use and required the submission, but not approval, of a New Drug Application (NDA) before pharmaceutical products could be marketed.

Human experimentation in Nazi concentration camps provoked international condemnation and resulted in the 1947 Nuremberg Code; modern consent traces much of its lineage to this document, which was developed by the military tribunals charged with judging the atrocities perpetrated by Nazi physicians as they carried out so-called 'medical experiments.' Of its 10 articles, 'Informed consent to research was the first and most prominent.'[4]

In the 1950s, the sedative thalidomide, widely used in Europe, was imported into the USA for testing of its safety and efficacy in treating nausea and vomiting of pregnancy – 'morning sickness.' Its use caused severe, irreversible damage to fetuses and led to US Senate subcommittee investigations that resulted in what are termed the Kefauver–Harris Amendments to the FD&C Act. This Act required informed consent, adherence to Good Manufacturing Practice (GMP), and approval of the NDA before marketing of a new drug.[5]

After years of discussion, the Declaration of Helsinki was first published in 1964. This policy statement of the World Medical Association (WMA) has been revised six times, most recently in 2008. Clarifying statements were previously added in 2002 and 2004. It is widely recognized as an authoritative statement on research ethics. It draws distinctions between therapeutic and non-therapeutic research, supports independent review of studies prior to enrolling subjects, and speaks directly to a requirement for written consent.

In 1974, the US Congress passed the National Research Act as a result of public reaction to research atrocities including what were most often called the Tuskegee Syphilis Study and the Willowbrook Hepatitis Study. The Tuskegee study, beginning in the 1930s and lasting nearly 40 years, collected data on African-American males in the rural south who were infected with syphilis. It was specifically designed to follow the subjects and observe the effects and progression of their untreated disease. Subjects were promised free medical care, but were informed neither of their condition nor of the true nature of the study; they were also denied access to treatment with penicillin when it became available in the 1940s.[6] Additional discussion of the Tuskegee Syphilis Study can be found in Chapter 1.

The Willowbrook Hepatitis Study, conducted at the Willowbrook State School, a New York state institution, was a study in which children of diminished mental capacity were purposely exposed to the hepatitis virus to gain an understanding of the natural history of infectious hepatitis. Children were initially fed virus samples from infected individuals; later subjects were injected with the virus. The researchers defended this practice by claiming that the children at Willowbrook would have been infected with the hepatitis virus anyway. The institution refused to admit new patients unless they agreed to participate in the hepatitis study. Parents were left with very little choice but to agree to the study in order for their children to attend the school.[7]

The National Research Act provided for additional regulations to protect the health and welfare of research subjects by requiring independent review by Institutional Review Boards (IRBs)/Independent Ethics Committees (IECs). It created the National Commission for the Protection of Human Subjects in Biomedical Research. This commission composed a document entitled *The Ethical Principles and Guidelines for the Protection of Human Subjects of Research*, otherwise known as the Belmont Report.[2]

The Belmont Report delineates the ethical principles upon which federal regulations for the protection of human subjects are based. It identifies three principles: respect for persons, beneficence, and justice. It is primarily the respect for the autonomy of the individual, or protection of those who are not fully autonomous, that supplies the ethical basis for informed consent.

Ethical behavior allows the objectives of clinical research (i.e., to develop generalizable knowledge, increase understanding of human biology, and improve health) to be met while using human subjects as its means. Provisions for informed consent lie at the center of these behaviors. The right of each subject, not the researcher, to choose to participate or not is paramount.

Later in this chapter we will explore the actual form of the consent; how it is operationalized; how it explains the purposes, methods, alternatives, risks, and possible benefits of the proposed research; and how it addresses special situations (e.g., the consent of children or adults with diminished mental capacity).

Regulations and guidelines

Informed consent is a process that defies precise measurement. Although it involves shared decision making between a medical professional and a potential research subject – a disclosure of (study) information and a sharing of its meaning (comprehension) by a medical professional – it is difficult to specify what consent (the process) consists of and requires. As a starting point, it is essential to understand the requirements detailed in the US regulations and widely accepted ICH Guidelines that govern informed consent.

Title 21 of the Code of Federal Regulations (CFR) Part 50.25 lists eight 'basic' and six 'additional' elements of informed consent. ICH E6 Guidelines Section 4.8.10 lists 20 elements of informed consent. These requirements are compared in Table 3.1. Although there are a few areas of where similar items are more detailed (underscored) in one listing, and a four instances where a specific item is not found in both sets of requirements (italic typeface), these lists of required content are nearly identical; in practice all elements are included in informed consent forms for trials conducted by the pharmaceutical industry.

Although this section has presented detail regarding the specific content requirements for informed consent forms, the reader is urged to consult the entire text concerning informed consent found in 21 CFR 50 Subpart D, the ICH E6 Guidelines section 4.8, the FDA Information Sheet entitled *Guidance for Institutional Review Boards and Clinical Investigators: A Guide to Informed Consent* and, for US federally funded research, 45 CFR 46 Subpart A, known as the Common Rule. Finally, in the USA, state and local laws may also apply to informed consent and may require additional elements, documents, or restrictions.

Introduction to form and process

Despite ethical, regulatory, and legal imperatives, significant deficiencies in the informed consent process persist. The recognition and resolution of these shortcomings are complicated by competing goals of consent: information, risk mitigation, and documentation.[3]

The communication of accurate, comprehensible information is a self-evident goal of consent. Informed consent documents pursuing this goal

Table 3.1 Comparison between FDA Regulations and ICH E6 Guidelines[a]

21 CFR 50.25	ICH 4.8.10
(a) *Basic elements of informed consent*. In seeking informed consent, the following information shall be provided to each subject:	Both the informed consent discussion and the written informed consent form and any other written information to be provided to subjects should include explanations of the following:
(1) A statement that the study involves research,	(a) That the trial involves research.
an explanation of the purposes of the research and	(b) The purpose of the trial.
Not specifically stated in US Regulations, but routinely included.	(c) The trial treatment(s) and the probability for random assignment to each treatment.
the expected duration of the subject's participation,	(s) The expected duration of the subject's participation in the trial.
a description of the procedures to be followed, and	(d) The trial procedures to be followed, including all invasive procedures.
Not specifically stated in US Regulations.	(e) The subject's responsibilities.
identification of any procedures which are experimental.	(f) Those aspects of the trial that are experimental.
(2) A description of any reasonably foreseeable risks or discomforts to the subject.	(g) The reasonably foreseeable risks or inconveniences to the subject and, *when applicable, to an embryo, fetus, or nursing infant.*
(3) A description of any benefits to the subject or to others which may reasonably be expected from the research.	(h) The reasonably expected benefits. *When there is no intended clinical benefit to the subject, the subject should be made aware of this.*
(4) A disclosure of appropriate alternative procedures or courses of treatment, if any, that might be advantageous to the subject.	(i) The alternative procedure(s) or course(s) of treatment that may be available to the subject, *and their important potential benefits and risks.*
(5) A statement describing the extent, if any, to which confidentiality of records identifying the subject will be maintained and that notes the possibility that the Food and Drug Administration may inspect the records.	(n) That the monitor(s), the auditor(s), the IRB/IEC, and the regulatory authority(ies) will be granted direct access to the subject's original medical records for verification of clinical trial procedures and/or data, without violating the confidentiality of the subject, to the extent permitted by the applicable laws and regulations and that, *by signing a written informed consent form, the subject or the subject's legally acceptable representative is authorizing such access.* (o) *That records identifying the subject will be kept confidential and, to the extent permitted by the applicable laws and/or regulations, will not be made publicly available. If the results of the trial are published, the subject's identity will remain confidential.*

(continued overleaf)

Table 3.1 (continued)

21 CFR 50.25	ICH 4.8.10
(6) For research involving more than minimal risk, an explanation as to whether any compensation and	(k) The anticipated prorated payment, if any, to the subject for participating in the trial.
an explanation as to whether any medical treatments are available if injury occurs and, if so, what they consist of, or where further information may be obtained.	(j) The compensation and/or treatment available to the subject in the event of trial-related injury.
(7) An explanation of whom to contact for answers to pertinent questions about the research and research subjects' rights, and whom to contact in the event of a research-related injury to the subject.	(q) The person(s) to contact for further information regarding the trial and the rights of trial subjects, and whom to contact in the event of trial-related injury.
(8) A statement that participation is voluntary, that refusal to participate will involve no penalty or loss of benefits to which the subject is otherwise entitled, and that the subject may discontinue participation at any time without penalty or loss of benefits to which the subject is otherwise entitled.	(m) That the subject's participation in the trial is voluntary and that the subject may refuse to participate or withdraw from the trial, at any time, without penalty or loss of benefits to which the subject is otherwise entitled.
(b) *Additional elements of informed consent.* When appropriate, one or more of the following elements of information shall also be provided to each subject:	
(1) A statement that the particular treatment or procedure may involve risks to the subject (or to the embryo or fetus, if the subject is or may become pregnant) which are currently unforeseeable.	**Not specifically stated in ICH Guidelines; however, see (g) above. Routinely included.**
(2) Anticipated circumstances under which the subject's participation may be terminated by the investigator without regard to the subject's consent.	(r) The foreseeable circumstances and/or reasons under which the subject's participation in the trial may be terminated.
(3) Any additional costs to the subject that may result from participation in the research.	(l) The anticipated expenses, if any, to the subject for participating in the trial.
(4) The consequences of a subject's decision to withdraw from the research and procedures for orderly termination of participation by the subject.	**Not specifically stated in ICH Guidelines.**
(5) A statement that significant new findings developed during the course of the research which may relate to the subject's willingness to continue participation will be provided to the subject.	(p) That the subject or the subject's legally acceptable representative will be informed in a timely manner if information becomes available that may be relevant to the subject's willingness to continue participation in the trial.
(6) The approximate number of subjects involved in the study.	(t) The approximate number of subjects involved in the trial.

[a] Underlining indicates areas where similar items are more detailed in one listing; bold type indicates instances where a specific item is not found in both sets of requirements.

will be brief, simple, and thoroughly reviewed with attention to comprehension rather than speed. Risk mitigation, however, is a concern for sponsors, investigators and IRBs. The goal of risk mitigation requires documents with characteristics that compete with those above – the forms are longer, more precise (i.e., detailed, technical), and often completed quickly. A third goal is appropriate documentation of consent. This minimalist objective merely requires inclusion of the required elements accompanied by appropriate dated signatures. It should be obvious that documentation alone does not address comprehension, language, or the time required for truly informed consent.

Interventions to improve patient understanding and thereby validate truly informed consent have unfortunately focused on the informed consent document. Preoccupation with form, however, has not yielded significant gains in participant understanding; the tide of interventions may be turning toward process.[8]

Threat of litigation increases the urgency of finding solutions. Virtually all clinical research litigations filed in the last quarter century have included claims of inadequate consent. Prevailing standards place a stricter duty and higher standard on research practitioners than on physicians in a therapeutic setting. In standard therapeutic practice, a patient can reasonably expect to receive generally accepted best standard of care. In a research setting, the participant must abandon this presupposition. The informed consent is the 'waiver that makes this change of circumstances legitimate.'[9]

A moral imperative, however, should both supersede and undergird legal considerations. The moral obligation to provide informed consent affirms human dignity, underscores the principle of respect for persons, distinguishes contemporary researchers from the many cited examples of the past, and protects both human participants and researchers.

Ethical pontification, however, fails to offer practical guidance in how the process should be operationalized. Despite the inestimable importance of appropriate consent, there is little guidance on acceptable thresholds of understanding. How do we evaluate capacity to consent? What constitutes appropriate information? Is it possible to quantify understanding? What is the 'gold standard' for informed consent?

Informed consent form

As we have discussed, regulations and both current and historical guidance documents unequivocally articulate the ethical and legal necessity for informed consent and differentiate the informed consent document (i.e., the form) from the process. The form is a documentation of the process, which represents an exchange of information – an interaction, a dialogue, a conversation.

Guidance from the *IRB Guidebook*[10] reiterates the basic and additional elements codified in 21 CFR 50.25 and evaluates 'adequacy' in terms of content of the form. Additional consideration is given to ensuring that 'information is presented to prospective subjects in a language they can understand' and that 'medical terms and complex sentences are presented in simpler terms – ordinary language should replace technical terms (e.g., venipuncture as taking blood from your arm with a needle).' IRBs increasingly request that informed consent documents be written at the sixth- to eighth-grade reading level.

As stated above, interventions to improve informed consent reflect an early focus on the form. Modifications of the consent form include considerations for readability, grade level, vocabulary and terms, definitions of concept, category and value words, and alterations of document format with adjustments of white space, bold headings, and the addition of graphs or charts.[8,11–19]

Exclusive focus on the form, however, results in longer, more technical documents with no demonstrable corresponding increase in understanding.[4,20–22] Similarly, no significant demonstrable improvements are noted with alternative media presentations.[8,12]

Informed consent process

To reiterate, the form is a documentation of the process, which represents an exchange of information – an interaction, a dialogue, a conversation. It is often forgotten that informed consent is an ongoing process, not a piece of paper or a discrete moment in time.

This concept is articulated in the Department of Health and Human Services' *Institutional Review Board Guidebook*:[10]

> It is essential that IRB members think of informed consent not as a form that must be signed, but as an educational process that takes place between the investigator and the prospective subject. No one can guarantee that another person has understood the information presented; one can only inform prospective subjects as clearly as possible. No one can guarantee that another's choice is voluntary; one can only attempt to remove obvious impediments to free choice by being alert to coercive aspects of the consent procedure.[10]

Interventions to improve understanding with an emphasis on process may include extended discussion, utilization of various media (video, computer), employment of various teaching aids, presentations of historical material and regulatory apparatus, in addition to an assortment of methods to assess understanding and solicit feedback.[8,12] Extended discussion interventions range from a 30-minute phone conversation to multiple counseling sessions lasting up to two hours.[8]

Analyses of proposed interventions reveal that direct human contact, one-on-one interactions with extended discussion and feedback, is the best way to improve understanding. Ideally, this process will begin long before the introduction of the consent document – perhaps at the first subject contact in response to advertisement or phone call – and continue long after the study has been completed, through resolution of adverse events, database lock, unblinding, and publication of results.

Extended discussion that includes person-to-person interactions between study staff and participants accompanied by an evaluation/feedback approach does result in statistically significant demonstrable increases in participants' understanding.[8] Potential participants benefit from dialogue over time, consent procedures that incorporate patient education, and layered information presented orally.[8,22,23] Comparative analyses conclude that one-on-one human interactive extended discussion is the most consistent intervention for improving understanding and thereby achieving valid, ethical, informed consent.

Roles, responsibilities, perspectives

Principal investigator

The ultimate ethical and regulatory responsibility for the informed consent process lies with the investigator. Notably, when signing the 'Statement of Investigator' (Form FDA 1572) the principal investigator commits to ensuring that the informed consent requirements detailed in 21 CFR Part 50 are met.

Henry K. Beecher, known for his article on unethical practices in medical experimentation, insists that 'intelligent, informed, conscientious, compassionate, responsible investigators' are essential to assure human subject protection.[24] Further, an informed and conscientious investigator establishes credibility, not authority. 'Credibility comes from knowing the study in detail, so that questions can be answered honestly and accurately, and from established expertise in the scientific area under study.[25] Informed investigators study the investigator's brochure and study protocol, and are well versed in federal regulations, historical documents, and the ethical imperatives of human subject protection.

The goal of the informed consent process for the investigator is the accurate communication of information coupled with appropriate understanding by the participant and solicitation of voluntary non-binding consent. Compassionate and responsible practitioners abandon paternalism and embrace the autonomy, competence, and empowerment of the research participant. The compassionate and responsible investigator remains sensitive to participants' inherent vulnerability and susceptibility to coercion or undue influence. Further discussion of the responsibilities of the investigator can be found in Chapter 4.

Institutional Review Boards and Independent Ethics Committees

Institutional Review Boards (IRBs)/Independent Ethics Committees (IECs) bear regulatory responsibility for human subject protection and share responsibility for assuring adequacy of consent. The IRB/IECs primary access to the informed consent process is through the informed consent document. The goal of the informed consent process for the IRB, then, is documentation. This access point and corresponding goal lead seemingly to inevitable and disproportionate emphasis on wordsmithing and thus preoccupation with form. Resnik[26] calls on IRBs/IEC, to actually observe, monitor, and audit the informed consent process. Education and continued dialogue on developing a 'gold standard' for assessing adequate consent are imperative. Further discussion of the role of the IRB/IEC in the evaluation of informed consent can be found in Chapter 8.

Sponsor

Although not a party to the consent, the sponsor is vitally concerned with the solicitation of informed consent and frequently dictates or approves content for the consent document template. The consent document may serve as the primary vehicle for sponsor guidance to the investigator in determining what information to communicate to potential subjects and how to communicate that information.[16,27] Although concerned with providing comprehensible information for research subjects, the primary goals of the informed consent process for the sponsor are risk mitigation and documentation.

In addition to ethical, regulatory, and legal considerations, the informed consent process affects recruitment, compliance, and retention, and as such, also becomes an economic concern for the sponsor. Spending on patient recruitment programs has increased exponentially as randomization rates inversely decline and dropout rates increase. Over 90% of clinical trials extend original study timelines to meet enrollment requirements.[28] Simultaneously, in the last decade, litigation alleging informed consent inadequacies has resulted in multimillion-dollar verdicts.[29] An informed consent process that exceeds minimal regulatory requirements, meets the stricter and higher reasonable person disclosure standard, and meticulously upholds the ethical standard of autonomy safeguards the research participant and potentially leads to increased enrollment, compliance, and retention. Further discussion of sponsor responsibilities can be found in Chapter 5.

Public

Ken Getz, founder of the Center for Information and Study on Clinical Research Participation (CISCRP), argues persuasively for greater public awareness and self-conscious partnerships to maintain a productive medical science and innovation engine: 'The public and volunteer communities know virtually nothing about clinical research and the important role that each party plays in the process. These stakeholders and others have limited to no context with which to understand and to easily access quality information about clinical research.'[28] Getz notes that this absence of contextual understanding leads to sluggish responses to recruitment campaigns and declining public trust in the clinical research enterprise, especially in the minority and lower-income communities. A concerted effort to provide a framework for understanding the clinical research enterprise by outlining the roles and responsibilities of the primary research entities, building a generalized knowledge of ethical principles and human subject protections while maintaining a conscientious platform of transparency and disclosure would serve to reestablish a public trust and provide a context for soliciting an informed consent.

Liability, understanding, therapeutic misconception

Liability: A higher legal and moral obligation

Pullman[4], Menikoff[9], Goldfarb[16], Resnik[26], Golec[27], and Mello[29] all detail a higher legal and moral standard for research practitioners. The prevailing Reasonable Person Standard, which obligates practitioners to disclose as much information as any reasonable person in a particular situation would expect to receive, supersedes the Professional Standard, which merely requires disclosure that would approximate the practice of one's peers.

The higher legal and moral standard derives from the investigational nature of the research protocol. In standard therapeutic practice, a patient can reasonably expect to receive generally accepted best standard of care. In a research setting, the participant must abandon this presupposition. It bears repeating that the informed consent is a 'waiver that makes this change of circumstances legitimate.'[9]

As stated earlier, clinical research litigation nearly always involves allegations of inadequate informed consent.[16,26,29] Researchers often respond with a myopic preoccupation on the informed consent document. Documents written with a legal eye trained on liability, however, fail to meet the moral purpose and ironically may undermine legal standing by documenting a process that is woefully inadequate.[4,16,26–28,30]

The moral nature of the consent and the essential particularities of each participant preclude attempts to precisely quantify the information required for adequate understanding.[4] The Reasonable Person Standard, then, does not attempt to quantify information elements but instead translates regulatory language into a dialogue of disclosure tailored to the individual needs and desires of the participant.[9] A golden-rule standard to 'disclose unto others as you would have others disclose unto you' provides a minimal ethical starting point for an adequacy of disclosure that would meet the Reasonable Person

Standard: when in doubt, it is imperative to err on the side of presenting more rather than less.[31]

Researchers must embrace comprehensive informed consent, not from fear of liability, but as a joyful and effective celebration of virtue, integrity, and intrinsic goodness. That is, researchers should ensure adequate consent because it is right, honorable, good, and an expressive appreciation of human dignity.[32] The appropriate posture for soliciting and obtaining informed consent involves treating subjects with a respect that promotes a climate of honesty, transparency, open communication, disclosure, and trust.[26,28]

Documented lack of understanding

Despite the absence of agreement or guidance on how to define or measure understanding, it is clear that research participants demonstrate pervasive misconceptions. Subjects may be unaware that they are even participating in a study or that they may withdraw at any time.[11,16,22] Subjects also demonstrate significant gaps in recall and understanding of treatment-related information.[33,34] More than 70% are unaware of treatment alternatives or the phase of the trial, and nearly 60% are unaware of personal involvement expectations;[22] 33% are unaware of additional risks or discomforts.[11,28] Table 3.2 shows the percentage of participants who were unable to appropriately define clinical research terms.

A major shortcoming in the analysis of participants' understanding is the lack of guidance in establishing a threshold of understanding. That is: What are subjects expected or required to know? What information is absolutely essential? What conspicuous deficiency would disqualify a subject from participation? What are appropriate tools for assessment? What constitutes adequate performance? There is no definitive guidance on how to measure understanding, what assessment tools to employ, or even acceptable terms to describe successful communication of information. This obvious lack of a 'gold standard' is universally acknowledged[8,9,11,12,21,35,36], but does not dissuade researchers from attempting to gauge participant understanding.

Researchers employ a variety of outcome measures to assess understanding from multiple-choice and true/false questions to structured interviews and open-ended questions. Some evaluate understanding at the conclusion of the consent process, while others assess throughout the process. Researchers assess both immediate and delayed recall. Critics argue that although various assessments intend to measure understanding or comprehension, what is actually measured is recall of presented information. There is little agreement on terminology with the terms comprehension, knowledge, understanding, and recall used interchangeably.[11] Although there is a great variety of outcome measures (from written examinations to informal questions), there is a general preference for oral assessments of understanding that include asking

Table 3.2 Percentage of participants who were able to define clinical research terms[17,18]

Term	Percentage able to define term
Concomitant medication	7
IRB	12
Titrate	12
Washout	15
Double-blind	17
Randomly	22
BID, TID, QD	24
Efficacy	33
Investigator	35
Protocol	41
FDA	42
Baseline visit	47
Concurrent medication	47
Sponsor	56

short answer or open-ended questions and allowing participants to describe a process in their own words.[23,35–37] Demonstrable misunderstandings should call not for disqualification but for reeducation, extended discussion, and clarification with repeated assessments for understanding. Any evaluative proposal that would judge or degrade a participant's motivation fails to appreciate the nature of autonomy; 'Bioethics does not demand that patients make "good" or "rational" decisions. Instead the ethical goal of informed consent is to give patients comprehensible information and let them make uncoerced choices. If patients make decisions that others consider irrational, that is their right.'[27] Autonomy embraces the principle that patients voluntarily agree to participate or decline participation according to their own value system. The researchers' obligation is to appropriately inform and allow the potential participant to choose freely.

Therapeutic misconception

A myriad of factors, cognitive and emotional, influence a subject's decision to participate in a clinical trial. A CenterWatch Survey of 749 Volunteers[38] reveals that the highest rated reasons cited for study participation were 'to find a better treatment' (79%), 'to help myself and others' (79%), with the third highest reason 'to receive higher quality medical care' (49%). The survey results underscore the importance of defusing therapeutic misconception for potential study participants.

This survey and the research of many others[11,12,39–42] reveal that subjects consistently exhibit a therapeutic misconception and confuse the dual role of the physician/investigator. Seventy percent of volunteers report that 'in the absence of context, they don't even know what questions to begin to ask' and 14% did not even bother to read the consent document prior to signing it.[28] Although participants overwhelmingly report satisfaction with the informed consent process, 75% of these same responders suffered from therapeutic misconception, 74% failed to recognize that they were receiving non-standard treatment, and 70% did not understand the investigational nature of treatment.[42] Participant naïveté precludes reliable assessment of the adequacy of the process through measures of 'satisfaction.'

Therapeutic misconception is the misunderstanding that research subjects may have that the primary purpose of research is treatment and potentially the 'best treatment' available. Research, by its very nature is investigational. The purpose of research is to evaluate a treatment, device or regimen; its therapeutic value is uncertain. The primary purpose of any protocol, then, is not to treat the patient, but to evaluate the treatment. The purpose is not to study the patient, but to evaluate the outcomes. The patient is the vehicle for evaluating the treatment. This is a crucial distinction. While eradication of therapeutic misconception is not a required element of consent by federal regulation, there is overwhelming consensus that it is a significant ethical issue that should be methodically explored as part of the consent process.[11,12,21,25,41,42] One study concludes that over 60% of research participants suffer from therapeutic misconception.[42]

The point of addressing therapeutic misconception is not to remove all hope of therapeutic effect, but to properly inform potential participants of the intent of the study and emphatically underscore the assertion that there can be no guarantee of therapeutic benefit.

Developing a 'gold standard'

FDA Guidance Sheets differentiate between form and process and include guidance to provide 'adequate' information and opportunity and to 'ensure' comprehension.[43] The regulations and guidelines clearly provide a moral and legal imperative but fail to quantify, qualify, or define assessments of adequacy.

The unanimity of dismay at and remarkable homogeneity of reported deficiencies underscores a pervasive belief about what constitutes adequate consent or understanding. Appropriate consent, according to these presuppositions, essentially includes the content discussed earlier. Conceptual understanding necessarily involves comprehension of the basic vocabulary of clinical research and necessitates specific definition of terms. Additional consensus exists for providing a context for understanding including education regarding the roles of the sponsor, FDA, IRB, investigator, and participant. There is a resounding chorus for defusing therapeutic misconception.

An important finding, one that strongly supports continued research, is that on average no one in any group or demographic correctly answered more than two-thirds of the knowledge questions. There is no 'gold standard' for understanding a protocol. Perfect recall of details of side-effects and procedures at the time of signing the consent form may not be necessary and/or it may not be sufficient. Profiles of responses suggested a distinction between understanding details of a specific research study, principles of research, and one's rights as a participant that may be important for refining measures in future studies.[33]

The development of a gold standard for assessing adequacy of informed consent will involve considerable debate and consideration and encompass both adequacy of disclosure and assessment of understanding. The Nuremberg Code requires capacity, free power of choice, sufficient knowledge and comprehension, and an affirmative decision.[44] The Belmont Report requires information, comprehension, and voluntariness[2], while the Declaration of Helsinki states that subjects must be volunteers and informed participants whose consent is obtained only after the researcher ensures understanding.[45] Morally valid informed consent requires the researcher to fully disclose relevant information, assess competence or capacity to make a decision, and ensure understanding and voluntariness of choice.[11,23,27,37,46]

Although beyond the scope of this chapter, there are several tools (e.g., Standardized Mini-Mental Status Examination [SMMSE], MacArthur Competency Assessment Tool for Clinical Research [MACCAT-CR], Aid to Capacity Evaluation [ACE]) to aid in the assessment of capacity to consent.

Despite the absence of a gold standard, widespread consensus appears evident for support of generalized understanding. An obvious starting point is the basic elements required by federal regulation and discussed in detail earlier: statement of research, risk/discomfort, benefits, alternatives, confidentiality, compensation for research-related injury, contact information, voluntariness. Within this list there are crucial elements, objective statements, and categories with broad latitude. Contact information and confidentiality are objective statements that stimulate little debate or discussion. Compensation for research-related injury is also an objective statement yet one that provokes considerable debate and criticism.[47] Crucial elements include voluntariness and statement of research or the investigational nature of the intervention. Elements with some latitude include treatment alternatives generally and risk/benefit disclosures specifically. Voluntariness distinguishes ethical research from the experiments conducted by Nazi doctors in concentrations camp and as such is preeminent. Full disclosure must satisfy the Reasonable Person Standard and be conscientiously individualized to meet the particular participant's needs and circumstances. Risk assessment and disclosure – what to disclose and how to disclose it – are joint responsibilities of the sponsor, IRB, and investigator.

While there is generalized consensus for ensuring understanding, there exists no universally recognized means of assessment or standard threshold of adequacy. There is strong consensus for open-ended, short-answer questions as a means of assessment with continued re-instruction where deficiencies are exposed and varying thresholds of comprehension for various elements. That is, voluntariness and statement of research (clarifying disparate roles of physician/investigator and therapeutic misconception) must be considered inviolate understanding requirements for participation. Risk analysis may be on a sliding scale with participants required to recall or to be able to locate the primary or top three identified risks. Alternative treatment understanding may be acknowledged with a generalized affirmative participant statement that other options exist outside the protocol. Knowledge of drug classification, preclinical testing, and roles and responsibilities of research entities (sponsor, FDA, IRB, investigator, Contract Research Organization [CRO]) all provide a framework for understanding but would not be mandated as a prerequisite threshold of understanding for participation.

Impact on recruitment, compliance, and retention

Sachs notes that an improved consent process that details risks may potentially lower enrollment rates while at the same time acknowledging the opposing possibility that improved informed consent might actually increase enrollment and retention if the improved process results in a better match between expectations and experience.[48] Golec similarly hypothesizes that value, respect, fully informed consent, and continued support for the participant may enhance compliance and future recruitment.[27] O'Mathiuna concurs; no empirical evidence shows that greater attention paid to informed consent leads to reduced enrollment.[42]

Attention to informed consent might instead improve enrollment. Potential subjects may be impressed by the researchers' openness and honesty. Well-informed participants may be more willing to complete studies, continue with follow-up, or participate in future research. Dropout may be related to participants' belated realization of therapeutic misconception. When this occurs, they may be angry or resentful, causing them to withdraw from the project. Then it will not matter whether the misconceptions arose with the researcher's description or the participants' understanding. This could negatively impact that particular project and have broader implications. People will talk about their bad experiences and 'may contribute to a general perception that researchers treat patients as guinea pigs.'[42]

Leadership

All research practitioners exercise leadership as they set the tone, define and refine the message, and reflect a commitment to ethical conduct and compliance. Values are promoted and uncompromisingly communicated through public statements, actions, policies, and financial decisions.[26] Effective leaders engage in well-coordinated, integrated, and consistent efforts to improve process and deliver quality. Leadership involves continuing education for all stakeholders, modeling openness to lifelong learning and ongoing teaching and sharing.

Communication is an essential priority. Effective communication with potential participants is the conduit for informed consent. Communication with collaborators, subordinates, and IRBs reduces error and in turn protects the rights and welfare of human subjects while defusing potential for litigation.[26,41]

An unremitting commitment to a higher consent standard is a reflection of integrity and inherent goodness: 'The education of patients for the sake of informed consent should be seen as virtuous rather than obligatory and as a result would become more effective and enjoyable.'[27] All stakeholders in the research enterprise would do well to embrace this joyful and virtuous standard.

Additional topics

This final section briefly introduces several consent-related issues: assent by minors, waivers and exceptions to informed consent requirements, and the consent of 'vulnerable subjects', and ends with a few words about impact of the US Health Insurance Portability and Accountability Act (HIPAA) on the informed consent process.

Assent by minors

Consent for a minor's participation in clinical research is normally comprised of the child's assent and the parent's or parents' permission. Although 45 CFR 46 defines assent as 'a child's affirmative agreement to participate in research,' this regulation, as well as 21 CFR 50, does little to help researchers operationalize the concept of assent. The IRB, local laws, as well as the research protocol must be consulted for specific requirements. Numerous authors, among them Erb[49] and Leiken[50], provide useful reviews of the assent/consent issues related to the participation of children in clinical research. Leiken helps with the understanding of issues related to the continuum of cognitive development, the ability of the child to reason, and expression of the child's right and personal volition.[50] Erb discusses various models of consent and proposes several methods of providing understandable information to children.[49]

Regardless of the model chosen, it is useful to remember that assent involves many of the components of consent, namely, the provision of information to the potential research subject, decision making (in this case shared with the parent(s) or legal guardian(s)) and documentation of the 'voluntariness' of the assent. This latter item necessitates consideration of the possibility of dissent by the minor. Under most circumstances, a minor should not be enrolled in clinical trials if they decline the invitation to participate. However, US regulations do allow for an IRB to decide that assent by minors is not required and when a child may be enrolled against their wishes. Specifically, in instances of severely limited capacity or when 'the intervention or procedure involved in the clinical investigation holds out a prospect of direct benefit that is important to the health or well-being of the children and is available only in the context of the clinical investigation.'[51]

Waivers and exceptions

There are several, though relatively uncommon, instances where informed consent requirements may be waived.

US regulations allow for exceptions to the general requirements for informed consent in two instances. In the first, the investigator must certify the existence of several specific items: a life-threatening situation; inability to communicate with or obtain consent from the patient or legal representative; and lack of alternative therapy with an equal chance of success. This same subsection also allows for the President of the United States to waive informed consent requirements prior to administration of an investigational product to members of the armed forces. This controversial section of the US regulations has been vigorously debated.[51]

Waiver of consent in emergency research is specifically addressed in 21 CRF 50.24. An IRB may approve an investigation where prior consent will not be obtained in very specific instances – life-threatening conditions, no acceptable alternative treatment, necessity to conduct the trial to obtain valid safety and efficacy data, or obtaining consent is not feasible. This section continues with a detailed description of information that the investigational plan must contain requirements for the IRB approval and additional methods/ guidelines for protecting the research subject.

ICH E6 also provides guidance, albeit limited, for the conduct of emergency research when prior consent cannot be obtained.[1]

Consent by vulnerable subjects

Respect for persons also requires protection of those who do not possess or are unable to express full autonomy. Although broadly stated, the Declaration of Helsinki provides much to ponder when it states:

> Some research populations are vulnerable and need special protections. The particular needs of the economically and medically disadvantages must be recognized. Special attention is also required for those who cannot give or refuse to give consent for themselves, for those who may be subject to giving consent under duress, for those who will not benefit personally from the research and for those for whom the research is combined with care.[45]

Generally, special protections are owed to those who are unable to understand the information or significance of consent and/or the significance of providing consent. These certainly include – but are not limited to – children, those who cannot read or speak the language of the investigative staff, some with psychological or neurological impairments, prisoners, individuals institutionalized against their will, and those who lack access to medical care outside of the research setting.

HIPAA and informed consent

The Health Insurance Portability and Accountability Act of 1996 (HIPAA) has added a layer of, some would say unnecessary, complexity to the informed consent process. We will leave that judgment to you, the reader. However, it is contrary to US law to collect Protected Health Information (PHI) without a HIPAA authorization in place. But is the HIPAA authorization part of the informed consent? It depends. First, a bit of terminology related to consent and HIPAA. It is important how the documents, the consent, and the HIPAA authorization are assembled. For the purposes of this discussion, a 'complex' document is one in which the HIPAA authorization is imbedded within the text of the consent form; whereas a 'standalone' document is one where the authorization accompanies, but is not part of, the informed consent document; it is a separate form or document. As you are aware, informed consent forms must be approved for use by a properly constituted IRB or IEC. Further, regulations and guidelines require IRB or IEC review of all information to be provided to research subjects. It would seem to follow that IRB review and approval of the HIPAA authorization is required. However, both the DHHS and FDA have said that they will exercise 'enforcement discretion' regarding this requirement.[52] The FDA's notice reads, in part, as follows:

> In order to ensure the continued enrollment of subjects in clinical investigations, and to encourage IRB flexibility with respect to

handling possible backlogs, FDA is announcing its intention to exercise ongoing enforcement discretion with respect to the requirements of Sec. 56.108(a) to the extent that an IRB's written procedures require the review and/or approval of standalone HIPAA authorizations. FDA is exercising this discretion in order to encourage IRBs to permit the continued enrollment of subjects in clinical investigations without IRBs' prior review and approval of standalone HIPAA authorizations ... FDA does not intend to take enforcement actions against IRBs that decide not to review standalone HIPAA authorizations even though the IRB's written procedures would otherwise require this review and/or approval.[52]

Summary

Our current understanding of informed consent has evolved and will continue to evolve. No study of consent should be undertaken without a detailed review of the Nuremberg Code, Belmont Report, Declaration of Helsinki, ICH E6 GCP Guidelines, and applicable laws and regulations. Nor should we ignore the competing goals of the consent process.

Successful, valid consent must be based on a conversation, on interaction between individuals. It is never just a form to be signed. It should not be rushed.

Informed consent is the ethical foundation on which all of clinical research rests.

References

1. International Conference on Harmonisation. *Guidance for Industry: Good Clinical Practice, Consolidated Guidance*, ICH-E6. Geneva, ICH, 1996.
2. National Commission for the Protection of Human Subjects of Biomedical and Behavioral Research [Online]. The Belmont report: *Ethical Principles and Guidelines for the Protection of Human Subjects of Research*. Washington, DC: US Government Printing Office, 1979. Available from: URL:http://ohsr.od.nih.gov/guidelines/belmont.html (accessed December 17, 2009).
3. Steinbrueck S. Was Belmont wrong: A critical analysis of informed consent comprehension; 2008.[Unpublished].
4. Pullman D. Subject comprehension, standards of information disclosure and potential liability in research. *Health Law J* 2001; 9: 113–127.
5. Stephens T, Bryner R. *Dark Remedy: The Impact of Thalidomide and Its Revival as a Vital Medicine*. Cambridge, MA: Perseus Publishing, 2001.
6. Jones JH. *Bad Blood: The Tuskegee Syphilis Experiment*. New York: The Free Press, 1993.
7. Murphy TF. *Willowbrook Hepatitis Studies*. In: *Case studies in biomedical ethics*. Cambridge, MA: The MIT Press, 2004.
8. Flory J, Emanuel E. Interventions to improve research participants' understanding in informed consent for research: a systematic review. *JAMA* 2004; 292(13): 1593–1601.

9. Menikoff J. Obtaining research consent: what tort law can teach us. *Research Practitioner* 2006; 7(5): 159–163.
10. Pensler RL (1993). *Basic IRB Review: Institutional Review Board Guidebook* [Online]. DHHS Office for Human Research Protections. Available from: http://www.hhs.gov/ohrp/irb/irb_chapter3.htm (accessed January 9, 2009).
11. Dunn LB, Jeste DV. Enhancing informed consent for research and treatment. *Neuropsychopharmacology* 2001; 24: 595–607.
12. Agre P *et al.* Improving informed consent: the medium is not the message. *IRB: Ethics and Human Research Supplement* 2003 Sept/Oct; 25(5): S11–S19.
13. Paasche-Orlow MK *et al.* Readability standards for informed consent forms as compared with actual readability. *N Engl J Med* 2003 Feb 20; 348(8): 721–726.
14. Hochhauser M. Concepts, categories, and value judgments in informed consent forms. *IRB: Ethics and Human Research* 2003 Sept/Oct; 25(5): 7–10.
15. Waggoner W, Hochhauser M, speakers. ICF: does one size fit all? [Audio recording]. Association of Clinical Research Professionals Annual Conference, 2003. Windsor, Berkshire, UK (European Office): Association of Clinical Research Professionals.
16. Goldfarb NM. Readable informed consent forms are not optional. *J Clin Res Best Pract* 2005 Sept; 1(9): 1–7.
17. Waggoner WC, Mayo DM. Who understands? A survey of 25 words or phrases commonly used in proposed clinical research consent forms. *IRB: Ethics and Human Research* 1995 Jan/Feb; 17(1): 6–9.
18. Waggoner WC, Sherman BB. Who understands? II: A survey of 27 words, phrases, or symbols commonly used in proposed clinical research consent forms. *IRB: Ethics and Human Research* 1996 May/June; 18(3): 8–10.
19. Padberg RM. The National Cancer Institute's recommendations on informed consent. *SoCRA Source* 2006 Feb; 18–21.
20. Hochhauser M. Why you can't write a consent form at a 6th grade level. *DIA Forum* 2002 Oct; 22–25.
21. Hochhauser M. Reading and understanding are not the same. *Appl Clin Trials* 2000 April 1; 1–9.
22. Brink S. Making informed consent work for all. *J Clin Res Pract* 2006 Dec; 2: 12.
23. Wirshing AD *et al.* Informed consent: assessment of comprehension. *Am J Psychiatry* 1998 Nov; 155: 1508–1511.
24. Beecher HK. Ethics and clinical research. *N Engl J Med* 1966; 69(4): 367–372.
25. Santana VM. Informed consent: an investigator's perspective. *SoCRA Source* 2005 Feb; 21–24.
26. Resnik DB. Biomedical Research litigation: lessons learned from human research litigation. *Research Practitioner* 2006 Jan/Feb; 7(1): 4–11.
27. Golec L. Are you truly informed about informed consent? *Monitor* 2004 Fall; 15–23.
28. Getz K. A public health need: informing and engaging stakeholders on the periphery of the clinical research enterprise. *Research Practitioner* 2005 Jan/Feb; 6(1): 4–8.
29. Mello M *et al.* The rise of litigation in human subjects research. *Ann Intern Med* 2003; 139: 40–46.
30. Wood A *et al.* *The Crisis in Human Participants Research: Identifying the Problems and Proposing Solutions.* Bethesda, MD: National Institute of Health, Department of Clinical Bioethics, September 2002.
31. Sharp SM. Common problems with informed consent in clinical trials. *Research Practitioner* 2004 Aug/Sept; 5(4): 133–137.
32. Davis B. *A Process for Consent: A Conversation.* Unpublished Master's Proposal, George Washington University, 2007.
33. Agre P, Rapkin B. Improving informed consent: a comparison of four consent tools. *IRB: Ethics and Human Research* 2003 Nov/Dec; 25(6): 1–7.
34. Siminoff LA. Toward improving the informed consent process. *IRB: Ethics and Human Research Supplement* 2003 Sept/Oct; 25(5): S1–S3.

35. Goldfarb NM. How well does the average U.S. adult read? *J Clin Res Best Pract* 2005 Sept; 1(9).
36. Hochhauser M. Consent forms: no easy read. *Appl Clin Trials* 2007 May 1.
37. Lavori PW *et al.* Improving informed consent: a duty to experiment. *Control Clin Trials* 1999 April; 20(2): 187–193.
38. McDonald D, Lamberti MJ (2006). *The Psychology of Clinical Trials: Understanding Physician Motivation and Patient Perception* [Online]. Available from: http://www.clinicaltrialstoday.com/2006/10/the_psychology_.html (accessed January 9, 2009).
39. Appelbaum PS *et al.* The therapeutic misconception: Informed consent in psychiatric research. *Int J Law Psychiatry* 1982; 5: 319–329.
40. Appelbaum PS *et al.* False hopes and best data: consent to research and the therapeutic misconception. *Hastings Center Report* 1987; 17(2): 20–24.
41. Motil KJ. Personal leadership protects research subjects. *SoCRA Source* 2005 May; 44: 15–19.
42. O'Mathiuna DP. Therapeutic misconception and research ethics. *Research Practitioner* 2006 May/June; 7(5): 80–88.
43. Food & Drug Administration [Online] (1998). Information Sheet. *Guidance for Institutional Review Boards and Clinical Investigators.* Available from: http://www.fda.gov/oc/ohrt/irbs/faqs.html#Informed%20Consent%20Process (accessed January 9, 2009).
44. Office for Human Research Protections (OHRP) [Online] (2009). *The Nuremberg Code.* Available from: http://www.hhs.gov/ohrp/references/nurcode.htm (accessed January 9, 2009). [Reprinted from *Trials of War Criminals before the Nuremberg Military Tribunals under Control Council Law No.* 10, Vol. 2, pp. 181–182. Washington, DC: US Government Printing Office, 1949.]
45. World Medical Association [Online] (2008). *Declaration of Helsinki: Ethical Principles for Medical Research Involving Human Subjects.* Available from: http://www.wma.net/e/policy/b3.htm (accessed January 9, 2009).
46. O'Mathiuna DP. Informed consent and gene therapy research. *Research Practitioner* 2003 Sept/Oct; 4(5): 180–187.
47. Vasgird DR *et al.* Protecting the uninsured research subject. *J Public Health Manag* 2000; 6(6): 37–47.
48. Sachs GA *et al.* Conducting empirical research on informed consent: challenges and questions. *IRB: Ethics and Human Research Supplement* 2003 Sept/Oct; 25(5): S4–S10.
49. Erb TO *et al.* Permission and assent for clinical research in pediatric anesthesia. *Anesth Analg* 2002; 94: 1155–1160.
50. Leiken SL. Minors' assent, consent, or dissent to medical research. *IRB: Ethics and Human Research* 1993; 15(2): 1–7.
51. Food & Drug Administration. *Protection of Human Subjects*, Title 21 Code of Federal Regulations Part 50.
52. Food & Drug Administration [Online] (2003). *Guidance for Industry: IRB Review of Stand-Alone HIPAA Authorizations under FDA Regulations.* Available from: http://www.fda.gov/ohrms/dockets/98fr/03d-0204-gdl0001.pdf (accessed January 9, 2009).

4

Investigator responsibilities

Jesse Goldman, Michael J. McGraw, and Adam N. George

Physicians have long functioned as investigators on clinical research studies involving human subjects in both the development of new products or therapies and for the assessment of existing treatments.[1] Strategies implemented by industry sponsors to identify qualified investigators have evolved in recent years. Academic medical centers are no longer the exclusive sites for the conduct of cutting-edge clinical research. The pharmaceutical industry has gradually developed a relationship with networks of physicians practicing in private offices in order to perform clinical research studies. In 1991, 80% of pharmaceutical industry funds for clinical research went to investigators in academic medical centers.[2] In 1998, that proportion had dropped by half to 40%. An outcome of this arrangement has been to transform thousands of private physicians into physician–investigators and their patients into patient–subjects.[3] This transformation has caused much debate because of the potential clash of the dual role played by the physician: first as a clinician with obligations to serve the well-being and interests of the individual patient, and second as an investigator whose goal is to further activities that contribute to the development of generalizable knowledge that can be related back to the population as a whole.[4] Although practice settings of investigators are varied, responsibilities of investigators in these environments continue to remain the same.

A principal investigator (PI) is the person responsible for the ethical conduct of a clinical trial at an investigational site. Due to the complexity and/or size of a clinical trial, it is often necessary for an investigator to seek the help of other qualified individuals to assist with the conduct of the study. These individuals are referred to as subinvestigators. They are designated and supervised by the investigator to perform critical trial-related procedures and/or to make important trial-related decisions.[5] It is important to emphasize that while subinvestigators play an important role in the conduct of a clinical trial, the overall responsibility for the conduct of a clinical trial lies in the hands of the investigator.

Table 4.1 Investigator responsibilities

- Proper training and experience in the conduct of clinical research
- Adequate assessment the of the research
- Communication with the Institutional Review Board/Independent Ethics Committee
- Communication with the sponsor
- Supervising the conduct of the investigation
- Responsibility for investigational product
- Proper safety reporting
- Retention of study documents
- Financial disclosure

An investigator has numerous responsibilities in the conduct of clinical trials, which are described in the International Conference on Harmonisation (ICH) E6 Consolidated Good Clinical Practice (GCP) Guidelines and various sections of the United States Code of Federal Regulations (CFR). These responsibilities are listed in Table 4.1.

In the United States, these responsibilities are also listed on FDA Form 1572 (Statement of Investigator), which is signed by the investigator to acknowledge compliance with GCP and accountability for the ethical conduct of a research study. The purpose of this chapter is to describe the responsibilities and obligations of an investigator throughout the conduct of a clinical trial.

Qualifications

It is vital to the success of any clinical trial to select investigators who are well trained and experienced in the conduct of clinical trials. According to regulatory requirements, sponsors are responsible for selecting investigators qualified by training and experience as appropriate experts to conduct clinical trials of an investigational drug.[5,6] See Chapter 5 for additional discussion of the responsibilities of a sponsor.

As proof of training and experience, investigators must provide documentation in the form of an up-to-date curriculum vitae and medical license to the sponsor, the Institutional Review Board/Independent Ethics Committee, and/or the appropriate regulatory authority. The PI must also demonstrate experience with the conduct of clinical trials, training in GCP, and understanding of local regulations pertaining to clinical research. The PI does not need to be a physician; however, in clinical trials that require medical decisions, if the investigator is not a physician, a qualified physician should be listed as a subinvestigator for the trial and should be responsible for all trial-related medical decisions.[5,7] Often, in practice, many sponsors require that the PI be a licensed physician for a clinical trial to ensure proper medical governance.

An investigator must be knowledgeable as a physician in the therapeutic area being studied. An investigator might consider an 'interesting' clinical trial protocol that involves therapeutics or medical management outside of the scope of his or her specialty. Without practical experience in the disease or condition under investigation, the investigator might inadvertently put research subjects at risk. He or she might misinterpret signs and/or symptoms of Adverse Events (AEs) or Serious Adverse Events (SAEs) or not recognize that a subject's clinical condition is worsening, thus jeopardizing the subject's safety and well-being.[8] The investigator must be thoroughly familiar with the appropriate use of the investigational product or device, as described in the protocol, in the current Investigator's Brochure (IB), in the product information, and in other reference documents provided by the sponsor.[5] He or she must also be thoroughly familiar with the potential risks and side-effects of the investigational product found in the IB.[6]

Assessment of the research

Important criteria for a potential investigator are enthusiasm and a true desire to evaluate the research question at hand. It is the driving force of the PI that motivates the performance of colleagues and associates who work with him or her. Without the passion of the study group leader, the trial may fail.[8] Therefore, it is important for the investigator to reasonably consider the protocol and all the information about the investigational product to adequately assess the validity and feasibility of conducting the research.

The first question that an investigator should ask is whether the protocol presents a sound scientific question. The investigator should feel comfortable with the design and hypothesis of the trial and determine whether the investigational product or the study assessments present undue risk to potential research participants.[8] If unsatisfied with the study design or the level of risk to research subjects, the investigator should not agree to participate in the study. A responsible investigator should reject such a study on this basis alone.

Next, an investigator should ask whether he or she has sufficient training and experience in the therapeutic area under study.[8] If the investigator is moving into unfamiliar territory, it may be best to conduct research in a therapeutic area where he or she has experience and knowledge so that prospective research participants are not subjected to unjustified risks. In some cases, it may be possible to suggest to the sponsor a colleague better suited to monitor an individual study.

Lastly, an investigator must decide whether the research study is designed to be compatible with the principle of equipoise. Ethical concerns during a clinical trial arise in human trials when the investigator(s) begin to believe that one arm of the trial is obviously superior to another. Clinical equipoise means that there is genuine uncertainty over whether or not a treatment will be beneficial. Once there is sufficient evidence that a treatment strategy is superior to another, research is usually stopped since clinical equipoise is not met.[9] The concept of equipoise is addressed further in Chapter 6.

Resources and feasibility

Before agreeing to conduct a clinical trial, it is also necessary that the investigator assess the adequacy of resources available to conduct the research. The investigator must determine whether he or she has appropriate support staff and facilities to conduct the study according to the protocol. An inadequate assessment of resources may adversely affect study execution, which, in turn, may compromise the scientific integrity of the research and possibly even the safety of trial subjects. The investigator should have an adequate number of qualified staff and adequate facilities for the duration of the trial to conduct the study properly and safely.[5] A sufficient number of well-trained subinvestigators, study coordinators, study nurses, phlebotomists, administrative staff, and others can assure that the clinical trial is conducted in a timely manner and according to the standards of GCP.

There may also be special facilities or equipment issues to be considered. Investigational drugs and records must be kept in a secure, locked area. Some trials require certain equipment such as a centrifuge, a freezer for storing biological samples, or a source of dry ice for shipping specimens. Blood samples or other specific laboratory tests may be required. An on-site catheterization laboratory, electrocardiogram machine, X-ray machine, or magnetic resonance imaging (MRI) machine may also be necessary for certain studies. All of these issues need to be carefully considered before one agrees to participate in a trial.[8] In most cases, the study sponsor will conduct an evaluation of the site to ensure that it has adequate staff and facilities to conduct the study according to protocol. Chapter 7 provides additional discussion of the resources required to conduct a clinical study and the evaluation of these resources.

In addition, the investigator must allocate sufficient time to oversee the conduct of the trial in order to assure the safety and well-being of study participants. This may be impossible if the PI and coordinators are performing too many studies or are strained by other responsibilities. It is also important that an investigator completes the trial within the period agreed with the sponsor.[5] This is often a function of resources and availability of clinical trial subjects.

Study recruitment

Recruitment and retention of clinical trial subjects is of the utmost importance to the sponsor and the investigator. Simply, data cannot be generated if subjects are not enrolled. The sponsor and investigator will negotiate the number of clinical trial subjects that can be recruited at the site and it is important that both parties are realistic with this estimation. The investigator should be able to demonstrate (e.g., based on retrospective data) a potential for recruiting the required number of suitable subjects within the agreed recruitment period.[5] Sponsors will often provide questionnaires or ask potential investigators to evaluate medical charts in a blinded fashion in order to provide an objective assessment of recruitment capabilities. An investigator should only agree to conduct a study if he or she is able to recruit a sufficient number of patients. Having access to patient data can be helpful, though it is not essential in identifying potential study subjects.

Communication with the Institutional Review Board or Independent Ethics Committee

IRB/IEC Review

An investigator is required to assure that an Institutional Review Board (IRB)/ Independent Ethics Committee (IEC) that complies with regulatory requirements is responsible for the initial and continuing review and approval of the proposed clinical study. The investigator is required to submit to the IRB/IEC for review: the study protocol, written informed consent form (ICF), Investigator's Brochure (IB), subject recruitment materials, and any other written information to be provided to the subjects. Before initiating a clinical study, the investigator must have written and dated approval of these documents from the IRB/IEC.[5] He or she is also required to promptly report to the IRB/IEC all changes in the research activity and all unanticipated problems involving risk to human subjects or other individuals. All amendments or changes to the protocol, ICF, or other materials, must be approved by the IRB/IEC before implementation, except where necessary to eliminate apparent immediate hazards to human subjects.[6] If the IB is updated during the trial, the investigator should supply a copy of the updated IB to the IRB/IEC as soon as possible.[5]

Annual review

The IRB/IEC is responsible for continual review of the trial to determine whether the risks and benefits of the trial have changed due to adverse events or other issues that may arise during the course of the study. The investigator should submit written summaries of the study status to the IRB/IEC annually, or more frequently if requested by the IRB/IEC.[5] See Chapter 8 for a discussion of the responsibilities of an IRB or IEC.

Final report

Upon completion of the trial, the investigator should inform the IRB/IEC of the completion of the study at the site and provide a summary of the trial's outcome.[5] This information may include a summary of the recruitment statistics at the site, a description of the AEs and SAEs, and any additional information that may be relevant to the safety of clinical trial participants.

Communication with sponsor

The primary liaison between the sponsor and the investigator is the clinical research associate (CRA) or site monitor. The investigator should be in frequent contact with the site monitor to provide updates on screening and enrollment and to discuss any issues that may arise during the course of the study.[6] The site monitor will visit the site on a scheduled basis to meet with the investigator and to ensure that the study is conducted according to the protocol and that the investigator is conducting the study according to GCP. See Chapter 7 for additional discussion of the responsibilities of the site monitor.

The investigator should promptly provide written reports to the sponsor on any changes significantly affecting the conduct of the trial, and/or increasing the risk to subjects.[5] Examples include staff changes (study coordinators, subinvestigators, etc.), changes in address or upgrades to the facility, changes in the clinical laboratory where biological samples are analyzed, changes in the IRB/IEC, or any other change that may affect the safety of subjects.

Protecting safety, rights, and welfare of subjects

Informed consent

An investigator must obtain adequate informed consent from potential study participants before conducting any study-related procedures. In obtaining and documenting a subject's informed consent, the investigator should comply with all applicable regulatory requirements, and adhere to GCP and other ethical principles pertaining to informed consent. Prior to the beginning of the trial, the investigator should have the IRB's written approval of the written ICF and any other written information to be provided to subjects. The investigator, or a person designated by the investigator, should fully inform the subject or, if the subject is unable to provide informed consent the subject's legally acceptable representative, of all important aspects of the trial.[5] Before informed consent may be obtained, the investigator, or a person designated by the investigator, should provide the subject or the subject's legally acceptable representative ample time and opportunity to inquire about details of the trial and to decide whether or not to participate in it. All questions about the trial should be answered to the satisfaction of the subject or the subject's legally acceptable representative.[5,10]

The written ICF and any other written information to be provided to subjects should be revised whenever important new information becomes available that may be relevant to the subject's consent. Any revised written informed consent form, and written information, should receive the IRB/IEC's approval in advance of use. All subjects participating in the trial should be informed in a timely manner if new information becomes available that may be relevant to subjects' willingness to continue participation in the trial. The communication of this information to the subject should be documented. Neither the investigator nor the trial staff should coerce or unduly influence a subject to participate or to continue to participate in a trial. No oral or written information concerning the trial, including the written informed consent form, should contain any language that causes the subject or the subject's legally acceptable representative to waive or to appear to waive any legal rights, or that releases or appears to release the investigator, the institution, the sponsor, or their agents from liability for negligence.[5]

Depending on the research setting, an investigator may choose to conduct the informed consent discussion in a group setting. This is often the case in Phase I studies of healthy volunteers. However, this setting may not be appropriate for an open question-and-answer period between the investigator and potential research subjects. See Chapter 3 for a further discussion of the informed consent process.

Medical care associated with a study

During and following a subject's participation in a trial, the investigator should ensure that adequate medical care is provided to a subject for any AEs that occur due to their participation in the research. The investigator is also responsible for informing a subject when medical care is needed for concomitant illnesses that develop or worsen during the course of the study.[5]

It is strongly recommended that an investigator notify the subject's primary physician about the subject's participation in a research study. This should occur if the subject has a primary physician and if the subject agrees to the investigator informing his or her primary physician.[5] It is considered professional courtesy and may be important if the study prohibits the use of certain medications or therapies during the course of the clinical trial. An investigator may choose to send a copy of the protocol to the subject's primary physician so that the primary physician is aware of potential issues that may prevent the prescribing of prohibited medications or therapies. Importantly, the primary physician may help report potential AEs associated with the drug if he or she is aware of the fact that the patient is in a trial. It is the responsibility of the investigator to evaluate and follow up on these potential AEs.

Medical care after study completion

In some cases it may be necessary for the investigator to provide follow-up care after the completion of the study or to refer the subject to another healthcare provider for care. This can be a complicated issue if the patient has a severe or life-threatening disease with few or no approved treatments. There is a often a time between the end of the study and approval of a new drug in which the patient has no alternatives. What therapies will be available to the patient during that time? This is another consideration for the investigator and these issues should be discussed with the sponsor prior to study start. Depending on the therapeutic area and specifics of the protocol, it may also be necessary for the investigator to follow-up on any AEs that may be ongoing at the end of the study.

Supervision of clinical trial conduct

As previously stated, the investigator may delegate responsibilities to other qualified individuals, but the ultimate responsibility for the conduct of the study lies with the investigator. Consequently, the investigator is responsible for supervising the activities of the individuals to whom responsibilities have been assigned. The investigator is required to maintain a list of the appropriately qualified persons to whom he or she has delegated trial-related duties. The investigator should ensure that all persons assisting with the trial are adequately trained and informed about the protocol, the investigational product, and their trial-related duties and functions.[5] This training should be documented appropriately. In order to ensure appropriate supervision of the trial, the investigator should have a detailed plan or standard procedures in place. This plan may include routine meetings to assess the current status of the study and the safety and well-being of the participants; procedures for correcting problems or issues that may arise; regular assessments of staff performance and re-training as necessary; frequent evaluation of the consent process to ensure that subjects are adequately informed; a quality assurance process with regard to Case Report Forms (CRFs) and source documents; and overall compliance with GCP. The overall goal of this plan should be to guarantee that the trial is conducted in accordance with the protocol agreed by the sponsor and the investigator and approved by the IRB/IEC and regulatory authorities, when applicable.

The investigator should not implement any deviation from, or changes to the protocol without agreement by the sponsor and prior review and documented approval from the IRB/IEC of an amendment, except when necessary to eliminate an immediate hazard to trial subjects, or when the changes involve only logistical or administrative facets of the study. The investigator or a designated person (often termed a 'designee') should document and explain any deviation from the approved protocol. As soon as possible, the implemented deviation, the reasons for it, and, if appropriate, the proposed protocol amendment should be submitted to the IRB/IEC, the sponsor and the regulatory authorities, if applicable.[5]

Investigational product

Investigational product accountability and reconciliation

Accountability for the investigational product at the trial site is the responsibility of the investigator.[5] An investigator should administer the investigational product only to subjects under the investigator's personal supervision or under the supervision of a subinvestigator. The investigator is not permitted to provide the investigational product to any person who is not part of the clinical trial.[6] The investigator may assign some or all of the investigator's duties for investigational product accountability at the trial site to an investigational pharmacist or another appropriate individual.[5]

The investigator, a pharmacist, or other appropriate individual should maintain records of the product's delivery to the trial site, the inventory at the site, the use by each subject, and the return to the sponsor or alternative disposition of unused investigational product. These records should include dates, quantities, batch/serial numbers, expiration dates (if applicable), and the unique code numbers assigned to the investigational product and trial subjects. Investigators should maintain records that document adequately that the subjects were provided the doses specified by the protocol and reconcile all investigational product received from the sponsor.[5] If the investigation is terminated, suspended, discontinued, or completed, the investigator should return the unused supplies of the drug to the sponsor, or otherwise provide for disposition of the unused supplies of the investigational product.[6]

Investigational product storage

The investigational product should be stored as specified by the sponsor and in accordance with applicable regulatory requirements.[5] If the investigational drug is a controlled substance, the investigator should take adequate precautions, including storage of the investigational product in a securely locked, substantially constructed cabinet or other securely locked enclosure, with limited access, to prevent theft or diversion of the substance into illegal channels of distribution.[6] If the investigational product is required to be stored under specific environmental conditions, then appropriate accommodations should be made, such as a refrigerator, and documentation of temperature and humidity should be kept, if applicable.

Randomization and blinding

Many clinical trials are randomized and/or blinded. See Chapter 6 for a definition of randomization and blinding. The investigator should make every effort to maintain the blind and follow the randomization scheme in the protocol. Numerous sponsors have moved to some form of interactive voice response system (IVRS) to determine the treatment allocation for a patient. IVRS is an automated telephone system that interacts with callers and gathers information. It accepts a combination of voice telephone input and touch-tone keypad selection and provides appropriate responses in the form of voice, fax, callback, e-mail and other media. IVRS can be used to track the investigational product and subject recruitment at a site. When the investigator receives a shipment, the investigator or designee must call the IVRS to activate the investigational product in the system. The system acknowledges the quantity and expiration date of the investigational product at the site and can assign the investigational product to patients in a randomized fashion. The investigational product label usually includes a code number to maintain the blind and the IVRS will allocate the drug to patients according to this code number.

Also included with the investigational product will be some method for breaking the study blind and revealing the treatment allocated to a patient in the event of a safety issue. Sponsors will often provide an emergency code-breaking envelope or will have a similar mechanism to allow an investigator to break the study blind, if necessary. Sponsors will have a procedure for this process or a description of code-breaking procedures will be included in the protocol. The investigator should follow the trial's randomization procedures, if any, and should ensure that the code is broken only in accordance with the protocol. If the trial is blinded, the investigator should promptly document and explain to the sponsor any premature unblinding (e.g., accidental unblinding, unblinding due to a SAE) of the investigational product.[5]

Investigational product administration

Based on the design of the study and the nature of the investigational product, the investigational product may be administered at the clinical trial site, on an in-patient basis, or it may be provided to the subject to administer at home. If the study medication is taken by the patient at home, the patient may be asked to return any unused study drug and the packaging that accompanied it in order to assess patient compliance with the investigational product. The investigator, or investigator designee should ensure correct administration of the investigational product by each subject. Additionally, follow-up should be provided at appropriate intervals during the trial to ensure that each subject is following instructions properly.[5] Depending on the investigational product and the phase of development, the investigator may be required to observe the patient for AEs shortly after the administration of the study drug. The specific requirements will be described in the study protocol.

Safety reporting

An AE is defined as any untoward medical occurrence in a patient or clinical investigation subject administered a pharmaceutical product and which does *not necessarily* have a causal relationship with this treatment (ICH E2A).[11] SAEs should be reported immediately to the sponsor according to the study protocol. See Chapter 9 for a detailed discussion of the definition of an AE and an SAE. The immediate reporting of SAEs should be followed by detailed, written reports. The immediate and follow-up reports should identify subjects by unique code numbers assigned to the trial subjects rather than by the subjects' names, personal identification numbers, or any other information that may identify the subject. The investigator should also comply with the applicable regulatory requirements related to the reporting of unexpected serious adverse drug reactions to the IRB/IEC. AEs or laboratory abnormalities identified in the protocol as critical to safety evaluations should be reported to the sponsor according to the reporting requirements and within the time periods specified by the sponsor in the protocol. For reported deaths, the investigator should supply the sponsor and the IRB/IEC with any additional requested information such as autopsy reports or terminal medical reports as required and permitted by local regulations.[5] See Chapter 9 for additional requirements for adverse event reporting.

Assessment of causality

Evaluating and assessing AEs is one way that an investigator monitors the safety and well-being of subjects or patients in his or her care. When the PI is assessing AEs, there are many issues to be considered. The determined causal relationship between an AE or SAE and the investigational product affects whether the AE or SAE is reported to the sponsor, the IRB/IEC, and the health authorities in an expedited fashion. It is essential to understand that assessing the causal relationship of an AE is a medical decision, which requires great care. It requires an understanding of the mechanism of action of the investigational product and the disease state being studied. An investigator must be aware of all AEs that are occurring in his or her subjects and must always consider the risk versus benefit. The investigator should be cognizant of the point at which he or she will consider the AEs excessive and discontinue the study. See Chapter 9 for a further discussion of the assessment of causality.

Documentation and record retention

An investigator is required to prepare and maintain adequate and accurate case histories that record all observations and other data pertinent to the investigation on each individual administered the investigational drug or employed as a control in the study. Case histories include the CRFs, supporting source documents such as signed and dated ICFs and medical records including progress notes of the physician, the individual's hospital charts, nurses' notes, laboratory reports, radiological test results, and other diagnostic test results. The case history for each individual should document that informed consent was obtained prior to participation in the study.[6] The investigator must ensure the accuracy, completeness, legibility, and timeliness of the data reported to the sponsor in the source documents, the CRFs, and all required reports. Data reported on the CRF that are derived from source documents should be consistent with the source documents or the discrepancies should be explained and documented as necessary.[5] Any change or correction to a CRF should be dated, initialed, and explained and should not obscure the original entry, to ensure that an audit trail is maintained. This applies to both written and electronic changes or corrections. Sponsors should provide guidance to investigators or the investigator's designated representatives on making such corrections. Sponsors should have written procedures to assure that changes or corrections in CRFs made by sponsor's designated representatives are documented, are necessary, and are endorsed by the investigator. The investigator should retain records of the changes and corrections.[5]

The investigator maintains the trial documents as necessary according to the applicable regulatory requirements. Essential documents are retained until at least 2 years after the last approval of a marketing application in an ICH region and until there are no pending or contemplated marketing applications in an ICH region or at least 2 years have elapsed since the formal discontinuation of clinical development of the investigational product. These documents should be retained for a longer period if required by the applicable local regulatory requirements or by an agreement with the sponsor. It is the responsibility of the sponsor to inform the investigator when these documents no longer need to be retained. The investigator should take measures to prevent accidental or premature destruction of these documents.[5] Investigators are permitted to store study documents locally or at an off-site storage facility. However, it is important that an investigator is able to retrieve the study documents in a timely manner in the event of an inspection by a regulatory authority.

The financial aspects of the trial should be documented in an agreement between the sponsor and the investigator/institution. Upon request of the monitor, auditor, IRB/IEC, or regulatory authority, the investigator should make available for direct access all requested trial-related records including the financial aspects of the trial.[5]

Financial disclosure

The investigator is required to provide the sponsor with sufficient accurate financial information to allow the sponsor to submit complete and accurate certification or disclosure statements in a marketing authorization application. The investigator should update this information if any relevant changes occur during the course of the investigation and for one year following the completion of the study.[6,12] See Chapter 2 for additional discussion of financial disclosures by clinical investigators.

Inspections by health authorities

An investigator should permit authorized health authorities to have access to, and copy and verify any records or reports made by the investigator with regard to the clinical trial under subject to the investigation. The investigator is not required to divulge subject names unless the records of particular individuals require a more detailed study of the cases, or unless there is reason to believe that the records do not represent actual case studies, or do not represent actual results obtained.[6]

Summary

An investigator is responsible for protecting the rights, safety, and welfare of clinical trial subjects under his or her care. When presented with a study protocol, an investigator should carefully consider all aspects of the study and determine whether he or she has adequate interest and resources to conduct the study according to the standards of GCP. Although the duties of an investigator may be delegated to other individuals, the investigator remains ultimately responsible for the ethical conduct of a clinical study.

References

1. Fisher JA. Practicing research ethics: private-sector physicians & pharmaceutical clinical trials. *Soc Sci Med* 2008 June; 66(12): 2495–2505.
2. Bodenheimer T. Uneasy alliance: clinical investigators and the pharmaceutical industry. *N Engl J Med* 2000; 342(20): 1539–1544.
3. Fleischman AR, Klein JE. Clinical research in the private office setting: ethical issues. *Trans Am Clin Climatol Assoc* 2002; 113: 126–136.
4. Levine RJ. Clinical trials and physicians as double agents. *Yale J Biol Med* 1992; 65(2): 65–74.
5. International Conference on Harmonisation [Online] (June 2006). *Guidance for Industry: Good Clinical Practice, Consolidated Guidance*, ICH-E6. Available from: http://www.ich.org/LOB/media/MEDIA482.pdf (accessed December 14, 2008).

6. Food & Drug Administration [Online] (April 2009). *Investigational New Drug Application, Title 21 Code of Federal Regulations Part 312.* Available from: http://www.accessdata.fda.gov/scripts/cdrh/cfdocs/cfcfr/CFRSearch.cfm?CFRPart=312&showFR=1 (accessed November 16, 2009).

7. Food & Drug Administration [Online] (July 2008). *Information Sheet Guidance for Sponsors, Clinical Investigators, and IRBs: Frequently Asked Questions – Statement of Investigator (Form FDA 1572).* Available from: http://www.fda.gov/OHRMS/DOCKETS/98fr/FDA-2008-D-0406-gdl.pdf (accessed December 14, 2008).

8. Lader EW *et al.* The clinician as investigator: participating in clinical trials in the practice setting. *Circulation* 2004; 109: 2672–2679.

9. Freedman B. Equipoise and the ethics of clinical research. *N Engl J Med* 1987; 317: 141–145.

10. Food & Drug Administration [Online] (April 2009). *Protection of Human Subjects. Title 21 Code of Federal Regulations Part 50.* Available from: http://www.accessdata.fda.gov/scripts/cdrh/cfdocs/cfcfr/CFRSearch.cfm?CFRPart=50&showFR=1 (accessed November 16, 2009).

11. International Conference on Harmonisation [Online] (October 1994). *Guidance for Industry: Clinical Safety Data Management: Definitions and Standards for Expediting Reporting,* ICH E2A. Available from: http://www.ich.org/LOB/media/MEDIA436.pdf (accessed November 16, 2009).

12. Food & Drug Administration [Online] (April 2009). *Financial Disclosure by Clinical Investigators. Title 21 Code of Federal Regulations Part 54.* Available from: http://www.accessdata.fda.gov/scripts/cdrh/cfdocs/cfcfr/CFRSearch.cfm?CFRPart=54&showFR=1 (accessed November 16, 2009).

5

Sponsor responsibilities

Donna W. Dorozinsky

The Sponsor of a clinical research study is an individual, group, or company that takes responsibility for the design, management, and financing of the study. This can be an individual, as in investigator-sponsored research; a commercial organization such as a pharmaceutical company or biotechnology company; or a federally funded agency such as the National Cancer Institute. The responsibilities of the sponsor can be retained by the original party or transferred to another organization such as a Clinical Research Organization (CRO). If delegation takes place, then the CRO assumes responsibility, but accountability remains with the original sponsor. Any transfer of responsibility should take place as a written agreement between the two parties. A CRO that assumes a sponsor obligation is required to comply with the local regulatory requirements.[1,2,3]

Quality

Overall responsibility for the quality of the study lies with the sponsor. Through the use of written Standard Operating Procedures the sponsor implements a quality control system to ensure that the trial is conducted and that data is generated, recorded, and reported in compliance with the protocol, Good Clinical Practice (GCP), and local regulatory requirements. It is important that quality control is applied at all steps of the research process.[4] A comprehensive quality system is critical to ensure that the study is conducted in compliance with GCP.

Quality systems

A quality system is a set of checks and balances that helps to ensure the quality of the data and the conduct of the study to standards of GCP. Quality systems include both quality assurance (QA) and quality control (QC). *Quality assurance* is a comprehensive review of processes to assess their compliance with standards and systems of GCP. *Quality control* is data-driven and done in real-time. It is done at the local level and is specific to a particular aspect of the business.

Quality assurance

QA is the cornerstone of success in GCP. The need for quality assurance in studies is increasing as the landscape of clinical research is changing. There are a greater number of studies being conducted at a greater number of investigator sites. The globalization of clinical research into countries without previous experience with GCP has created a need for stronger QA programs in clinical trials. The addition of electronic record keeping has only heightened this need. Sponsor organizations must strive for building quality in trials from the beginning, assuring quality throughout the conduct and establishing an infrastructure that is committed to continuous improvement as a part of the sponsor organization as well as the investigator organization.[5]

Quality control

A QC plan is usually prepared for a specific trial that specifies the standards to which quality control will be measured. Generally it includes the following topics: sampling plan to be used for data QC; data sources to be used at each stage of QC; planned metrics to be documented with acceptable variances; a plan for reporting and distributing results.[1,6]

The site management organization within a sponsor may also develop a QC plan that includes: investigator selection; monitoring; source document verification by the monitor; query resolution; compliance with regulatory regulations to the local area.

Data management QC includes an acceptable standard of error for data transcription. Data QC is performed by an independent person who did not participate in the initial data management activities. Often this is achieved through duplicate data entry, when two individuals enter the same data into the database. Then a variance analysis is performed to identify the percentage of inconsistencies. If the inconsistencies are within the pre-established parameters then the data is accepted. Variance beyond the acceptable level requires additional steps to ensure quality of the final database.

Medical expertise

The sponsor is responsible for designating individuals with appropriate training and qualification who will be responsible for providing guidance and direction on all trial-related medical issues. Since it is important that the physician have experience in the particular therapeutic area being studied, consultants may be necessary. This individual is active in the safety review of data. During early development, this individual is a key member of the team evaluating the safety of the drug being studied and decisions around dose escalation.

Each protocol has a designated medical representative or representatives assigned who will be involved in the study from design to data completion. A medical representative is involved in the review of the study protocol to ensure that the safety of the trial subjects is taken into consideration in the study design. During the conduct of the study, all serious and non-serious adverse events (AEs) are reviewed by a medical representative and pharmacovigilance personnel. As the study progresses and data is entered into the database, a medical representative is available to answer medical questions related to the data. As the study concludes, a medical representative reviews the final report on the trial.

A medically qualified individual is also involved in the review of the Investigator's Brochure. Although it is written by individuals with expertise in each of the content areas, it is often reviewed and edited by a medically qualified person.[4]

Medical representation is critical throughout the development process. A sponsor medical representative is a critical sponsor contact for the investigator and should be available for answering questions related to the conduct of the study. See Chapter 4 for more information about the responsibilities of an investigator.

Study design

The study design is driven by the information that the sponsor desires to obtain. Examples of study designs include parallel design, factorial, dose escalation, dose–response, and drug–drug interaction.[7] The trial is designed by a qualified group of individuals that include representation from biostatisticians, physicians, and clinical pharmacologists. Many factors go into the design of a clinical trial. The key factor is determining the objective of the trial. The primary objective of the trial drives all aspects of the design. The phase of development will also drive the overall study design. Drugs in early development are designed around safety and tolerability, while later phase studies focus on efficacy as well as safety. Other key factors include: sample size; blinding; choice of controls; treatment design; randomization; pharmacokinetics; use of a Data Review Committee and/or Data Safety Monitoring Board; dosages and formulations; and plan for data analysis.[8] Once these factors have been decided, the design can begin to take form. A key component of an effective study design is feasibility. A perfect study design is of no use if the study cannot actually be conducted. It is important that the population selected is actually available, that the inclusion/exclusion criteria are not so stringent as to completely limit enrollment, and that the study is designed to answer the primary objective. The key to a successful study lies in the study design. See Chapter 6 for more information about clinical trial design.

Data management

The clinical data from an investigative site are reported using Case Report Forms (CRFs) that are either paper-based or electronic. This collection of data is managed through a clinical data management system. Data management is critical to accurate reporting of the results of a clinical trial.

Safety data

The management of data related to safety is critical in conducting a study to GCP standards. Safety data drives decision making within the protocol itself and also the development plan of the compound. It is important that standard definitions and terminology are developed for reporting of clinical safety data to create data harmonization. Data harmonization allows for cross-study summarization, which is important when submitting data for regulatory approval.

Electronic data management

Electronic data management is becoming the standard in drug development. Data management must be conducted in a validated environment in order to maintain GCP compliance. Data management is a function that is often out-sourced by sponsors to a CRO. Although this is outsourced, the sponsor organization retains responsibility for ensuring that the data management system is GCP compliant. Electronic data capture (EDC) allows for rapid decision making, especially in trials that include adaptive design. Turnaround time for data review when using EDC is significantly reduced and the quality of data is higher, allowing for more aggressive drug development timelines and higher-quality decision making. Data is available in real time, which allows for much quicker decision making based on actual data. Data queries can be generated immediately, which results in cleaner data being readily available for decision making.

It is important that the sponsor place controls over how the system is utilized. This is best achieved through Standard Operating Procedures (SOPs). SOPs should include database access processes that define level of access, control of access, and training required prior to using the system. A list of individuals who are permitted to access the system must be maintained. Processes for database lock and archiving should also be defined. Well-defined processes are critical to all data management systems and to maintaining GCP compliance.

Record keeping

Study records must be maintained in accordance with local regulatory requirements for the region in which the product is approved. Sponsors should define the standard for record retention and formally advise all investigators of this standard. If a sponsor permanently discontinues development of a compound then they should advise all investigator sites and regulatory authorities.[4] This notification should be done in writing. Essential files should be retained for at least two years beyond final regulatory submission or longer if required by local regulatory authorities. For studies that do not involve regulatory submissions, files should be retained for at least five years or longer if required by local regulatory authorities. Any destruction of trial documentation should be documented and signed by the individual destroying the files.[9]

It is expected that the sponsor will make all records related to the clinical investigation available to the regulatory authorities upon request. Regulatory inspections often take place as part of the approval process.

Essential study documents

A Trial Master File is maintained by the sponsor to allow for the evaluation of both the conduct of the trial and the quality of the trial. It is comprised of essential study documents that demonstrate that the trial was conducted to standards of GCP. This master file is the foundation of the clinical trial audit.[10]

Trial master files are established at both the sponsor and investigator sites. Essential study documents are grouped into three sections: before the trial starts, during the conduct of the trial, and after completion of the trial. The majority of documents in the investigator's file are duplicated in the sponsor file. The study monitor is responsible for ensuring that the site file is complete at the end of the study. See Chapter 7 for a description of the responsibilities of a site monitor.

Before the trial begins

The trial master file is established at the beginning of the trial as soon as documents become available. The Investigator's Brochure (IB) is a part of the file and should be updated at least annually. It includes documentation of the scientific and clinical information about the investigational product. A copy should be provided to anyone involved in investigational product accountability. All signed protocols, amendments, and CRFs are maintained by both the sponsor and investigator. Any information that is given to the subject is included in the file, along with evidence of approval by an Institutional Review Board (IRB) or Independent Ethics Committee (IEC).

Copies of all signed agreements are retained by both parties. This includes agreements between the sponsor and CROs, between sponsor and investigator/institution, and between CROs and investigator/institution. This serves as evidence of agreed responsibilities. All IRB/IEC communications and approvals are included along with the composition of the reviewing ethics committee. This serves as evidence that the committee functions within the scope of GCP. A copy of the curriculum vitae (CV) provides evidence of the training and experience of the investigator and subinvestigators. Normal values and reference ranges for all tests and procedures are also retained. These documents are updated during the conduct of the study if any changes occur. Evidence of certification and validation of tests and assays is retained as evidence of data quality. The sponsor retains validation documentation for any assays that are developed specifically for the trial. Samples of labels for investigational product, certificate of analysis, instructions for handling, and copies of all shipping documentation are retained by the sponsor as evidence of compliance with GCP labeling requirements. Blinded studies should include procedures for breaking the blind. The master randomization list is retained as evidence that the randomization process was in compliance. Pre-trial monitoring and trial initiation reports are retained as evidence that the trial has been reviewed with the investigator and investigator's staff. It is acceptable to combine these two visits into one.[4]

Active trial conduct

Any revisions that are made to the above documents once the trial has started are retained in addition to the original documents. CVs for any new investigators or subinvestigators are added. All monitoring reports are retained by the sponsor as evidence that monitoring was conducted in compliance with GCP. Any communication by the monitor with the site is retained as evidence that the investigator has been kept appraised of all findings and outstanding issues. All safety-related communications are retained, including communications related to serious adverse events (SAEs). This includes information received from the investigator site, notification to all investigators of SAE information from other sites, and all communications with regulatory authorities and IRBs related to safety findings.[6]

After trial completion

The sponsor retains all documentation related to destruction or return of investigational product. Unused drug must be accounted for in drug accountability documentation. If an audit is conducted at the end of the study, a copy of the audit certificate is retained by the sponsor. The final monitoring report for all investigator sites documents that all activities related to study close-out have been performed. All documentation related to randomization is part of the file, including any decoding of randomization that has occurred. When the final study report is issued, this completes the trial master file.[10]

At the conclusion of the trial, this master file is archived in a manner that allows rapid retrieval of documents in the event of an audit or inspection.[4] Archiving of study files is done under conditions that ensure that documents remain legible. Sponsors should audit vendors of off-site storage facilities to ensure that document storage is in alignment with the sponsor's standards and GCP.[6]

Safety reporting

Safety evaluation of a drug is the responsibility of the sponsor from early development through post-marketing. Safety is not something that is proven. It requires continuous evaluation through the life cycle of development through post-marketing. The sponsor is the individual most qualified to analyze safety information and communicate it to all involved parties.[11] Complying with GCP, it is the sponsor's responsibility to ensure that safety information is communicated to all parties involved in the research of the drug. This includes regulatory bodies, investigators, ethics committees, and research participants. Guidance for reporting of AEs is given by the individual regulatory bodies. Sponsors should have SOPs in place that are in alignment with the local regulatory agency reporting requirements. It is expected that sponsors keep detailed documentation of all AEs reported by investigators[3] and promptly review all safety data received from investigators.[12] Methods of communication include the IB, investigator letters, regulatory notices, and amendments to the informed consent document. See Chapter 9 for further discussion of safety reporting and pharmacovigilance.

Investigator's Brochure

The Investigator's Brochure (IB) is written by the sponsor and includes both the clinical and non-clinical information on the investigational product that is relevant to human testing. It is also used to communicate the known or anticipated risks or reactions to the drug, to the investigators. It communicates data from previous testing in both animals and humans. The IB is a resource for the investigator in understanding potential risks to humans involved in research. This information can be used by the investigator to write the safety portion of the informed consent document. It is also submitted to the regulatory agencies as part of the initial regulatory submission. It is updated annually by the sponsor to include any new information regarding the safety of the drug. It is also given to the ethics committee that reviews the protocol as an aide in making an unbiased risk–benefit assessment of the appropriateness of the proposed trial.

The IB content is guided by GCP and includes a summary of non-clinical studies with information regarding species, dosing, systemic distribution, and results. The results summary should include the nature, frequency, severity, and intensity of toxic effects with further description of timing, reversibility, and duration of effects. It also includes a summary of the most important findings from non-clinical pharmacology, pharmacokinetics, and drug metabolism in animals and toxicology. Data associated with the effects in humans is presented as a thorough discussion of the known effects in humans. Important safety information includes pharmacokinetics and product metabolism in humans and safety and efficacy. It includes a description of the possible risks and AEs that might be expected during the study. In addition, the IB should include a description of marketing experience with the drug in other countries where the drug has been approved. A summary of data and guidance for the investigator provides a discussion of the data, both clinical and non-clinical, and summarizes the available information about the drug under study.[4]

Investigator letters and safety reports

The sponsor should notify all investigators of all unexpected AEs (not presented in the most recent IB) as soon as possible. Notifications are submitted to the investigators as written summaries of the event. The written report should include an analysis of the significance of the event. The investigator is expected to review all reports and determine whether a change in the informed consent is warranted based on the information presented. In addition, the investigator provides a copy of the information to the ethics committee approving all active protocols for that drug. If a central ethics committee has been contracted by the sponsor, then the sponsor may submit the information directly to the central ethics committee. It is generally not expected that the investigator would submit it a second time.[12]

Post-marketing reporting

Sponsors are expected to continue to report post-marketing unexpected safety findings to regulatory authorities. Unexpected safety findings are those SAEs that are reported to the sponsor but do not appear in the labeling of the approved drug product. These events may be identified through scientific journals, presentations, or direct reporting, or through post-marketing trials.[13] Sponsors should have written procedures for identifying and reporting such events. This includes events that occur as a result of continued research on a drug after initial approval has been given. It is anticipated that with the increasing requirements of registering clinical trials, regulatory authorities will examine trials on approved drugs with closer scrutiny.

In addition, Periodic Safety Update Reports (PSURs) are issued by the sponsor. The main purpose of a PSUR is to summarize and evaluate the safety data for a specific period, to determine whether it is in agreement with previously reported information, and to provide an update to the clinical program. It is especially useful in keeping the public advised of new or trending safety issues. It is prepared for drugs held under an Investigational New Drug Application (IND) as well as marketed drugs.[14]

Monitoring for safety

Data and Safety Monitoring Plans (DSMPs) are an important component of planning and demonstrating compliance with safety requirements. The DSMP serves as a guide to individuals responsible for the monitoring the study. A key aspect of this plan is safety monitoring. Table 5.1 provides a listing of the potential components of the DSMP. Different members of the study team may assume responsibility for different tasks associated with the safety of the study. Responsible parties may include the Principal Investigator, the safety monitor, an independent physician, or Data Safety Monitoring Board.[15]

Data Safety Monitoring Board or Data Monitoring Committee

The purpose of the Data Safety Monitoring Board (DSMB) or Data Monitoring Committee (DMC) is to protect participant safety and to give credibility and validity to the results of the study. Trials sponsored by government agencies in the USA and Europe have been using DSMBs for many years. Federal guidelines indicate the need to establish independent monitoring boards for multi-site clinical trials where the study interventions entail potential risk to participants. This oversight is different from that provided by an IRB/IEC.[16] The DSMB assesses the progress of a study and subsequently recommends whether to continue the trial, modify the protocol, or stop the study altogether. The DSMB functions with written operating procedures and documents all meetings. It is generally appointed by the sponsor with qualified representatives from outside of the organization. The DSMB evaluates the data at regular intervals and makes recommendations regarding the continuation of the study. If data suggests increased risk to any group of subjects, changes are made to the trial to address these risks. The DSMB has a critical

Table 5.1 Potential elements of a Data Safety Monitoring Plan

- Safety data parameters
- Timing of review
- Individual responsible for review
- Safety rules for discontinuing subject

role in conducting the study to the standards of GCP and ensuring the rights and well-being of study participants.

Investigator selection

Investigator selection is the responsibility of the sponsor. Sponsors should have in place a GCP-compliant process for selection of qualified investigators based on education, training, and experience. It is also critical that the investigator has the resources and infrastructure to conduct the study in accordance with the sponsor's requirements and standards of GCP. The investigator should have an opportunity to review the IB and protocol prior to making a commitment to conduct the study. Generally the sponsor or sponsor representative conducts an initial site assessment to confirm that the investigator is appropriate for the conduct of the study once the investigator expresses an interest in serving as an investigator site. The sponsor confirms that the investigator has proper GCP training, experience in conducting clinical research trials, access to an adequate sample of subjects who potentially qualify for participation, and an infrastructure that can adequately resource the conduct of the study. Once this has been confirmed, then the sponsor and investigator enter into a formal agreement to conduct the study as outlined in the protocol.[4]

Investigational product

Manufacturing, packaging, labeling, and coding of the Investigational Product (IP) is the responsibility of the sponsor.[4] The sponsor should ensure that adequately packaged drug and placebo supply are available for the life cycle of development. Packaging of the IP is relative to the phase of development. Early in development, the drug supply may be packaged and shipped as bulk. This is especially the case for single-center early Phase I studies. Later in development, the IP is usually packaged for a single subject. Timing of shipment of IP is determined by local regulation; however, at a minimum, a filing with the local regulatory agency is required.[4]

The sponsor must ensure that the Principal Investigator and other key study staff members (e.g., study coordinator, pharmacist) have received adequate training on IP, IP storage conditions, and expectations regarding drug accountability. This facilitates investigator compliance with GCP requirements of IP accountability.

Key sponsor investigational product responsibilities

The commitment to GCP requires that the sponsor ensure that IP is available at the site for the start of the study. Adequate time should be given to the site to prepare the drug for administration. All records relative to the handling of the IP should be maintained as part of the Trial Master File. There should be a system in place for retrieval of IP for purposes of product recall, study completion, or expired IP. In addition, the sponsor should maintain a system for drug destruction and documentation of drug destruction. Stability testing should be conducted by the sponsor to ensure that all IP used in the study is in compliance with stability requirements. Every effort should be made to ensure stability of IP under conditions of administration. For example, if IP is to be given as an IV infusion, there should be evidence of stability with the reconstitution solution and administration supplies. Local regulations may require the retention of drug samples for bioavailability and bioequivalence studies. The sponsor should make arrangements with an outside party to retain these samples and ensure access to these samples if required by the local regulatory agency.

Supplying investigational product to the investigator sites

The IP is not supplied to the investigator site until the sponsor has received all documentation as specified by the local regulatory agencies. This may include a favorable opinion from an IEC or IRB approval, financial disclosure information, and signed regulatory commitments by the investigator.

For studies that require special drug preparation activities prior to administration of the drug, a detailed set of instructions should be given to the investigator site. The site should be given adequate time to review these documents to ensure that information is clear and understood. The sponsor should confirm that written procedures are in place for documenting receipt, storage, handling, and return of supply at the investigator site. The sponsor should also maintain copies of all shipping and receiving receipts.[4] These documents allow for the re-creation of study activities and ensure evidence of compliance with standards of GCP.

Blinding of investigational product

Blinding of the IP occurs throughout development. A double-blind study is one in which both the investigator and the subject do not know which study drug the subject is receiving. Generally the different study drugs look exactly the same. The protocol should contain directions for breaking the blind should it become necessary in the safety management of the subject. All steps in breaking the blind should be documented and a system should be in place at the investigator site to ensure that only the blind for the one subject is broken. During study initiation, the investigator should be trained on the procedure for breaking the blind and the monitor should ensure that site procedures will adequately protect the blind of the study and prevent undetectable breaking of the blind.

Labeling and packaging of investigational product

Labeling of drug supply is determined by local regulation. The sponsor determines the storage temperature and conditions of the IP on the basis of drug stability data available. If special storage conditions are required, then the sponsor confirms that the investigator can maintain these storage conditions. Storage conditions should be monitored to ensure compliance. It is the sponsor's responsibility to inform all parties (investigator, pharmacist, and monitors) of special storage or temperature requirements.[4] The IP should be properly labeled to ensure that the right drug is given to the right subject at the right time.

Drug accountability

The investigator must only administer drug to subjects who qualify for and are enrolled in the study for which the drug is authorized.[1] Through regular monitoring visits, the sponsor ensures that the investigator is in compliance with this requirement. At the conclusion of the study, the unused IP is returned to the sponsor. The sponsor may elect to have the investigator destroy the IP. In such circumstances, clear documentation of the destruction is required. Destruction should be performed in such a way as to prevent the risk of exposure to humans.[1]

Registration of clinical trials

In 2005, the International Committee of Medical Journal Editors required that a clinical trial must be posted in an acceptable registry prior to initiation in order for the trial to be considered for publication. In 2007, the Food and Drug Administration Amendments Act (FDAAA) required that all clinical trials be registered through the National Institutes of Health clinical trial registry at www.clinicaltrials.gov. While this is similar to WHO requirements, the FDAAA requires a greater level of detail. It applies to any 'controlled clinical investigation other than Phase I that is subject to section 505 of the Federal Food, Drug and Cosmetic Act or to section 351 of this Act.'[17] The sponsor is responsible for posting the information unless the investigator is so specified in an agreement and also the investigator has the ability to publish the clinical trial results.

Reporting of clinical trial results

The FDAAA also required the registration of clinical trial results for drugs and devices, both approved and unapproved. These results must be made publicly available through the internet. It is not clear how this regulatory requirement will fully impact future standards of GCP; however, it is clearly a first step in making this information accessible to the lay public.[18]

Clearly this aspect of clinical research is changing at a rapid rate and it is the sponsor's responsibility to remain informed of local regulatory requirements regarding reporting of clinical trial results. See Chapter 10 for additional information regarding clinical trial registration and reporting.

Summary

The sponsor retains ultimate responsibility for ensuring that the study is conducted according to the standards of GCP. The sponsor is responsible for the oversight of the trial at the investigative site and also the study design, monitoring of the trial, and reporting of the clinical trial data. Compliance is achieved through processes that are in alignment with local regulatory requirements. It includes the availability of medical expertise, good study design, timely evaluation and reporting of safety data, study documentation, IP accountability, and reporting of results. The eventual approval of the compound to market is rooted in the sponsor's compliance to the standards of GCP.

References

1. Food & Drug Administration [Online] (April 2009 Apr. *Investigational New Drug Application, Title 21 Code of Federal Regulations Part 312.* Available from: http://www.accessdata.fda.gov/scripts/cdrh/cfdocs/cfcfr/CFRSearch.cfm?CFRPart=312&showFR=1 (accessed November 16, 2009).
2. European Commission. *Commission Directive of European Communities.* 2005/28/EC. Official Journal of the European Union L 91/13.
3. European Commission. *Directive 2001/20/EC of the European Parliament and of the Council of 4 April 2001 on the approximation of the laws, regulations and administrative provisions of the Member States relating to the implementation of good clinical practice in the conduct of clinical trials on medicinal products for human use.* Official Journal of the European Communities L 121/35.
4. International Conference on Harmonisation [Online] (June 2006). *Guidance for Industry: Good Clinical Practice, Consolidated Guidance, ICH-E6.* Available from: http://www.ich.org/LOB/media/MEDIA482.pdf (accessed December 14, 2008).
5. Lepay DA [Online] (2001) *GCP, Quality Assurance, and FDA.* Available from: http://www.fda.gov/oc/gcp/slideshows/lepay2001/SQAWeb.ppt (accessed May 5, 2007).
6. Valania M (2006). Quality control and assurance in clinical research [Online]. *Applied Clinical Trials Online.* Available from: http://appliedclinicaltrialsonline.findpharma.com/appliedclinicaltrials/CRO%2FSponsor+Articles/Quality-Control-and-Assurance-in-Clinical-Research/ArticleStandard/Article/detail/310811 (accessed May 6, 2009).
7. International Conference on Harmonisation (ICH). *Guidance for Industry: General Considerations for Clinical Trials,* ICH-E8. Geneva: ICH, 1997.
8. Spilker B. *Guide to Clinical Trials.* Baltimore: Lippincott, Williams and Wilkins, 1991: 7.
9. O'Donnell PA. New GCP bible is born. *Applied Clinical Trials* 2005 Jun 5.
10. O'Donnell PA. Checking in on children, checking up on files. *Applied Clinical Trials* 2002 Aug 1.
11. Office for Human Research Protection, Department of Health and Human Services. *Guidance on Reviewing and Reporting Unanticipated Problems Involving Risks to*

Subjects or Others and Adverse Events. Washington, DC: Office for Human Research Protection, Department of Health and Human Services, January 2007.

12. *Guidance for Clinical Investigators, Sponsors, and IRBs Adverse Event Reporting – Improving Human Subject Protection, Draft Guidance* [Online] 2007. Available from: http://www.fda.gov/downloads/RegulatoryInformation/Guidances/UCM126572.pdf (accessed February 12, 2010).

13. Food & Drug Administration. *New Drug Application, Title 21 Code of Federal Regulations Part 314.*

14. International Conference on Harmonisation (ICH). *E2F Development Safety Report.* Geneva: ICH, June 2008.

15. White S *et al.* Monitoring the monitors. *Applied Clinical Trials* 2007 Sep: 52–60.

16. National Institutes of Health (NIH). *Policy for Data and Safety Monitoring.* Bethesda, MD: NIH, June 1998.

17. Food and Drug Administration Amendments Act of 2007 [Online]. Available from: http://frwebgate.access.gpo.gov/cgi-bin/getdoc.cgi?dbname=110_cong_public_laws&docid=f:publ085.110 (accessed February 12, 2010).

18. DeAnglis C *et al.* (2007). *Is This Clinical Trial Fully Registered? A Statement from the International Committee of Medical Journal Editors* [Online]. Available from: http://www.icmje.org/clin_trialup.htm (accessed June 4, 2008).

6

Clinical trial design

Steven Gelone and Patrick Scoble

Introduction

Clinical trials represent the most critical and important part in development of investigational drugs. According to the FDA, the clinical data and analyses generated from these studies account for up to 80% of the standard New Drug Application (NDA) for a New Molecular Entity (NME).[1] It is the most complex, most time-consuming, and most expensive part of the drug development process. A clinical trial requires the coalescence of several parts that begins with a sponsor undertaking the responsibility for funding the trial, and maintaining the legal and regulatory responsibilities associated with such an undertaking. Added to this is the commitment of the research subjects and the health care professionals; the physicians, nurses, pharmacists, study coordinators who participate in the study and, ultimately, delve into whether a new experimental drug is safe and effective.

What is clinical research?

In 1999, the American Medical Association (AMA) and the American Association of Medical Colleges (AAMC) Task Force on Clinical Research convened a clinical research summit. The output of this gathering was a national call to action that included a working definition for clinical research that states that clinical research is

> a component of medical and health research intended to produce knowledge essential for understanding human diseases, preventing and treating illness, and promoting health. Clinical research embraces a continuum of studies involving interaction with patients, diagnostic clinical materials or data, or populations, in any of these categories: disease mechanisms; translational research; clinical knowledge; detection; diagnosis and natural history of disease; therapeutic interventions including clinical trials; prevention and health

promotion; behavioral research; health services research; epidemiology; and community-based and managed care research.[2]

In the Code of Federal Regulations (45 CFR 46), research is defined as a systematic investigation, including research development, testing, and evaluation, designed to develop or contribute to generalizable knowledge. Activities that meet this definition constitute research for purposes of this policy, whether or not they are conducted or supported under a program that is considered research for other purposes. For example, some demonstration and service programs may include research activities.[3]

Historical perspective on clinical research

The first clinical trials were conducted in 1747 on board the *Salisbury*, a British Navy vessel at sea with 12 seamen who were critically ill with scurvy. An officer and surgeon named James Lind evaluated six potential cures for scurvy and rapidly came to the conclusion that the daily consumption of citrus fruits would bring the seamen back to health in six days.[4] In the late nineteenth century, Dr. Robert Koch published the 'Koch postulates,' which were designed to establish a causal relationship between a microbe and disease.[5] The twentieth century brought with it amazing advances in the medical sciences, the establishment of medical colleges in Europe and the USA, and the discovery of such drugs as penicillin and insulin. In 1910, Abraham Flexner, a noted medical educator, wrote that 'research can no more be divorced form medical education than can medical education be divorced from research.'[6] Like many advances, progress in clinical research also brought with it troubling events, including human experimentation by the Nazis and the Tuskegee syphilis experiments as discussed in Chapter 1. These events led to the development of several key measures to insure the ethical conduct of clinical research including the Nuremberg Code, the Harris–Kefauver amendment to the Food, Drug and Cosmetic Act, the Declaration of Helsinki, and the Belmont Report. Implicit in the conduct of all clinical research are ethical principles and integrity, which are discussed in greater detail in Chapter 1 and Chapter 3 of this book. The remainder of this chapter will focus on clinical research involving drug products intended for use in humans.

Why is clinical research needed?

Given the uncertain nature of diseases and the potentially large variation that exists in biological systems and measures, it is extremely difficult on the basis of uncontrolled observation to determine whether a new treatment or intervention makes a difference to a patient's outcome. In addition, a true risk-versus-benefit analysis cannot be conducted outside the context of a controlled situation. The randomized, controlled trial is considered the gold

Table 6.1 Types of evaluations of medicines

- Safety
- Efficacy
- Pharmacokinetic/pharmacodynamic
- Mechanism of action
- General population
- Clinical methodology
- Clinical pharmacology
- Post-marketing

standard in establishing the effects of a therapeutic intervention, especially when the level of uncertainty about its efficacy makes a trial both ethical and practical. Although the controls that are sometimes employed in clinical research may not exactly mimic clinical practice, they do provide a standardized manner in which to evaluate the safety and effectiveness of interventions to treat or prevent disease. The bulk of observational associations sought out in clinical research are inconclusive, which leads to the formation of clinical trials. Randomized clinical trials determine the effectiveness of the independent variable factor within the study. These studies should be performed until enough data are available to suggest the benefits of one treatment, but not so much that providing treatment in one arm of a study would mean putting those in the other treatment arm at risk with an inferior agent. The types of evaluations of medicines or interventions are outlined in Table 6.1.

The phases of drug development

The development of drug products is generally divided into four phases, Phases I to IV. Phase I studies are exploratory clinical research designed to evaluate the safety of new medicines to determine whether further investigation is appropriate. Phase I studies involve the first administration of a new therapy to humans (first-in-human studies) and are often conducted in normal, healthy subjects. In addition to evaluating safety, Phase I studies are commonly designed to describe the clinical pharmacology of a new drug. They may evaluate single- versus multiple-dose exposure, establish a maximum tolerated dose (MTD), describe drug–drug or drug–food interactions, or evaluate the pharmacokinetics of a drug in special patient populations such as those with renal insufficiency. Phase I investigations are conducted throughout the development life cycle of a drug, the earliest of which evaluate safety and pharmacokinetics, while drug–drug interaction studies and special patient population studies may be conducted later in the development cycle.

Phase II studies are the first attempt to evaluate the safety and efficacy of a drug in patients *with the disease* to be diagnosed, treated, or prevented.

The overall objectives for Phase II evaluations are to acquire information on dose–response relationship, estimate the incidence of adverse reactions, and provide additional insight into the pathophysiology of disease and the potential impact of new therapy. Some have divided Phase II studies into Phase IIa, which comprises small, pilot-type studies, and Phase IIb, which comprises larger studies and sometimes what can be considered a pivotal trial (key studies used for application to regulatory authorities). Regardless of whether termed Phase IIa or IIb, this phase of clinical research often evaluates dose–response or different patient types (e.g., young versus old or different ethnicities).

Phase III studies are considered the definitive evaluation of a new therapy to determine the safety and efficacy of new medicines in patients with the disease to be diagnosed, treated, or prevented. These clinical investigations most commonly compare a new therapy with the standard of practice at the time and involve large numbers of patients, including special patient populations. A standard of therapy may not exist, in which case, a placebo would likely be used as the comparator. Phase III studies are often called 'pivotal' or 'registration trials' in that they are the clinical research backbone of a NDA or Biologics License Application (BLA) to the Food and Drug Administration (FDA) and will ultimately provide the basis for labeling of a new medicine. Phase IIIb studies are clinical trials conducted after the submission of an NDA or BLA and may supplement earlier studies and add new information to the labeling of a medicine.

Phase IV studies are trials conducted after a medicine has been approved and marketed. These studies monitor the use of a new therapy in clinical practice and are designed to gather additional information on the impact of a new therapy on the treatment of disease, the rate of use of a new therapy, and a more robust estimate of the incidence of adverse events of a new therapy. Phase IV trials are post-marketing studies and may be required by a regulatory authority as a condition of approval of a new product. Phase IV research can be observational in nature and is often not as well controlled as Phase I–III investigations. A summary of the phases of the drug development life cycle is present in Figure 6.1.[7]

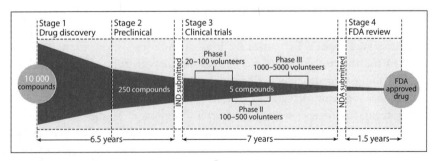

Figure 6.1   The drug development life cycle.[7]

Where does clinical research begin?

All clinical research begins with an unanswered question and the development of a concise and specific primary objective. The objective is the springboard for all of the analysis to occur from the data generated from the clinical research study. Although one can theoretically change the primary objective of a clinical research study after initiation, this usually results in major problems with analysis and interpretation of the data obtained, as well as the acceptability of the data by the medical community. As such, it is critical that prior to initiating a clinical research study one invests the time upfront to explore and develop a primary objective that will allow for the most robust analysis to occur.

Critical concepts in clinical research

The two fundamental aspects of all clinical research are whether or not the results are valid and generalizable. The most compelling evidence in research is the ability to replicate the outcome of an investigation. As not all studies undergo replicate analysis, one should critically evaluate the study design and analysis utilized as a surrogate marker of the validity of a study. If one concludes that a study result is valid, it is equally important to consider whether the findings of the study are generalizable to multiple clinical practice settings. Again, replication of a study is very helpful in this assessment, but often is not conducted. In the absence of a replicate study, one should evaluate the inclusion and exclusion criteria utilized in the clinical study to assess the generalizability of the results. Researchers from McMaster University have developed a series of questions that are useful in interpreting the results of clinical research studies. These questions can be found in Table 6.2.[8]

Approaches to the design of clinical research studies

As noted above, the design of a clinical study is critical to the analysis, interpretation, validity, and generalizability of clinical research. Although an in-depth review of statistical approaches to clinical trial design and all of the permutations a clinical research study can take on are beyond the scope of this text, the following represents an overview of the approaches to clinical research design.

Clinical research design can be divided into one of a couple of broad categories: retrospective versus prospective studies and those involving a single group versus multiple groups. In short, retrospective studies evaluate events that occurred in the past and as such are limited by the data that were collected. As a result, retrospective studies are unable to definitively answer research questions. Although these limitations are a reality, retrospective studies are easier to conduct, usually require less resources and time than

Table 6.2 Interpretation of clinical trial results[8]

Are the results of the study valid?

Primary guides

Was the assignment of patients to treatments randomized?

Were all patients who entered the study properly accounted for at its conclusion?

Was follow-up complete?

Were patients analyzed in the groups to which they were randomized?

Secondary guides

Were patients, clinicians, and study personnel blinded to treatment?

Were the groups similar at the start of the trial?

Aside from experimental intervention, were the groups treated equally?

What were the results?

How large was the treatment effect?

How precise was the treatment effect (confidence intervals)?

Will the results help me caring for my patients?

Does my patient fulfill the enrollment criteria for the trial? If not, how close is the patient to the enrollment criteria?

Does my patient fit the features of a subgroup analysis in the trial report? If so, are the results of the subgroup analysis in the trial valid?

Were all the clinically important outcomes considered?

Are the likely treatment benefits worth the potential harm and costs?

prospective studies, and are very useful for generating hypotheses. Prospective studies evaluate events in the present time and forward. As such, these studies' greatest strengths are the ability to more effectively control bias and to have more robust data collection than retrospective studies (Figure 6.2).

In single-group studies, all subjects are treated with the same intervention or medicine. In multiple-group studies, subjects in each group are treated with different interventions and the results are compared between groups. The major study designs employed for two groups of subjects are cross-sectional and longitudinal trials. Cross-sectional studies are usually short-term trials (weeks) in which a cross-section of the patient population is evaluated and data are obtained from each group is compared. Most safety and efficacy studies conducted are cross-sectional trials. Longitudinal trials are typically longer in duration (months) and patients' data are generally compared with

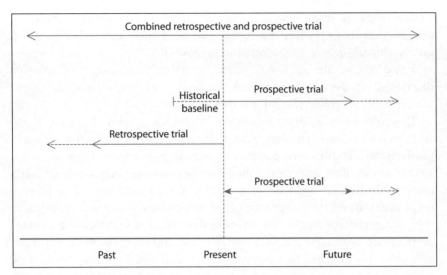

Figure 6.2 Timeline of retrospective and prospective studies.[8]

the patient's baseline data to identify any changes. Many epidemiological studies and Phase IV studies are longitudinal trials.

The two most commonly utilized prospective study designs comparing two groups of subjects are the parallel and crossover designs. In a parallel design, subjects are randomized into one of two groups and typically receive one of two potential treatments as assigned for the entire duration of the study. These studies are applicable to most experimental situations. In crossover studies, subjects receive both treatments being compared. In order for a crossover design to be effectively utilized, subjects should have a stable, chronic condition during both treatment periods and a similar baseline condition at the start of each treatment. Examples of diseases for which a crossover-designed study may be conducted include migraines, epilepsy, and glaucoma. For the same sample size, the parallel design is less sensitive in detecting differences between the two groups, while the analysis of crossover studies is more greatly affected by patient dropouts and missing data.

Two other designs comparing two groups of subjects are matched pairs and historical control studies. Neither is as robust as parallel or crossover studies. Matched-pairs design is a type of parallel design in which subjects who are identical with regard to relevant factors are identified. One subject within each matched pair would receive one treatment, while the other receives the other treatment. The obvious limitations of this design are the difficulty in identifying well-matched pairs and that all relevant factors for matching pairs may not be known.

In historical control trials, all subjects receive the same treatment and the control group is composed of a similar group of subjects who were previously treated, often by different investigators. The advantage of historical control trials is that enrollment may be easier, but this must be counter-balanced by the fact that it is very difficult to have an adequately controlled historical group with all the relevant information required.

Phase IV study designs can be divided into five broad categories including descriptive studies, cross-sectional studies, case–control studies, cohort studies, and controlled clinical research studies.

Descriptive studies provide information on the pattern of disease occurrence in populations. The data used in descriptive studies are often collected passively to describe rare events or generate hypotheses. Cross-sectional studies involve data from a random sampling of a target population and data are classified based upon exposure and observed outcomes. This type of study can provide the prevalence of an event and as such is a snapshot in time. Case–control studies are retrospective research in which the patients representing cases have the disease in question and the controls do not. Each case subject is matched to a control subject on the basis of relevant factors, which is often difficult. Case–control studies can evaluate multiple exposures and uncommon diseases, and are logistically easy. A cohort study follows a group of subjects who have been exposed to an event or intervention and they are followed forward in time. The outcomes in the cohort are then compared retrospectively with a control group that was not exposed to the event or intervention. Cohort studies can evaluate multiple outcomes and uncommon exposures. Lastly, controlled clinical trial designs have been presented above and are the most convincing clinical research design.

Bias in clinical research

Bias is error that enters into a clinical research study and may distort the data collected. Bias may be introduced by anyone involved with the design, conduct, or analysis of clinical research. As the introduction of various forms of bias into a clinical research study may significantly affect the validity and generalizability of a study, one of the primary goals in designing a clinical research study is to eliminate or minimize the introduction of bias. In 1979, D.L. Sackett described seven different places where bias may occur:[9]

1 examining the literature in the field
2 specifying and selecting the clinical trial sample
3 executing the experimental maneuver
4 measuring exposures and outcome
5 analyzing the data
6 interpreting the analysis
7 publishing the results.

As described above, some clinical research designs will inherently introduce bias (e.g., case–control or retrospective designs), but the best way to avoid

Table 6.3 Types of bias in clinical research[9]

Type of bias	Description
Selection bias	Occurs during recruitment and selection of potential subjects
Information bias	Information collected directly from subjects can be biased based on beliefs or values
Observer bias	Clinical investigator objectivity for measuring outcomes varies greatly
Interviewer bias	The expectation of the interviewer may influence how information is collected

bias is to identify its potential during the design of a clinical research study. The types of bias to be considered in clinical research are summarized in Table 6.3.[9]

The main methods used to control bias in clinical research include blinding, randomization, and, when possible, the administration of placebo to the control population in the study. Blinding is a method used to keep the identity of the treatment used in a group unknown. Groups that can be blinded include patients, investigators, data review committees, ancillary personnel, statisticians, and monitors. With regard to blinding, clinical research studies can be described as outlined in Table 6.4.[8]

Randomization is a process by which patients in a clinical research study are randomly assigned to receive one of the potential treatments using a predetermined randomization code. Randomization decreases the effect of interjecting an investigator's bias, allows for breaking a blind on one patient while keeping it on the remaining subjects, and permits statistical testing to be conducted on resulting data in a valid manner.[8] Examples of randomization methods are provided in Table 6.5.[8]

Table 6.4 Clinical trial blinding schemes[8]

Type of blinding	Description
Open-label	No blinding is used. Both patient and investigator know the identity of the treatment being used. Least rigorous design
Single-blind	Patient is unaware of the treatment being used
Double-blind	Neither the patient nor the investigator is aware of what treatment is being used
Full double-blind	The patient and anyone that interacts with the patient group is aware of the treatment being used
Full triple-blind	The patient, the investigator, and anyone who interacts with the patient or investigator are unaware of the treatment being used
Full clinical trial blind	The patient, and anyone who interacts with the patient or the data are unaware of the treatment being used

Method	Description
Simple randomization	Uses a predetermined code to assign patients to one of two or more treatments
Block randomization	A block size is chosen and the number of patients assigned to each treatment is proportional (e.g., $1:1, 2:1, 3:1$)
Systematic randomization	Patients are assigned to receive treatment based on a random order in the first block, whose pattern is repeated in subsequent blocks or by a sequential assignment to treatment

Table 6.5 Randomization methods[8]

Type I error, Type II error, and sample size

The purpose of testing in clinical research is to indicate whether the hypothesis of the study should be accepted or rejected. From a purely statistical perspective, one typically develops a null hypothesis that states that the result of the test intervention is expected to be no different from that of another intervention. Type I error (alpha) is defined as the probability of rejecting the null hypothesis when it is in fact correct – a false positive. For a given statistical test, the probability of a Type I error is equal to the value set for the 'alpha' (α). In most clinical studies, the α usually set at 0.05. Type II (beta) error is the probability of incorrectly accepting the null hypothesis when a difference in outcome truly exists – or in other words, a false negative. Type II error (β) is typically dealt with through the selection of the 'power' of a clinical trial, which is defined as $(1 - \beta)$. In most clinical trials, an acceptable β is 0.1–0.2 (in other words, the power is 80–90%). There are a number of ways to affect the power of a study including but not limited to: (1) the sample size selected for the study; (2) the number of primary end points in the trial; and (3) the accuracy and precision with which the primary end point can be measured. Figure 6.3 shows the association between outcome and Type I and II error.[8]

Underpowered clinical trials have a decreased chance of demonstrating a true difference between the treatment arms. The converse is also applicable; here when the observed effect trends toward what is expected, but the p-value is >0.05, the reason may be due to an inadequate sample size. These problems can generally be minimized by thoughtful planning during the design of clinical studies.

Sample size is a critical component in the design of a clinical trial and is important in helping make statistical inferences from the data collected. A sample size calculation utilizes the assumed α, β, and estimates of the effect expected of the investigational intervention and the standard intervention to determine an appropriate estimated sample size for testing a research

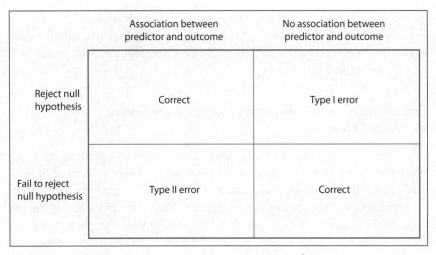

	Association between predictor and outcome	No association between predictor and outcome
Reject null hypothesis	Correct	Type I error
Fail to reject null hypothesis	Type II error	Correct

Figure 6.3   Association of outcomes and Type I and Type II error.[8]

hypothesis. Importantly, the estimated sample size needed for a research study refers to the number of patients who complete the study, not of those who enter. Patients who stop the study prematurely or who drop out altogether need to be taken into account when calculating the estimated size of the sample.

There are two types of sample size that can be chosen: (1) fixed and (2) sequential. When a fixed number is employed, the patients can be fixed a number of ways:

- at a defined number
- within a range
- by a minimum number
- by a maximum number.

With a sequential study design, the overall tally of subjects enrolled in the study is dependent upon analysis done throughout the study, with results able to be obtained more quickly. Generally, fewer patients are needed when the patients are enrolled sequentially than with a fixed sample. A required sample size is often determined by statisticians with three points in mind:

1   the magnitude of the effect expected or desired
2   the estimated randomness of the variables being investigated
3   power of the study.

Another point to consider in determining the sample size of a trial is establishing a ratio of patients between the two or more treatment groups. There are two choices that can be employed: (1) equal-size samples and (2) unequal but proportional-sized groups (e.g., a 2:1 or 3:1 ratio). Equal-sized groups are preferable from a statistical point of view in a clinical study, but both have advantages. With the equal-sized treatment groups, an advantage is that the trial itself will likely gain power. An advantage of an unequal-sized treatment is that more subjects are exposed to an experimental therapy, which will provide additional safety data.

Equivalency/non-inferiority versus superiority in clinical trials

Selection of an appropriate study design is principally dependent upon the objectives of the study. The trial can be designed to show equivalence or non-inferiority; the study can also be designed to show superiority. Regulators want to know whether an investigational new drug is effective – as a result, the bulk of the study protocols submitted to the FDA by the pharmaceutical industry are placebo-controlled, superiority trials.[10] Health care professionals frequently want to answer the question how much more effective a new drug is in comparison with the current treatment options. A superiority trial is an attractive option in this instance as well. The alternative to a superiority trial is an equivalency trial. The focus changes in that the comparison is of the study drug with a standard therapy. A placebo obviously cannot be used here, since it would never be advantageous to be equivalent to placebo, or essentially no treatment. Investigator-initiated trials (IITs) are often performed as equivalency studies to evaluate the standard of care treatment with the investigational drug. Often, this is done with the intent of studying a new or 'off-label' use of the new agent. While the two styles of clinical trials have a resemblance to each other in a number of areas (blinding and randomization to minimize bias), they are fundamentally different.

An equivalence (or more often in research, non-inferiority) clinical trial is typically conducted to demonstrate that there is no clinically significant difference between a standard treatment and an experimental treatment. The study is designed with the desired outcome being equivalence in efficacy, while immediate toxicity, long-term adverse effects, or cost-effectiveness may be demonstrated to be advantageous for the experimental treatment. For such experiments, the usual hypothesis-testing framework, which tests the null hypothesis of no difference in efficacy, is inappropriate. Instead, researchers test for the presence a specified difference between the efficacies of the two treatments to be no more than a predetermined value called the delta (δ). The delta is defined as the maximum margin of difference between the study intervention and the control intervention such that the study intervention would be deemed clinically equivalent to the control. In order to test precisely for the equivalence of two treatments, the alternative hypothesis must reflect that the treatments are the same. This requires a role reversal in defining the null and alternate hypotheses; in other words, the hypothesis testing structure for an equivalence trial requires the specification of no difference in the alternative hypothesis and a difference in the null hypothesis. Importantly, for a non-inferiority study design to be appropriate, both the study drug and the comparator drug need to have shown efficacy in the same population for the same end point at the same time point in other clinical trials.[10]

There are drawbacks of equivalency/non-inferiority trials. For example, when such a trial shows that two treatment arms have a similar effect, one can interpret the result in several ways:

1 Both treatment arms are equally effective.
2 Both treatment arms are equally ineffective.
3 The power of the study may be inadequate.

Superiority trials are designed with the intent to show a difference between the experimental drug and the control, which can be either a placebo or an active comparator.[10] Similarly to an equivalency trial, the structure of a superiority trial can be described by the null and alternative hypotheses. Efficacy is demonstrated when the difference between the experimental drug exceeds some preset threshold compared with that of the standard of care – which is considered clinically relevant. Figure 6.4 provides a graphic representation of the various outcomes possible in equivalence and superiority studies. The bars represent the 95% confidence interval (CI) around the point estimate of the difference between the test and control groups, while the outer bounds represent the predetermined delta used for the purposes of analysis.

One way to assess the data generated in a study is to evaluate the breadth of the CI. Figure 6.4 shows a 95% CI for three hypothetical, placebo-controlled superiority trials. Whenever the CI crosses some threshold (defined in Figure 6.4 as 0), the study drug is not different from placebo

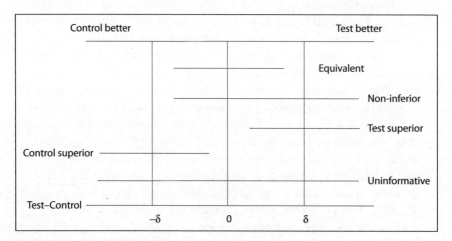

Figure 6.4 Potential outcomes in equivalence and superiority trials.

(see 'equivalent' and 'non-inferior' in Figure 6.4). When the CI does not cross 0 and is wholly greater than 0 (see 'superior' in Figure 6.4), the study intervention is considered superior. When the CI does not cross 0 and is wholly less than 0 (see 'control superior'), the study intervention is consider to be inferior to the comparator arm.

Clinical equipoise in controlled clinical trials

Equipoise in clinical research is defined as a state of genuine uncertainty on the part of the clinical investigator regarding the comparative therapeutic merits of each arm in a trial.[11] Equipoise has been proposed as the conceptual foundation for the ethical conduct of randomized clinical trials. This principle maintains that such a trial is acceptable only if there is reasonable uncertainty with regard to the overall outcome of the trial. In the event that the investigator discovers that one treatment is superior therapeutically, they are ethically obliged to offer that treatment. The current understanding of this requirement, which entails that the investigator have no 'treatment preference' throughout the course of the trial, presents nearly insurmountable obstacles to the ethical commencement or completion of a controlled trial and may also contribute to the termination of trials because of the failure to enroll enough patients. According to the concept of 'clinical equipoise,' the requirement is satisfied if there is genuine uncertainty within the expert medical community – not necessarily on the part of the individual investigator – about the preferred treatment. Clinical equipoise identifies that it is the community of physicians, rather than the individual physician, that establishes the medical standards of practice.

According to Benjamin Freedman:

> The ethics of medical practice grant no ethical or normative meaning to a treatment preference, however powerful, that is based on a hunch or anything less than evidence publicly presented and convincing to the clinical community. Persons are licensed as physicians after they demonstrate the acquisition of this professionally validated knowledge, not after they reveal a superior capacity for guessing. Competent medical practice is defined widely as that which falls within the bounds of standard care; that is practice endorsed by at least a respectable minority of expert practitioners. The innovation of clinical equipoise is the recognition that study treatments, be they the experimental or control treatments, are consistent with the standard of care. Thus a physician, consistent with his or her duty to the patient, may offer trial enrollment when there exists an honest, professional disagreement among expert clinicians about the preferred treatment.[11]

Comparison of placebo versus the best-available control group in controlled clinical studies

The rationale for the use of a control group in clinical studies has been well delineated by the Council for International Organizations of Medical Sciences. The council established that a clinical trial 'cannot be justified ethically unless it is capable of producing scientifically reliable results.'[12] A converse of this would be that scientifically invalid research would be unethical by putting subjects at unnecessary risk without benefit. As discussed earlier in this chapter, there are valid considerations to justify the choice of a control group in a clinical study. The options available to investigators are to have no control group, a placebo or sham control group, an active control group using an approved therapy, or an active control group that receives 'the best available therapy.' Placebo-controlled trials are acceptable when either no standard of care exists and the study does not impose unnecessary risk of harm to subjects or when the interruption is critically necessary such as when the benefit outweighs the risk of the use of placebo. When available as a control option, the use of a placebo in a double-blind, randomized, controlled trial is considered 'the most rigorous test of treatment efficacy' for evaluating an investigational drug.[12]

The use of best-available-therapy or standard-of-care control groups is common in Phase II and Phase III trials whose objective is a new treatment in the proposed mode in the general population. The best-available-therapy control group can also provide pivotal evidence of the agent's efficacy and additional data on the adverse effect profile – allowing comparison between two active drugs to be made. There are several drawbacks to this type of control group. Importantly, without a placebo-control arm, it is plausible that equivalence between two interventions is found when neither has been more effective than no intervention at all.

Challenges in conducting clinical research

After a clinical research idea is developed more fully into a study protocol, one must consider the complexity and various 'moving parts' that are critical to the efficient conduct of a clinical research study. The overall roles of the functional groups involved in a clinical research study are to provide intellectual and scientific leadership for the study (e.g., investigators, medical directors), selection and management of investigational sites (e.g., clinical operations, study managers, research associates), data gathering and analysis (data management, programming, biostatisticians), and infrastructure support (e.g., finance, human resources, information technology). It is only through collaboration of all of these functional groups that one can efficiently conduct clinical research that is scientifically and ethically sound.

The interpretation and integration of clinical research into clinical practice

The ultimate goal of conducting clinical research is to improve patient care. To this end, the results of clinical research must be integrated into clinical practice. The interpretation of the results of clinical research studies is therefore a critically important part of the process and must be undertaken with great care. In an effort to adequately synthesize empirical information, a variety of methods are currently in use to aid clinicians in effectively integrating clinical research study results into clinical practice (Figure 6.5).[13]

In particular, national and international societies and other organizations, most notably the Centers for Disease Control and Prevention (CDC), the Cochrane Collaborative Group, and the World Health Organization (WHO), regularly prepare evidenced-based guidelines derived from the available clinical research results to aid clinical decision making and improve patient care. Ultimately, for the results from a clinical research study to influence medical practice, they need to be published in a peer-reviewed journal and be interpreted by clinicians as positive, and must be generalizable to the clinician's specific patient population. It is worth noting that many well-designed trial results have had little effect on medical practice and many poorly designed studies have had a major influence. In the end, it is the

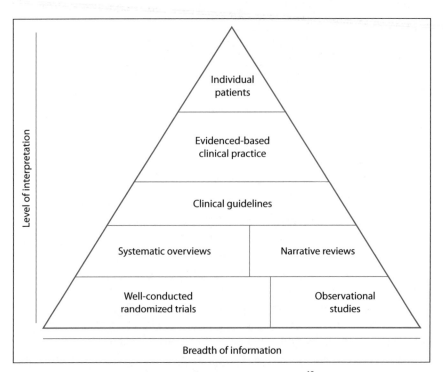

Figure 6.5   Integration of clinical trial results into clinical practice.[13]

responsibility of each clinician to make his or her own assessment of new clinical research data. Critical evaluation of such studies requires one to pose questions related to the end points, methodology, and data obtained from the study. Only after answers to these questions are generated and with an understanding of the strengths and limitations of a study can a clinician proceed to integrate the results into clinical practice.

References

1. United States Government Accounting Office. *New Drug Development: Science, Business, Regulatory, and Intellectual Property Issues Cited as Hampering Drug Development Efforts* [Online]. Washington, DC: United States Government Accounting Office, November 2006. Available from: http://www.gao.gov/new.items/d0749.pdf (accessed February 12, 2010).
2. Association of American Medical Colleges and the American Medical Association [Online] (November 1999). *Breaking the Scientific Bottleneck: Clinical Research: A National Call to Action.* Available from: https://services.aamc.org/Publications/showFile.cfm?file=version54.pdf&prd_id=147&prv_id=173&pdf_id=54 (accessed January 10, 2009).
3. *Public Welfare: Protection of Human Subjects* [Online]. 45 Federal Register 46 (August 18, 1991), p.7. Available from: http://www.hhs.gov/ohrp/humansubjects/guidance/45cfr46.htm#46.102 (accessed February 20, 2010).
4. Sutton G. Putrid gums and 'Dead men's cloaths': James Lind aboard the Salisbury. *J R Soc Med* 2003; 96(12): 605–608.
5. Fredericks DN, Relman DA. Sequence-based identification of microbial pathogens: a reconsideration of Koch's postulates. *Clin Microbiol Rev* 1996; 9(1): 18–33.
6. Flexner A. *Medical Education in the United States and Canada.* New York: Carnegie Foundation for the Advancement of Teaching, 1910.
7. Pharmaceutical Research and Manufacturers of America (PhRMA) [Online]. *Innovation.* Available from: http://www.phrma.org/innovation/ (accessed January 10, 2009).
8. Spilker B. *Guide to Clinical Trials.* Philadelphia: Lippincott, Williams, & Wilkins, 2000.
9. Sackett DL. Bias in analytic research. *J Chronic Dis* 1979; 32(1–2): 51–63.
10. Landow L. Current issues in clinical trial design: superiority versus equivalency studies. *Anesthesiology* 2000; 92: 1814–1820.
11. Freedman B. Equipoise and the ethics of clinical research. *N Engl J Med* 1987; 317: 141–145.
12. Council of International Organizations of Medical Sciences [Online] November 2002. *International Ethical Guidelines for Biomedical Research Involving Human Subjects.* Available from: http://www.cioms.ch/frame_guidelines_nov_2002.htm (accessed January 10, 2009).
13. Gallin JI. *Principles and Practice of Clinical Research.* San Diego: Academic Press; 2000.

7

Site monitoring

Vickie T. Payne

The primary purpose of monitoring a clinical trial is to ensure that the safety and well-being of subjects has not been compromised while ensuring that the study protocol has been followed and the data are accurate.[1]

While the Food and Drug Administration (FDA) requires in the Code of Federal Regulations (CFR), Title 21, Part 312.56(a) that 'the sponsor shall monitor the progress of all clinical investigations being conducted under its Investigational New Drug (IND) application,' it does not specify how the monitoring is to be conducted. For this, the International Conference on Harmonisation (ICH) Consolidated Guidance for Good Clinical Practice (GCP), ICH E6 Section 5.18 provides more direction.[1]

Selection and qualifications of the monitor

Monitors should be appointed and approved by the sponsor. They should be appropriately trained, and should have the scientific and/or clinical knowledge needed to monitor the trial adequately. A monitor's qualifications should be documented. Monitors should be thoroughly familiar with the investigational product(s), the protocol, the written informed consent form, and any other written information to be provided to subjects, the sponsor's Standard Operating Procedures (SOPs), GCP, and the applicable regulatory requirement(s).[1]

While a monitor may have a variety of educational backgrounds, typically a monitor will have a science background, often in pharmacy, medicine, or nursing. In addition, the monitor will be thoroughly familiar with ICH Guidelines as well as the local and/or regional regulatory requirements.

The sponsor should select a monitor after confirming that his or her qualifications are appropriate for the clinical trial. At this point, the monitor will be trained by the sponsor on the investigational product, how it relates to the therapeutic area being studied, and its mechanism of action. The sponsor will also train the monitor on the intricacies of the protocol and will review all documents to be used in the protocol, including the Informed Consent Form (ICF), subject diaries (if used), investigational product accountability forms and documents used to collect the data from the sites.

Finally, the sponsor will ensure that the monitor is trained on the SOPs that will be followed for the study. These could be the sponsor's SOPs or the Contract Research Organization's (CRO) SOPs, if the monitoring is delegated to a CRO. It is also important to ensure that monitors are trained according to ICH GCP guidelines and local laws or regulations. This will ensure consistency with procedures among all monitors on a clinical trial.

Once the monitors have been selected and trained, they are considered to be the sponsor's representative to the sites. At this juncture, the monitor will begin to evaluate, train, and assist the sites to conduct the clinical trial, encouraging and reinforcing their efforts to recruit and enroll eligible subjects, helping to resolve any issues that may arise, and ensuring that the data collected from the site are complete and accurate.

The evaluation visit

The purpose of the evaluation visit is to verify that the investigator has adequate qualifications and resources to conduct a clinical trial and that the staff and facilities, including laboratories and equipment, are adequate to safely and properly conduct the trial and remain adequate throughout the trial period.[1] It is also vital to ensure that the investigator has an adequate database of eligible patients to be enrolled in the proposed clinical trial.

The evaluation visit is the sponsor's opportunity to verify that the investigator is qualified and has adequate resources to conduct the study. It is also used as an interview for both the sponsor and the site to determine whether each party and the study will be a good fit.

This visit should occur after a search has been conducted to determine whether the principal investigator (PI) has had any disciplinary action taken against him or her by any regulatory agency. This would include a search of the FDA's website to determine whether the investigator or any of the site staff have been debarred. The FDA's debarment list is a list of individuals or companies that have been disqualified from conducting research for a given period. In addition, the sponsor will often require that a Confidentiality and Disclosure Agreement (CDA) be signed by the PI. The CDA is often required because the sponsor will provide proprietary information to the PI so that he or she can evaluate the study. After the CDA has been signed and received by the sponsor, a synopsis of the protocol will be sent for the PI to review in advance of the visit. A feasibility questionnaire should also be sent to the PI to be completed. The purpose of the feasibility questionnaire is to determine whether the investigator has the appropriate resources and capabilities to execute the clinical trial. It may include questions regarding the number of eligible patients that are available at the site, a description of specific facilities and equipment available at the site, and a list of all the site staff. Once these have been completed, an on-site evaluation visit will be scheduled if preliminary requirements are met.

During the evaluation visit, the monitor will meet with the PI to discuss the protocol to determine the PI's interest and ability to recruit and enroll subjects into the study. The study objectives and study procedures will be reviewed, as well as enrollment expectations, inclusion and exclusion criteria, safety and efficacy parameters, and data collection.

If one was completed, the information provided in the feasibility questionnaire will be reviewed with the site. The PI will be asked about the patient population, their patients' receptiveness to participating in clinical trials, how the site plans to find patients for the study, and whether they foresee any barriers to recruitment. The monitor will ask how new patients are evaluated, pre-screened, approached, consented, and selected for a study in order to determine whether these procedures are in compliance with ICH guidelines and local regulatory requirements.

The monitor will try to ascertain how the facility will function as a research site. Some common questions associated with this assessment are listed in Table 7.1.

Finally, a tour of the facilities will be conducted to ensure that the site has the resources and ability to perform all aspects of the study. Included in this

Table 7.1 Common questions relating to the site evaluation process

- How many practitioners are at the site?
- How supportive are these practitioners to clinical trials and who would be listed as a subinvestigator for the study?
- How long has the principal investigator been conducting clinical trials?
- Has the principal investigator or subinvestigator ever been audited by a regulatory agency?
- Who will be the study coordinator and what is his or her experience?
- Does the site have the time and resources available to conduct the study?
- Does the site have any studies that would compete for the same patient population?
- Who will be responsible for preparing the regulatory documents?
- Who will be responsible for submitting documents to the Institutional Review Board (IRB) or Independent Ethics Committee (IEC)?
- What IRB/IEC will be used and how often does it meet?
- How long does it typically take for documents to be submitted to, reviewed by, and approved by the IRB/IEC?
- Who will conduct the consenting of the subjects and what is the process?
- Who will perform the required study procedures and where will they be conducted?
- How and where will the required data be documented for the study?
- What data will be available to the monitor for review during monitoring visits?
- Will the principal investigator and subinvestigator(s) be available to the monitor during the course of the study?
- What is the involvement of the principal investigator in the day-to-day conduct of a study?
- How is the principal investigator kept informed of subject status if the study procedures are delegated?

tour are patient care areas, laboratory facilities, biological sample and investigational product storage facilities, document storage facilities, and space for the monitor during the monitoring visits.

At the conclusion of the visit, the monitor will discuss the site selection and contracting processes with the PI and will answer any remaining questions. He or she will often collect a signed and dated copy of the PI's and sub-investigators' curriculum vitae (CV) and the site's contact information. This would also be an appropriate time to collect information regarding meeting dates for the Institutional Review Board (IRB) or Independent Ethics Committee (IEC).

After the visit, the monitor will review the information obtained from the evaluation visit to determine whether the site is qualified and interested in participating in the study. He or she will evaluate the site's strengths and weaknesses, assess whether they have demonstrated the potential to recruit and enroll subjects into the study and decide whether the site would be a good match for the study. The monitor will then write a report, documenting the visit and submit it to the sponsor for their review. The sponsor will then decide whether the site will be selected for the study and will notify the site of the decision.

The initiation visit

Once the site has been selected for the study, the contract has been signed, IRB approval has been obtained, and all essential regulatory documents have been received by the study sponsor, the study supplies will be shipped and a study initiation visit will be scheduled with the site. The purpose of the initiation visit is to ensure that the study staff has been thoroughly trained on all the nuances of successfully conducting the study.[1]

Under certain circumstances, study initiation activities can be completed at an Investigator Meeting, but usually the study initiation is done by the monitor at an on-site visit to the study site. An Investigator Meeting is a meeting conducted by the sponsor to train investigators and Study Coordinators (SC) about the clinical protocol and to prepare them for participation in the upcoming study.[2]

Prior to the initiation visit, the monitor should ensure that he or she has a thorough understanding of the investigational product, the therapeutic indication being treated, the protocol, and the study procedures required for the protocol. The monitor should then contact the site to schedule the initiation visit. A written confirmation of the visit and an agenda should be sent to the site, noting that all key study staff should be present at the visit. At a minimum, this would include the PI and SC but may also include additional staff that would be designated to perform certain required study procedures.

During the visit, the monitor will meet with the PI and study staff to review the protocol and Investigator's Brochure (IB), focusing on the inclusion and exclusion criteria, study design, objectives, schedule of events, study procedures, prohibited medications, and safety considerations. Often, the progress of a potential subject, from identification to consenting, screening, determination of eligibility, randomization, and completion of the study will be discussed with the staff to ensure that the site is knowledgeable about the study and with GCP guidelines as they relate to the study. It will also help to identify potential roadblocks and issues as they relate to the conduct of the study at this site.

The monitor will discuss the obligation of the PI to retain oversight and control of all activities at the clinical site(s) used for the study at all times and that he or she is required to comply with the protocol, GCPs, and all applicable regulations. Any study-related activities and responsibilities delegated to other staff personnel should be clearly documented on a list, noting the appropriately qualified individuals who will perform these activities. The monitor will also point out that the PI is responsible for ensuring that these individuals have been properly trained to perform these activities as it relates to the study.

The monitor will inform the PI and SC of the need to have direct access to original source documents, including electronic records, if utilized at the site. The need to meet with the PI at the monitoring visits will be discussed as well as the monitoring frequency.

The pharmacy binder and investigational product will be inspected and reviewed with the staff, noting storage, preparation, dispensation, administration, unblinding, and accountability requirements, as well as expected Adverse Events (AEs) associated with the use of the product. If the investigational product will be transported to other satellite study sites, the site should document their procedure for ensuring that the chain of custody and storage requirements are maintained.

A definition of AEs as it relates to the study will be reviewed to ensure that all study staff are aware of what is to be considered an AE and the period over which this data will be collected for each subject. Documentation and reporting requirements of these AEs and Serious Adverse Events (SAEs), as well as any pregnancies that may occur on the study, will be discussed. See Chapter 9 for further discussion of the definition and reporting requirements for AEs and SAEs. Study materials, including laboratory kits, will be checked to confirm that they have been received intact and that the study staff is familiar with their use. The procedure for obtaining, processing, storing, and shipping of biological samples will be reviewed as well.

The study file binder will be reviewed with the site staff to ensure that all essential documents have been filed and that the staff understands that all documents must be kept current, including IRB/IEC notifications and approvals, study correspondence, laboratory certifications and reference ranges, as well as PI and study staff CVs.

Finally, the monitor will confirm that the clinical site facilities have not changed since the evaluation visit. If changes have occurred, the monitor will tour the facilities again to ensure that they remain adequate for the clinical trial.

Once these activities have been completed, the monitor and the PI will usually sign a document that affirms that all initiation activities have been completed, that all essential study staff members have been trained on the protocol, and that screening for the study may begin at the site. A copy of this document is left on file at the site.

After the visit, the monitor will write a report and submit it to the study team, documenting the information covered in the initiation visit and listing any outstanding issues or questions raised by the site that require a response. The monitor will then write a follow-up letter to the site summarizing the visit, listing any outstanding issues, and also noting answers to any questions raised at the initiation visit.

The monitoring visit

The sponsor is required to monitor the progress of all clinical investigations being conducted under its IND.[3] The monitor, in accordance with the sponsor's requirements, should ensure that the trial is conducted and documented properly.[1]

The bulk of a monitor's time is spent monitoring clinical trials in order to ensure that the trial is conducted properly. While some studies may allow for monitoring to be done centrally, in the majority of studies this is done by on-site monitoring. In the course of these activities, the monitor will act as the main line of communication between the investigator and the sponsor, ensuring that the rights and well-being of the subjects are protected, the data collected is being documented accurately and completely, the site is following the currently approved protocol, and the site is in compliance with all applicable laws and regulations.[1]

The frequency of monitoring visits will be determined by the sponsor on the basis of many factors, such as the complexity and size of the study as well as the speed of subject enrollment. Typically, the monitoring visits will begin once the site has begun enrolling subjects into the study. However, if a site is having difficulty enrolling, the monitor may visit the site periodically to review screening activities at the site and discuss the study with the PI to identify any recruitment barriers that may exist at the site.

Prior to the monitoring visit, the monitor will contact the site to schedule the visit and will usually send a written confirmation, noting what will be reviewed at the visit. The monitor will then review any previous monitoring reports, study documents, and site correspondences, noting any outstanding issues, study updates, or upcoming data timelines for the study.

Upon arrival at the site, the monitor will inquire whether there have been any changes at the site regarding the study, subjects, enrollment, or site staff. Ideally, he or she will meet with the PI at the beginning of the visit to discuss the objectives of the visit, but typically the monitor will mostly interact with the SC. The monitor will meet with the PI at some time during the visit to discuss the study status, resolution of any outstanding issues, and any concerns that may have arisen during the course of the monitoring visit.

During the visit, the monitor will review the study file binders and sign a sponsor visit log. He or she will confirm that the most recent study documents (protocol, protocol amendments, ICF, IB, and any IND safety reports) have been submitted to and approved by the IRB, if necessary, and that all documents have been filed in the appropriate binders. He or she will also ensure that the sponsor's files are consistent with the site's files and will obtain copies as needed for the sponsor or site so that they remain consistent for the duration of the study.

The monitor will confirm that all study staff have been entered on a delegation of authority form and that they have received appropriate training for their role in the study. This specific form may differ between sponsors or investigative sites, but this form documents that the PI has delegated study responsibilities to specific members of the study team. He or she will confirm that all essential documents are up-to-date, including CVs, medical licenses, laboratory certificates, laboratory reference ranges, and IRB continuing review documents.

Drug accountability will be performed at the monitoring visit. In completing this task, the monitor will verify that all investigational product shipped to the site has been received in good condition and acknowledged properly by the site. He or she will ensure that the investigational product has been stored under the protocol-specified conditions; that it has been prepared, dispensed, or administered to the appropriate study subject; and that all required documentation of these activities is completed and filed in the investigator or pharmacy files. The monitor will confirm that there is sufficient investigational product on site and that it has not expired. All used or expired investigational product will be accounted for and returned for destruction according to the sponsor and study guidelines.

The largest and most important part of the monitoring visit will be spent reviewing the subjects screened and enrolled into the study. The monitor will confirm that all subjects screened for the study have been entered onto a subject screening log and that each one has been properly consented, using the most recently IRB-approved version of the ICF. The subject's consent should have been obtained before any study procedures were performed and the ICF should have been personally signed and dated by the subject (or legally authorized representative) and the person who obtained the consent. The monitor will check to see that the consent process has been properly documented in the subject's source documents. If during the course of the study the informed consent form has been revised and updated, the monitor will verify that each subject has been reconsented in a timely manner, according to the process described above. Refer to Chapter 3 for a further discussion of the informed consent process.

The monitor will review the eligibility of each subject, confirm that the site is following the approved protocol and all protocol amendments and verify that all study procedures are being followed. If any deviations from the protocol have occurred, these deviations will be documented and discussed with the PI and site staff to determine the explanation and the site will report these deviations to their IRB according to their procedures. Such deviations are often defined in the protocol or in a separate document generated by the sponsor.

Each subject will be monitored to ensure the accuracy and completeness of the data generated during the completion of the study procedures. Case Report Forms (CRFs) are the tools used by a sponsor to collect data about study subjects during the course of a clinical trial. The monitor will compare the original source data to the CRF entries to ensure that they match and that all investigational product usage, AEs, and concomitant medications have been captured as required by the protocol. Any missed visits or procedures will also be documented on the CRFs.

If an SAE has occurred, the monitor will confirm that the SAE has been reported promptly and completely to the sponsor and to the IRB/IEC according to their procedures. He or she will reconcile the SAE report with the CRF entries to confirm that they are consistent.

If the study is blinded, the monitor will verify that the blind has not been broken. If a blind break device is used for the study, the monitor will confirm that the device remains intact and is readily available, either in the pharmacy or in the study file binder. If the blind has been broken, the monitor will confirm that the sponsor has been properly notified, the event has been documented and the IRB has been notified according to their procedures.

Ideally, the monitor will meet with the PI again at the conclusion of the monitoring visit to discuss the study progress and to notify the PI of any significant findings, such as protocol deviations, GCP violations, significant CRF completion issues, or missing essential documents. If needed, a corrective action plan will be discussed and documented to resolve any outstanding issues. Usually, at this time the monitor will also schedule the next monitoring visit with the site.

After the monitoring visit, the monitor will write a report to summarize what was completed at the monitoring visit and submit it to the sponsor. This report will document who was present at the visit, what was reviewed, any deviations from the protocol, any significant findings, actions to be taken to resolve any issues or to ensure compliance with the protocol, and resolution of issues noted at previous monitoring visits. The monitor will also note any activities that were not completed at this visit.

Finally, the monitor will provide a written summary of the monitoring visit to the PI in the form of the follow-up letter. This document will note any significant findings and deviations from the protocol or GCPs. It will also note any actions the site should take to document these findings and to return to compliance in the future. Often this letter will document the date agreed upon for the next monitoring visit as well.

The close-out visit

A clinical trial site can be closed when the last subject has completed the study, all data has been verified, and the database has been locked. It is assumed that, once this visit has been completed, no further contact with the site will be needed. In the event that the study has been prematurely discontinued, the same procedures will be followed.

Prior to closing-out a site, the monitor will verify that all CRFs have been retrieved from the site, all queries have been resolved, all biological samples have been shipped, and all investigational product has been reconciled and returned for destruction, if applicable. Queries are sent to investigative sites in response to data entered onto CRFs that must be clarified or explained. The clarifications are documented and kept with the CRF to ensure that any changes to data are documented. Once the monitor has confirmed that no further queries will be issued and the database has been locked, the monitor will contact the site to schedule the close-out visit.

Prior to the close-out visit, the monitor will obtain a listing of all essential documents in the sponsor's study- and site-specific files, as well as a listing of all queries and protocol deviations for the site. The monitor will also review previous monitoring reports to determine whether there are any outstanding issues and arrange to resolve these issues at the close-out visit.

The monitor will send the site a close-out visit confirmation letter which will specify the visit date and advise the investigator to inform their IRB of a summary of the study at their site. This summary should include the number of subjects screened, enrolled, withdrawn, and completed at their site. It should also include a listing of any deaths and/or SAEs among their subjects and should inform the IRB that the study is being closed at their site. A copy of this document will be retrieved for the sponsor's files.

During the close-out visit, the monitor will review all CRF pages to ensure that the copies at the site are present and legible. He or she will verify that copies of all data queries or data clarification forms issued for the site are present and filed with the CRFs. This will ensure that the site's data remains consistent with the sponsor's data.

The monitor will also review the site's study file binder and compare it with the listing of all essential documents in the sponsor's study and site-specific files. If there are any documents at the site that are not listed in the sponsor's files, the monitor will retrieve a copy of those documents to be forwarded to the sponsor. Likewise, if a document listed in the sponsor's files is missing from the site's files, the monitor will obtain a copy for the site to ensure that the sponsor's and site's files remain consistent. The monitor will also obtain a copy of the sponsor visit log, subject screening log, delegation of authority forms, all investigational product accountability logs, and investigational product storage temperature logs (if applicable).

The monitor will review all IND safety reports at the site to confirm that the site has a copy of each report issued for the investigational product. Each of these IND safety reports should have documentation of submission to the IRB (if required by their IRB) and documentation that the PI has reviewed each one. If any IND safety reports are missing, the monitor will obtain a copy for the site.

If an emergency blind break device was used for the study, the monitor will confirm that it remains intact and will collect it so that it can be returned to the sponsor. This will ensure that the blind remains unbroken at the site. If the blind has been broken at the site, the monitor will retrieve a copy of all documentation referencing the blind break and forward it to the sponsor.

All investigational product should have been returned to the sponsor or destroyed prior to the close-out visit, but if any remains at the site, the monitor will do a final accountability and return at this time. In addition, a document that lists all investigational product shipped to the site and all product returned for destruction will be prepared for and signed by the PI. This will complete the final investigational product reconciliation for the site. A copy of the document will be retrieved and forwarded to the sponsor.

The monitor will confirm that all biological samples have been shipped, including back-up specimens. If any remain on site, the monitor should have the site ship the samples to the appropriate laboratory immediately and the monitor will notify the sponsor of their shipment.

Once all the above activities have been completed, the monitor will usually assist the site with preparing the study documents for archiving, usually in boxes labeled with the sponsor, study number, and contact information for whom to contact in the event that the study records are moved or prior to destruction. In addition, the monitor will confirm that any unused study supplies, such as CRFs or laboratory kits, have been returned to the sponsor or destroyed on site.

At some time during this visit, usually at the conclusion, the monitor will meet with the PI to review the activities completed at the visit and the PI's responsibilities regarding record retention requirements of study documents, medical records, and subject identification information. The monitor will confirm where the records will be stored and how long they must be stored and will advise the PI to notify the sponsor if the storage location changes.

The monitor will advise the PI to notify the sponsor immediately if the site is to be audited by any regulatory agency and, if the study required financial disclosure, that all required staff will report any changes in their financial disclosure status for up to one year after the study ended. See Chapter 2 for a discussion of other regulatory requirements.

If the study was prematurely discontinued, the monitor will discuss the reasons for premature discontinuation and any additional requirements for following the study subjects, as defined by the study sponsor.

The monitor will advise the PI to notify the IRB/IEC that the study is closed at the site and will request that a copy of the letter be forwarded to the monitor so that it can be added to the sponsor's files.

Finally, the monitor will review the publication policy as defined by the sponsor and the protocol and remind the PI that all data generated in the course of the study is confidential and is the property of the sponsor.

Once the close-out visit has been completed and all outstanding issues have been resolved, the monitor will write a report summarizing the close-out visit and submit it to the sponsor. All documents retrieved at the visit will be forwarded to the sponsor. If there are any documents that need to be obtained for the site's files, the monitor will forward these documents to the site along with the follow-up letter.

Summary

As demonstrated by the list of activities above, site monitors have an enormous responsibility for overseeing clinical trials and being the 'eyes and ears' of the sponsor. A monitor's responsibilities are based on the ICH Guidelines, which provide direction for all clinical investigations that involve human subjects. For more detailed information about the responsibilities of the monitor, the reader should refer to the ICH Guidelines E6, *Good Clinical Practice: Consolidated Guidance* (ICH-E6), section 5.18.

References

1. International Conference on Harmonisation [Online] (June 2006). *Guidance for Industry: Good Clinical Practice, Consolidated Guidance, ICH-E6*. Available from: http://www.ich.org/LOB/media/MEDIA482.pdf (accessed December 14, 2008).
2. Lake E. Inside Investigator Meetings: why this age-old industry staple is missing the mark for many and what can be done to remedy the situation. *Appl Clin Trials* 2008 Jun 1. [Online]. Available from: http://appliedclinicaltrialsonline.findpharma.com/appliedclinicaltrials/Sites/Inside-Investigator-Meetings/ArticleStandard/Article/detail/522054 (accessed February 12, 2010).
3. Food & Drug Administration [Online] (April 2009). *Investigational New Drug Application, Title 21 Code of Federal Regulations Part 312*. Available from: http://www.accessdata.fda.gov/scripts/cdrh/cfdocs/cfcfr/CFRSearch.cfm?CFRPart=312&show FR=1 (accessed November 16, 2009).

8

Institutional Review Boards and Independent Ethics Committees

Michael R. Jacobs

Institutional Review Boards (IRBs) and Independent Ethics Committees (IECs) are charged with protecting the rights and safety of clinical trial participants. The regulations that guide the review, approval, and conduct of human research refer to these independent boards as IRBs or IECs. In 2001 the Association for the Accreditation of Human Research Protection Programs (AAHRPP) was formed. Since that time many institutions have reorganized the various support and review services connected with human subject research including the IRB as one component of their Human Research Protection Program (HRPP). Similarly to the IRB, these programs have as their primary mission the protection of human research subjects. Some IRB responsibilities such as clinical trial monitoring, investigator and research participant education, and auditing of research records may be shifted to specialized units within the HRPP. These programs may also facilitate investigator–sponsor relationships to promote safe, ethical research practices. In many institutions in the USA the committee also serves as the Health Insurance Portability and Accountability Act of 1996 (HIPAA) privacy board for research-related activities.

There are at least three systems used by institutions to fulfill human research ethics review requirements.[1] It is important to determine the IRB that will be responsible for reviewing and approving the research. Some institutions require their own IRB to review all research, while others rely solely on the use of a central IRB, or permit central IRB review for certain types of studies. Central IRBs are particularly useful for multicenter studies because only one IRB is responsible for approval of the protocol and informed consent form. This can make meeting this regulatory requirement more efficient. The possible advantages and disadvantages of central versus local IRB review have been well described by Fitzgerald and Phillips.[1] A potential concern when using a central IRB surrounds the ability of that committee to understand relevant local issues. Local issues typically relate to the capabilities of the Principal Investigator (PI) to carry out the research, the adequacy of institutional resources to safely perform the research, and any considerations that should be given to potential study participants such as cultural or economic factors. In the European Community where a national health agency can attest to the capabilities of the clinician and institutional resources, some argue that there are no local issues related to whether the research is ethical or not.[2] The premise is, in theory, true; yet it is founded on the assumption that all good clinicians will be good researchers. Considering the current regulatory mandates, it is unlikely that the requirement for review and approval of research by local IRBs will be abandoned in the near future. Given this, sponsors and investigators should make certain which IRB review process applies to their study.

Composition, procedures, and function

Composition

The IRB must consist of at least five members reflecting diversity of scientific and non-scientific backgrounds and professional specialties and also cultural interests, include both sexes, and have at least one member who is not affiliated with the institution directly or through a family member (usually referred to as the community member). While the minimum number of members is set at five, most IRBs will consist of slightly more to accommodate additional expertise and to assure that a quorum can be convened to conduct the meeting. A factor that drives committee composition is the nature of research that is reviewed. Through regulations, the International Conference on Harmonisation (ICH), the Department of Health and Human Services (DHHS), and the Food and Drug Administration (FDA) require that IRBs consist of members who collectively have sufficient expertise to evaluate the quality of the science, medical aspects of the proposed research, and the ethics of conducting a study. The net effect of this regulation is to require that at least one member of the committee be a physician, since there is no other way to obtain the expertise required to evaluate the study's medical aspects. IRBs are permitted to use an alternate member system, where the alternate member may attend if the primary member is not available. Also, the IRB may invite outside consultants if necessary to provide insight into scientific or ethical issues that are beyond the expertise of the convened committee. While consultants can assist in the review of a protocol, they cannot participate in the voting for approval of the research.

IRB membership is also influenced by the population eligible to participate in the protocol. Vulnerable populations specifically addressed in the DHHS, FDA, or ICH regulations include children, prisoners, pregnant women, fetuses, and the handicapped and mentally impaired. In order to review research that includes these participant groups, the regulations require that individuals with expertise about those populations and who understand how they might be vulnerable be included on the committee. However, these are by no means the only potentially vulnerable groups of study participants. Students can be vulnerable if participating in research being conducted by a faculty member. Similarly, employees and staff members might be considered vulnerable if asked to participate in research directed by the department head. The IRB needs to be cognizant that there are a number of social, economic, and cultural reasons that might make an individual vulnerable. Furthermore, the underlying disease state and clinical prognosis can affect how the patient perceives the planned intervention and may create vulnerability.

Unlike the ICH and DHHS, the FDA requires committee membership that can assess the proposed research according to 'acceptability ... in terms of institutional commitments.' The effect of this section of the regulations is to allow an institution to restrict research that falls outside of its standards or places an undue burden on institutional resources. While an institution might prohibit IRB-approved research from being conducted, the institution cannot permit the conduct of research that has not received IRB approval.

Procedures and functions

The requirements for IRB operations and procedures are described in 21 CFR Part 56, Subpart C, and ICH E6 Sections 3.2 and 3.3. These sections identify what must be accomplished to be in compliance with the regulations, and does not recommend specific methods that must be implemented. Thus, each institution establishes its own policies and procedures to achieve the goal of protecting the rights and safety of human research participants. Because of this, it is in the best interest of the sponsor to work with investigators experienced with the IRB submission requirements of the institution. FDA and ICH regulations both require that IRBs follow written procedures for initial and continuing reviews, the frequency of continuing reviews, prompt reporting of changes to the research, prompt reporting of unexpected events, adverse reactions, and deviations from or non-compliance with the protocol. Under FDA and ICH regulations, IRBs can approve a research protocol, require modifications to the protocol in order to gain approval, disapprove the research, or suspend or terminate research that has already received approval. The IRB's determination must be communicated in writing within a 'reasonable time' and should provide specific recommendations for changes needed to secure approval, or if approved, the conditions of approval.

The ICH E6 *Guideline for Good Clinical Practice* is written primarily for research that requires full board review at a convened meeting. Expedited review (i.e., review conducted by the IRB chairperson or designee) is mentioned only as it relates to 'minor changes' to a protocol that has already received full board approval. In contrast, FDA regulations identify categories of research that can be exempted or follow an expedited review process and do not go to full committee. Of the four categories of research that qualify for a review exemption, the one most pertinent to IRBs that review biomedical research concerns the emergency use of an investigational drug or device. The first use of an investigational drug or device in an emergency situation is exempt from IRB review; however, such use must be reported to the IRB within 5 working days. Any subsequent use of the drug or device at that institution requires the approval of the protocol at a convened meeting of the full IRB. Research that qualifies for expedited review and approval is no more than minimal risk or for minor modifications of research that has already receive full board approval. Examples of research that is exempt from review or may be expedited under DHSS regulations are found

Table 8.1 Categories of exempt research
1   Research conducted in established or commonly accepted educational settings, involving normal educational practices, such as (i) research on regular and special education instructional strategies, or (ii) research on the effectiveness of or the comparison among instructional techniques, curricula, or classroom management methods.
2   Research involving the use of educational tests (cognitive, diagnostic, aptitude, achievement), survey procedures, interview procedures, or observation of public behavior, unless: (i) information obtained is recorded in such a manner that human subjects can be identified, directly or through identifiers linked to the subjects; and (ii) any disclosure of the human subjects' responses outside the research could reasonably place the subjects at risk of criminal or civil liability or be damaging to the subjects' financial standing, employability, or reputation.
3   Research involving the use of educational tests (cognitive, diagnostic, aptitude, achievement), survey procedures, interview procedures, or observation of public behavior that is not exempt under paragraph (b)(2) of this section, if: (i) the human subjects are elected or appointed public officials or candidates for public office; or (ii) federal statute(s) require(s) without exception that the confidentiality of the personally identifiable information will be maintained throughout the research and thereafter.
4   Research, involving the collection or study of existing data, documents, records, pathological specimens, or diagnostic specimens, if these sources are publicly available or if the information is recorded by the investigator in such a manner that subjects cannot be identified, directly or through identifiers linked to the subjects.
5   Research and demonstration projects which are conducted by or subject to the approval of department or agency heads, and which are designed to study, evaluate, or otherwise examine: (i) public benefit or service programs; (ii) procedures for obtaining benefits or services under those programs; (iii) possible changes in or alternatives to those programs or procedures; or (iv) possible changes in methods or levels of payment for benefits or services under those programs.
6   Taste and food quality evaluation and consumer acceptance studies, (i) if wholesome foods without additives are consumed or (ii) if a food is consumed that contains a food ingredient at or below the level and for a use found to be safe, or agricultural chemical or environmental contaminant at or below the level found to be safe, by the Food and Drug Administration or approved by the Environmental Protection Agency or the Food Safety and Inspection Service of the US Department of Agriculture.

Table 8.2 Categories of research that may be reviewed by expedited procedures

Research activities that present no more than minimal risk and fall into one of the following categories are eligible for review expedited by the IRB through the expedited review procedure.

1 Clinical studies of drugs and medical devices only when condition (a) or (b) is met.
   a Research on drugs for which an investigational new drug application (21 CFR Part 312) is not required. (Note: Research on marketed drugs that significantly increases the risks or decreases the acceptability of the risks associated with the use of the product is not eligible for expedited review.)
   b Research on medical devices for which (i) an investigational device exemption application (21 CFR Part 812) is not required; or (ii) the medical device is cleared/approved for marketing and the medical device is being used in accordance with its cleared/approved labeling.
2 Collection of blood samples by finger stick, heel stick, ear stick, or venipuncture as follows:
   a from healthy, non-pregnant adults who weigh at least 110 pounds. For these subjects, the amounts drawn may not exceed 550 mL in an 8 week period and collection may not occur more frequently than 2 times per week;
   b or from other adults and children, considering the age, weight, and health of the subjects, the collection procedure, the amount of blood to be collected, and the frequency with which it will be collected. For these subjects, the amount drawn may not exceed the lesser of 50 mL or 3 mL per kg in an 8 week period and collection may not occur more frequently than 2 times per week.
3 Prospective collection of biological specimens for research purposes by non-invasive means.
4 Collection of data through non-invasive procedures (not involving general anesthesia or sedation) routinely employed in clinical practice, excluding procedures involving X-rays or microwaves. Where medical devices are employed, they must be cleared/approved for marketing. (Studies intended to evaluate the safety and effectiveness of the medical device are not generally eligible for expedited review, including studies of cleared medical devices for new indications.)
5 Research involving materials (data, documents, records, or specimens) that have been collected, or will be collected solely for non-research purposes (such as medical treatment or diagnosis).
6 Collection of data from voice, video, digital, or image recordings made for research purposes.
7 Research on individual or group characteristics or behavior (including, but not limited to, research on perception, cognition, motivation, identity, language, communication, cultural beliefs or practices, and social behavior) or research employing survey, interview, oral history, focus group, program evaluation, human factors evaluation, or quality assurance methodologies.
8 Continuing review of research previously approved by the convened IRB as follows:
   a where (i) the research is permanently closed to the enrollment of new subjects; (ii) all subjects have completed all research-related interventions; and (iii) the research remains active only for long-term follow-up of subjects; or
   b where no subjects have been enrolled and no additional risks have been identified; or
   c where the remaining research activities are limited to data analysis.
Continuing review of research, not conducted under an investigational new drug application or investigational device exemption where categories two (2) through eight (8) do not apply but the IRB has determined and documented at a convened meeting that the research involves no greater than minimal risk and no additional risks have been identified.

in Table 8.1 and Table 8.2. Most research that involves a drug or device will exceed the criteria for minimal risk and will require full board review.

Protection of human subjects

The process for the protection of human research subjects is multifaceted. The underlying principles for the protection of research subjects are found in the Nuremberg Code, the Declaration of Helsinki, and the Belmont Report, which were discussed in Chapter 1. The charge to IRBs is to apply these principles in the evaluation of every aspect of the proposed research activity to protect the rights, safety, and well-being of study participants. Concurrent with this, the IRB staff assists investigators in maintaining adherence to regulatory mandates and institutional policies. It is not surprising, therefore, that when a research protocol is submitted to multiple IRBs the final determinations of the committees, their questions, and requests for additional information can vary greatly.[3,4]

Stress has been placed on the IRB by 'mission creep': the real or perceived need to consider all potential risks, not just to study participants but potential risks to researchers and the institution itself.[5] As part of the research approval process, IRBs will also consider issues that might not appear directly related to research risks such as investigator and/or institutional conflicts of interest, the scientific validity of a study, as well as the secure storage of and appropriate access to research records. Increasingly many sponsored trials request (or require) the collection and storage of biological specimens for future research, which presents another series of challenges for IRBs. This may be particularly problematic when studies using DNA are reviewed because of the potential to stigmatize certain ethnic or cultural groups.[6] It has been suggested that IRBs consider the risks to third parties (individuals not directly involved in the research) depending on the degree of risk to them.[7,8]

For many situations encountered by the IRB, there is little in the way of regulatory guidance. As a result, IRBs may establish substantially different submission requirements and review processes to fulfill regulatory mandates. The ultimate impact of these added responsibilities and diversity of review approaches is the potential for delays in starting the research. The effort required to ensure the adherence with regulatory and institutional policies also diverts IRB efforts from its primary mission of protecting the rights and welfare of human research participants.[5]

The materials that the IRB should obtain and review to make an approval determination are listed in Table 8.3. It should be noted that FDA regulations do not explicitly require that the committee obtain the Investigator's Brochure (IB). The need to review the IB is inferred from CFR 21.56.111, where the IRB is required to assess risks and determine that the risks are reasonable in relation to the anticipated benefits. Sponsors and investigators do a remarkable job in making these materials available to investigative teams and the IRB. The process may be particularly onerous in some institutions where 'hard copies' (as opposed to electronic copies) must be submitted. Despite providing all of this information, sponsors and investigators still encounter difficulties in obtaining IRB approval. This suggests that the major problem is not a lack of information, but failure to provide the information in the format and detail the IRB needs to conduct its review. Alternatively, sponsors and investigators may not understand the IRB review process or the IRB may not

Table 8.3 Documents the IRB/IEC should obtain

Materials submitted	IRB considerations	Potential problems
Trial protocol(s) and amendment(s)	The protocol is current and all amendments have been incorporated or appended.	All protocol elements are not adequately detailed. This frequently occurs when biosamples are being collected. See Table 6.3.
Investigator's brochure	Currently approved IB	IB lacks required information. Studies referred to in the protocol not detailed in the brochure. Is the brochure submitted the most current?
Written informed consent form(s) and consent form updates	Reading level. Adherence to local IRB requirements for the format and any standard language.	Failure to follow local IRB consent form template. Use of consent form language that differs substantially from institutional standards. Incorporating HIPAA language into the consent when the institution uses a standalone HIPAA authorization.
Subject recruitment materials	Provides sufficient detail to inform the potential participant of study requirements, duration, and compensation.	The recruitment process does not protect the patient's confidentiality, and/or privacy. Will patients receive unsolicited phone calls or letters?
Written information to be provided to subjects	Reading level. Not coercive. Indicate that the materials are related to a research activity.	Reading level is appropriate, but problems exist with type size and ease of use.
Available safety information	All of the available information regarding preclinical studies and sufficient safety data to support the use of the test article for the expected duration of participant enrollment.	Although usually provided in the IB, additional preclinical and clinical data, or safety reports may exist that have not been incorporated into the IB.
Information about payments and compensation to subjects	Compensation should not create an unfair inducement for study participation. Timing and method of payment should be clear. Pro-rating for partial study completion should be explained.	The process should be clear to the IRB and the study participant. Some institutions require that a W-9 be completed before processing a check. This should be reflected in protocol and consent form.
Investigator's current curriculum vitae and/ or other evidence of qualifications	Licensure and training necessary to safely perform all study-related activities. Inclusion of other study team members where special expertise is required.	There are many laboratory tests and clinical procedures that are used for screening and monitoring. It should be clear that qualified individuals are being used to interpret this information.
Any other documents required by the IRB/IEC	Completion of an IRB-approved course in human subjects' research.	Not all investigative team members have completed IRB training. This will delay study start.

have done a sufficient job of communicating its needs to those seeking to conduct the study. Further complicating matters is the lack of research and guidance on how IRBs should approach the review and approval of research.[9] The sections that follow are not intended to provide the details of the various documents reviewed by the IRB. Instead, they highlight the kind of information generally expected to be available to IRB members when protocols are discussed.

Review of the protocol, Investigator's Brochure, and informed consent

The IRB bases its decisions largely on the review of the documents provided by the sponsor and the PI. While the sponsor provides the bulk of materials that need to be submitted to the IRB, it is up to the investigator to ensure that the application is made in accordance with local IRB policies and procedures. Failure to 'follow the submission guidelines' occurs frequently and may result in delays in starting the study.[10] Some IRBs may invite the PI to the IRB meeting to present the research protocol and to clarify study-related issues, but even with this additional input, written documentation will be needed to support the basis of IRB's decision.

For industry-sponsored trials the protocol and IB are developed by experts in their field of research. As a result the need for the study, the design, and procedures required by the protocol most often have a sound scientific basis. Roadblocks may be encountered when these documents are submitted to the IRB for 'local review.' Regulatory authorities require local review to ensure that research subjects' rights are protected, taking into account the unique characteristics of the population served by the institution (e.g., religious, cultural, or economic) as well as the ability of the investigators and the institution to provide the care and services required by the protocol in light of existing commitments and resources. The problems encountered as a result of the local review of research are well documented.[2,11–13] Yet, for the foreseeable future it is not likely that the requirement for local review will change. Given this, there are steps that can be taken by study sponsors and investigators to minimize these difficulties as discussed below.

Protocol review

The research protocol is the principal document the IRB uses to determine whether the research should be approved at all. Depending on institutional requirements, one or more copies of the sponsor's full protocol will need to be submitted. The protocol should be the most current version and should have already incorporated any preexisting amendments. Many IRBs use a primary reviewer system whereby one member receives a copy of all original study documents. When this process is used, the IRB usually requires the submission of a protocol summary, which highlights the key aspects of the trial and is distributed to all committee members. The protocol summary is not as detailed as the full protocol but provides sufficient information for the committee to understand the key components of the research. These components include a brief overview of the condition being treated, inadequacies of current therapeutic interventions, the rationale of the study, the purpose of the study, identification of the primary outcome parameter, eligibility requirements, the treatment plan, the risks and how these have been minimized, the benefits, alternative treatments, sample size estimation, the primary and secondary outcome parameters, and plans for statistical analysis.[14] Because IRBs consist of members with scientific and non-scientific backgrounds, as well as community representatives, protocol summaries need to be written in uncomplicated language and avoid technical jargon. Sponsors and investigators should not assume that what is clear to them will automatically be clear to all IRB members.

Background

A short section providing the background of the condition being treated should be included. Most committees will not need extensive education about commonly encountered disease states such as hypertension, heart failure, or diabetes. But even in these conditions the proposed intervention might be directed at one component of the disease such as peripheral neuropathy, management of edema, or preserving renal function. In these circumstances, the background material should provide a basis for the committee to conclude that the intervention has the potential to improve or favorably alter the course of the disease. The FDA or the European Medicines Agency (EMA) may have published a guidance document that impacts on the design of the study. The guidance might suggest the need for a placebo arm, or recommend specific efficacy or safety criteria. IRB members, and sometimes the local investigators, are not always aware that the protocol was designed to conform to a specific guidance. A simple statement in the background that informs the committee of the guidance will facilitate their review.

Lack of details within the protocol can generate questions from the IRB and slow the process. While the purpose of the study might be clear (compare new drug A with established drug B), the rationale for conducting the study may not be readily apparent. Is the rationale that not all patients respond to the established drug so a new drug is needed? Or does the new drug have a better side-effects profile or offer the prospect of a more convenient dosage form or less frequent dosing? This information helps IRB members to understand why the study is important and should be conducted. It also introduces the prospects for potential benefit for study subjects and others with the underlying condition. The committee will want to see the rationale presented to study subjects in the consent document.

Primary outcome parameter

Identification of the primary outcome is essential to the conduct of the research, and should be clearly defined. The protocol should provide the basis for selecting the primary outcome variable and how it will be accurately measured. Some studies may use a primary outcome parameter that is a surrogate for the benefit the intervention is expected to achieve. For example, a study of an antihypertensive agent might use blood pressure lowering as an outcome although the real goal is to reduce cardiovascular morbidity and mortality. The sponsor should provide the rationale as to how the outcome is associated with the disease process being investigated. For comparative studies, the protocol should not only address the differences in outcome measures that can be shown to be statistically significantly different, but should also explain whether those differences have any clinical significance.

Eligibility criteria

IRBs look carefully at the eligibility criteria for the study. Inclusion and exclusion criteria are the first step the sponsor and investigator make in protecting study subjects. Again, adequate details should be provided to define the study population. The eligibility criteria should not be expressed in generalities (normal renal function) when specific criteria can easily be defined. Some protocols might define normal renal function as a serum creatinine <1.5 mg/dL; others as a creatinine clearance >80 mL/min. If the later definition is applied, how is this determined? Was it a 24-hour urine collection or an estimated creatinine clearance? If estimated, which formula is being used? The protocol should clearly state when eligibility assessments will be performed in relation to obtaining informed consent from the subject. The committee will look to determine whether eligibility is based on clinical and demographic information that already exists as part of the usual care the individual receives or whether eligibility will be determined on the basis of information collected and procedures performed solely for the purpose of the research. These and other issues will impact on inconveniences to the subject and may result in having to withdraw a subject who is no longer eligible to participate.

Study intervention and procedures

While the background, purpose, and eligibility criteria of the research generally raise few questions from the IRB, the procedures and interventions identified in the study methodology represent potential sources of risk, and thus receive very careful IRB attention. The IRB should consider all possible sources of risk. Some of these, such as the use of an investigational device or drug and research-related procedures, are easily recognized. Others such as inconveniences due to travel, emotional harm, and loss of confidentiality may be difficult to ascertain or may result from local conditions and therefore not be fully addressed in the sponsor's protocol. It is particularly helpful to the committee if the protocol identifies the interventions that are standard of care and those that are done solely for the purpose of the study. Input from the PI at each site is essential in making this determination since what represents standard of care at one institution may not at another. IRB members look for specific information in the protocol as it relates to the source of risk. In biomedical research, IRBs frequently consider the risks of drugs, devices, and study-related procedures. When the drugs and devices are investigational, the sponsor must assume the primary role for informing the committee. Individual investigators generally are not familiar enough with the drug or device to answer specific questions even if they have attended an investigators' meeting. Some of the information that IRBs will want to review may exist in the IB, but as mentioned above, not all members may receive a copy of the IB prior to the meeting. Furthermore, some elements of the methodology result from decisions made internally by the sponsor during protocol development or may be required by regulatory guidances and it may not be easily discernible why they were included.

Drug-related risks

In the case of a drug not yet approved for marketing, the extent of information available can vary considerably. Findings may be limited to the results of animal testing (for first-in-human studies) or may be much more substantial, reflecting the drug's tolerability and efficacy based on the exposure of thousands of study participants. To facilitate protocol review, the sponsor should incorporate the main findings of the pre-clinical and clinical studies reported in the IB into the protocol. The committee will be looking for justification of the dose and duration of treatment. For example, how did the pre-clinical studies influence the selection of the dosage that will be tested in humans? How does tolerability shown in a two-week human safety study support the transition to a six-month efficacy study? Most IRBs will not have the expertise to make an extrapolation of the results of animal testing to first-in-human studies and conclude that the dose being tested is safe. In order to facilitate the review process, it is worthwhile for the sponsor to address these issues in the protocol to educate the IRB about the regulatory guidances and scientific basis for the dose and duration of drug exposure. Issues surrounding dose selection for early clinical trials will become more complex if sponsors more actively pursue microdose studies or other FDA drug development initiatives.[15]

While not an infallible method for predicting Adverse Events (AEs), identifying similarities in structure or pharmacological activity of the investigational drug to those of marketed products with established side-effect profiles provides valuable information to the committee. The question raised by Cohen, 'Should we tolerate tolerability as an objective in early drug development?' relates directly to the drug safety concerns of the IRB.[16] Early-phase trials provide the opportunity to characterize a drug's kinetics and dynamics, which can then be used to inform the next series of human trials. Most committees review early-phase clinical trials with the understanding that rare, but serious, AEs are not likely to be identified even after substantial numbers of subjects have been studied.[17] While it is unlikely that an absolutely safe drug will ever be marketed, IRB members are very aware that a number of medications have been approved and marketed only to be withdrawn shortly thereafter because of rare, but serious side-effects. If the medication is not withdrawn from the market, regulatory authorities might require the addition of warning statements or restrict the types of patients who should receive the drug. Lacking any information to the contrary, these warnings might be extended to the whole class of drugs. This can impact on the IRB's assessment of risks for investigational drugs that are pharmacologically or structurally similar to the drug that was withdrawn. For this type of drug, the sponsor should not only include but highlight the portions of the protocol that identify and minimize the potential for this AE.

Device-related risks

Regulatory approval prior to the initiation of a device trial is required in the USA and Japan as opposed to the European Union, which has been suggested to impact development costs and the rapidity of bringing new devices to market.[18] Most countries have established criteria for classifying medical devices based primarily on the potential for risk. Some of the factors that are considered in making this determination include the characteristics of the device (invasive vs. non-invasive), duration of use (short-term vs. long-term), and the need for specialized training for safe and effective use of the device. The FDA identifies devices as 'significant risk or non-significant risk.' However, this determination applies only to the device and not to the manner in which the device will be used in the study. It is possible, therefore, that a non-significant-risk device could be determined by the IRB to be a significant-risk device on the basis of its intended use, the patient population being studied, or the consequences of device failure. In the USA, IRBs are also responsible for the approval of humanitarian use devices (HDEs) within their institutions. These are devices intended for use in conditions likely to affect fewer than 4000 patients yearly, making the conduct of a clinical trial nearly impossible. Many IRBs will have little or no experience with this type of device, so the sponsor should be prepared to educate the committee members by providing regulatory guidance information and identifying the sponsor's responsibilities.

Procedure-related risks

Study-related procedures contribute to the overall risks associated with the protocol, even if they are not experimental in and of themselves. It is of great value to the committee if the sponsor and PI clearly delineate those procedures that are considered standard of care from those performed solely for the purposes of the study. Making this determination is not always easy and can vary among research sites depending on local practices and the expertise available.[19] For example, the standard of care for certain conditions might be to obtain a chest radiograph at yearly intervals. The protocol might require that the study participant have had a chest radiograph performed within the previous six months. If a patient's last radiograph was obtained nine months ago, a radiograph will be required to qualify for the study. This is not part of the standard of care, so the radiation burden, though minimal, is still attributable to the research. Depending on the institution, the PI may be required to submit the protocol to a committee separate from the IRB for an assessment of radiation risks. The number and frequency of study visits might also be in excess of what would be considered standard of care; thus contributing to the inconveniences experienced within the study. It is imperative that the sponsor work closely with the site's PI to identify local issues related to study procedures.

Another kind of procedural risk relates to the need to withdraw other therapies in order to qualify a patient for the study. Today, most diseases have at least one drug, and sometimes dozens of drugs, indicated for the treatment of that condition. It is not unusual, therefore, to have potential participants discontinue medications in order to meet eligibility criteria. While it might be possible to restrict eligibility to newly diagnosed patients, this approach severely hampers study enrollment. Most IRBs are experienced with studies that require withdrawal of what might be very effective therapy for a patient in order to participate in a clinical trial. When effective therapy is withdrawn, the underlying condition would be expected to deteriorate, which might lead to the return of minor annoying symptoms or a disease flare of substantial clinical significance. For those studies in which withdrawal of other therapies is required, the protocol should explain in detail how participants will be monitored to detect worsening of the underlying condition and minimize the duration of poor disease control. In addition, some method of rescue therapy or rescue medication may be included in the protocol as an additional safety measure for patients.

The use of a placebo control group will receive careful attention from the IRB. A complete discussion of the ethical use of placebos in clinical research goes far beyond the purpose of this chapter; however, it is important to recognize that including a placebo control arm in a clinical trial can result in a clash of scientific, ethical, and regulatory principles.[20] As mentioned above, multiple therapeutic options exist for most medical conditions. Given this, why should a placebo control group ever be used? Amdur and Biddle have proposed an algorithm for the ethical use of placebos.[21] They suggest a number of factors that IRBs should consider in evaluating the ethical use of a placebo control in clinical research. Among these are the effectiveness and tolerability of current treatments, the long-term and short-term harms that might result from placebo use, and the potential value for the treatment of future patients with that condition. Consideration of the ethical use of placebos is not restricted to clinical drug trials. A similar concern exists for studies that might require a sham surgical procedure[22] or the insertion of a device that is not activated.[23] Once again, communication between the sponsor and the site investigator is critical, as is providing the rationale for using a placebo in the trial.

Methodology

Separate from study-related procedures is the study methodology. In addition to the general design of the trial (superiority, equivalence, non-inferiority), other aspects of the trial that are important to the IRB include the manner of randomization, stratification based on one or more patient characteristics, blinding procedures, choice of comparator, use of placebo, sample size estimation, and planned data analysis. It might appear that many aspects of the study methods fall outside of the purview of the IRB because they do not relate directly to individual participants' risks. However, they frequently do relate to the collective risks of study participants. For example, the lower boundary for non-inferiority trials must be established in order to estimate sample size.[24] The rationale for selecting this boundary should be explained. It might be acceptable to the committee if the inferiority boundary is set at 30% less effective if the comparator is associated with significant toxicities and the consequences of treatment failure are not life-threatening. On the other hand, this margin would likely not be acceptable if the comparator was highly effective and caused minimal toxicity. In either case, the sponsor should provide the rationale for why this lower limit was selected. Individual clinical investigators generally cannot provide a satisfactory answer to the committee, resulting in delays in starting the study.

Sample size estimations are important to the committee. Most often sample size calculations are based on an efficacy end point because it can be clearly defined and the variability in participant response to the intervention can be estimated from responses observed in similar studies of the same disease state. Though possible, it is impractical to base the sample size estimation on safety outcomes due to their unpredictability and low rates of occurrence, which would necessitate a large study population. Despite the relative ease with which a sample size can be determined for most studies, many investigator-initiated trials, and even those supported by NIH funding, may be underpowered to detect a significant treatment effect.[25,26] Studies conducted by the pharmaceutical industry rarely suffer from this problem but may appear to enroll an excessive number of participants. Studies like this might be 'overpowered' for the primary end point; that is, the clinical question could be answered with fewer participants enrolled. Overpowered studies can create problems during the review process because each of the study participants will still need to complete all of the study-related procedures (which might include blood sampling and radiation exposure) or be randomized to a less-effective treatment even though the study outcome could be determined based on a smaller number of subjects. Nonetheless, a case can be made for enrolling more than the number of participants required to ensure efficacy in order to better detect rare AEs and improve safety.

The regulatory landscape is changing with regard to the design of clinical trials, driven by the high costs of conducting human research and difficulties in recruiting and retaining study participants. Alternative strategies such as microdosing are being advocated by regulatory agencies.[15] In addition, adaptive trial designs are being suggested that will permit changes in the method of randomization, the doses being evaluated, and even modification of the primary outcome parameter.[27–30] Many IRBs do not have access to statisticians or others who are well versed in these types of clinical trial methodologies. It is in the best interest of the sponsor to assist committee members by providing the basics behind the design of these trials.

Special concerns related to biobanks

Any experienced clinician is aware that patients differ in their response to a drug. A clinically effective dose in one patient may result in serious toxicity in another. With the development of sensitive analytical techniques, demographic and clinical characteristics such as age, weight, and renal and hepatic function were identified that influence the pharmacokinetic profile of a variety of drugs. Although the kinetics of a drug are still of major importance in understanding the factors that contribute to the efficacy and safety of a drug, differences remain among individuals that cannot be explained by kinetics alone. Increasingly, industry-sponsored protocols are asking study participants to provide a blood or tissue sample to identify genetic polymorphisms that result in a different response among drug recipients. Other uses of banked materials include proteomic and biomarker studies that might be useful in the identification of new therapeutic targets. Despite the extensive detail provided in the sponsor's protocol regarding eligibility criteria, randomization procedures, safety monitoring, and possible adverse effects, the procedures for collection and use of biological samples sometimes receive less than a paragraph within the protocol. This lack of information may result in delays in the approval of this portion of the research. Because the procedures and risks of genetic research are different from other research-related risks, some IRBs require a separate consent form for genetic research. Questions frequently posed by the IRB related to research on stored blood or tissues that should be addressed in the protocol are listed in Table 8.4. Sponsors are responsible for providing this information to the committee as the local investigator will generally not be well versed in how the biobank will be operated and the steps taken to protect the confidentiality of the donor.

Table 8.4 Protocol elements and tissue banks

1.1 Title

- Should state that it is a tissue bank

1.2 Objectives

- Purpose of the bank, why is it important?
- Who is it for?
- What kind of testing will be performed?

1.3 Background

1.4 Eligibility criteria

- How are participants identified?
- Will normals be used?
- Samples from outside sources?

1.5 Treatment plan

- How will samples be collected? Departures from standard of care?
- Consider how clinical and demographic information will be handled.
- What types of testing will be performed?
  - Only for the disease the patient has or unrelated? Alzheimer's?
  - Genetic testing?
  - Other disease states? Hep. B, Hep. C, HIV?
- What happens to future test results?
- Procedures for releasing samples to other investigators.
- Plans to compensate for new product development.

1.6 Risks

- Major concern – confidentiality.
- Inaccurate pathological diagnosis.
- Due to alterations in procedures to accommodate specimen collection.

1.7 Benefits

- Generally none for the participant.
- It is fair to include potential to benefit patients with similar conditions; societal benefits.

1.8 Alternative treatments

- Don't participate.

1.9 Data collection and statistics

- Generally not an issue.

1.10 Other issues that should be addressed

- Coded samples – possibility to identity participant.
- Certificate of confidentiality.

Investigator's Brochure

ICH= International Conference on Humanisation. [handwritten annotation]

The ICH E6 *Guideline for Good Clinical Practice* describes the recommended content of the IB. Although the protocol describes what will be done during the study and how it will be done, it is the IB that provides the insight as to why certain procedures and monitoring parameters have been incorporated into the protocol. The IB serves as a resource for the IRB and the investigator to determine everything that is known (and what is not known) about the drug or device being studied. For drugs and devices in early development, there may be little or no published literature regarding the product's efficacy or safety. Consequently, in making its judgment for approving a protocol the IRB will rely heavily on the information provided in this document. As with the protocol, questions will be raised based on information that is referred to but not provided or that is not clear. For example, it is not unusual for participant accrual to proceed at a slower than expected rate, which may open the study to sites well after the original start date. Or the IB version submitted by the investigator may be dated two years prior to the date the protocol is scheduled for IRB review. How can the committee know that this the current version? The IB might also state that extended dosing studies in humans have been started and that long-term toxicity studies in rats are pending. Has this work been completed? Even IBs that are up to date may not include important information. For the IB to state that the chemical structure of the drug is well characterized, while no structure is provided, is a disservice to the committee. Most IRB committees will not have the expertise of a medicinal chemist available to them, but the ability of a clinician to compare the structure with that of a marketed agent with a known side-effect profile can provide a context for expected efficacy and toxicity. Sponsors can help themselves by keeping the IB current and by providing local investigators with information to be shared with the IRB related to studies that are in progress but not yet appearing in the IB.

Informed consent

While considerable attention is given to the consent document, the IRB is equally concerned about the process and timing for obtaining consent. Informed consent is discussed in Chapter 3. The material conveyed here relates primarily to potential barriers that may be encountered by sponsors and investigators to getting the consent form approved.

Some problems are easily predicted and thus avoidable. One of the frequently encountered problems is the inclusion of HIPAA language within the consent document. Some institutions require that HIPAA authorizations be obtained on a separate, study-specific document. The research consent informs participants of the study rationale, procedures, risks, and alternatives, and their rights and responsibilities. The HIPAA authorization informs parti- cipants that as a consequence of their involvement in the study, private health information will be shared with the sponsor, the IRB, and regulatory author- ities. Another theoretical reason for separating the HIPAA authorization from the research consent is to minimize institutional liability if either of these documents is found to be deficient in some manner. The local investigator should be able to provide some guidance to the sponsor as to which approach the institution uses.

Another common problem with consent forms lies within the injury state- ment. This is no doubt the result of the increase in litigation surrounding clinical research, which exposes sponsors, researchers, institutions, and even members of the IRB.[31] The IRB should make sure that the injury statement conforms to the language in the contract with the site. The contract will likely contain specific methods for allocating liability to the sponsor or the institu- tion at which the research is being conducted. This process, although essential to describe before the trial is initiated, is of little concern to the research participant and should not be included in the consent form. Trials sponsored by the pharmaceutical industry are more likely to offer coverage for medical expenses resulting from a research-related injury than those supported inter- nally or through government funding.[32] Injury statements tend to be written at a higher level than other portions of the consent and few meet the Institute of Medicine guidelines for compensation for research-related injuries.[32] Injury statements may contain wording that waives or appears to restrict the rights of the participant to receive treatment for research-related injuries. Language is sometimes included that places a certain level of responsibility on the research participant, such as, 'if you followed your doctor's instructions' or 'if you followed all study-related procedures.' In some cases even the PI and the institution are included through further modifications such as 'procedures that were properly performed ... .' Since study participants do not give up their rights to pursue a legal remedy in the event of an injury, it is unclear why these apparent restrictions appear in the consent form, except to inhibit participants from reporting problems. The language is so vague that study participants might feel that they have no recourse for treatment as a result of a missed appointment or failure to complete a study procedure. While all involved in the research enterprise are concerned about potential liability, the risks assumed by research participants are real and are usually accepted with no guarantee of benefit.

Qualifications of the investigator and investigative team

Patients expect that the clinical care they receive will be provided by physi- cians, nurses, and other health professionals who are qualified to deliver these services. Clinical researchers must meet this standard and fulfill other obligations to the sponsor, regulatory authorities, and IRBs. The significance of the additional obligations relates to the protection of study participants and the credible use of new drugs or devices in future patients. Stated another way, the research team must be committed to patient care and scientific integrity. Ultimately one individual at the site is responsible for meeting these commitments – the PI.

The process by which the IRB determines that an investigator is qualified to conduct a clinical study relates to their ability to meet criteria established by the IRB, the institution hosting the research, the sponsor, and regulatory authorities. Investigator responsibilities are outlined in the ICH E6 *Guideline for Good Clinical Practice* and in an FDA *Guidance for Industry*. The IRB needs evidence that the PI (usually a physician, podiatrist, or dentist) is capable of providing the medical care required by the study and can facilitate access to specialists in the event of a Serious Adverse Event (SAE). Evidence for this typically comes from the investigator's curriculum vitae. If the investigator is expected to perform a procedure as part of the research, the IRB may seek evidence that the investigator is authorized by the institution to carry out the procedure. Most IRBs will require the investigator to submit an FDA 1572 form or clinical trial agreement to demonstrate that the investigator intends to fulfill commitments made to the sponsor, and agrees to permit the sponsor and regulatory authorities access to records assuring adherence to the study protocol and to verify data collected during the study. Investigators will need to establish that they have received training in the conduct of human research and that it is in date. The IRB will usually ask the investigator to identify the total number of trials in which they are participating, the number of participants enrolled, and personnel who will be committed to the trial. Additional discussion of investigator qualifications can be found in Chapter 4.

Risk–benefit analysis

One of the first decisions made by the IRB chairperson, or designee, is determining the level of risk associated with the proposed research. Occasionally, industry sponsors are interested in de-identified data extracted from medical records, which could qualify for an exemption from IRB review. Examples of these kinds of studies include retrospective evaluations of prescribing patterns for certain conditions, or a meta-analysis of existing data. The FDA regulations are silent with regard to exempt research related to drug or device studies, except for the special case where emergency use of a drug or device is required. In the USA, adherence to HIPAA regulations is required and can influence the manner in which data is collected.

Prospective studies that are found to be of minimal risk may qualify for expedited review and approval. Minimal risk is defined in these terms: 'the probability and magnitude of harm or discomfort anticipated in the research are not greater in and of themselves than those encountered in daily life or during the performance of routine physical or psychological examinations or tests.' Differences in interpretation of 'minimal risk' can result in vastly diverse determinations among IRBs. This is particularly true in the application of the FDA standards for research involving children.[33] Some kinds of survey research might lead to the identification of issues that clearly are not minimal risk.[34] The difficulties encountered in applying the minimal risk standard have resulted in some IRBs abandoning this category in favor of a full board review for all prospective studies.

Most drug or device research exceeds minimal risk and requires full board review. The criteria for IRB approval of FDA-regulated research are found in Table 8.5. While the criteria are clear and succinct, problems with approval can occur because each ethics committee, consciously or unconsciously, develops a working definition for words such as 'minimized,' 'benefits,' 'risks,' 'equitable,' 'reasonable,' 'appropriate,' and 'adequate.'

Furthermore, even within the committee definitions can and do change from protocol to protocol depending on the drug or device being evaluated, the research team, the research location, the condition under study, and the population being studied. Better consistency within and among IRBs could be achieved if the words mentioned above could be assigned a relative value. Being able to quantify benefits and risks offers the possibility of manipulating these 'values' to establish whether benefits outweigh risks.[35] The viability of this approach related to the benefit–risk assessment for a population has been described.[36] While useful in the context of societal benefit–risk, it is not clear how this can be consistently applied to measure benefit–risk for individual research subjects. Being unable to quantify benefits and risks does not necessarily mean that sponsors and investigators are helpless and subject to the whims of the individual IRBs. Methods are available, although they are not always employed, that can help the IRB better understand exactly what benefits might come to participants and that the risks are appropriate and have been minimized to the extent possible. The following paragraphs, based on the FDA criteria for approval of

Table 8.5 Requirements for approval of research

- Risks to subjects are minimized
- Risks to subjects are reasonable in relation to anticipated benefits
- Selection of subjects is equitable
- Informed consent will be sought
- Informed consent will be documented
- Where appropriate, adequate provisions for data monitoring to ensure subject safety
- Where appropriate, adequate provisions to protect subject privacy and confidentiality
- Adequate safeguards to protect the rights and welfare of vulnerable subjects

research, describe what sponsors and investigators can do to educate IRB members and facilitate the review process.

Risks to subjects are minimized

The first step the sponsor and investigator can take is to identify all the risks and inconveniences associated with participating in the protocol. Most often the identification of risks is restricted to those related to the drug or device under investigation. While the IRB, the sponsor, and investigator might consider the investigational intervention the most important risk, as discussed above it is only one of the risks and inconveniences associated with the protocol. Once all of the risks are identified, the sponsor and investigator can facilitate the IRB review process by making a candid assessment of risks that the participant would experience as part of routine care, and those that are solely related to the research. Some risks undoubtedly result from research, such as use of placebo, surveys, and additional blood sampling; others might be less clear. If two radiographs are standard of care, are three? Some studies do not permit the use of medications that are considered as standard of care and investigators will implement a washout period in order to qualify patients for the study. Have the risks of withdrawing effective treatments been addressed? Similar considerations need to be given to every aspect of the protocol, including the amount of blood being drawn over the course of a study and the number of office visits.

Once all the risks have been identified, the sponsor and investigator can begin to address how these risks have been minimized. The specifics of how risks have been minimized will vary according to the research, but fall into three broad areas: selection and qualification of study participants, study-related methods and procedures, and monitoring and follow-up. Ultimately the sponsor can facilitate the review process by demonstrating how the protocol selects participants appropriately, and avoids enrolling individuals who are at higher risk of experiencing an AE; how study visits and procedures are scheduled to coincide as much as possible with usual clinical care activities; and for those risks that cannot be entirely eliminated, that appropriate monitoring methods have been included to reduce AEs. As local investigators usually will not have the insight to answer questions about how the protocol was developed, the sponsor should provide this information.

Risks to subjects are reasonable in relation to anticipated benefits

This is the only requirement for approval that mentions potential benefits to research participants. Most drug and device protocols are quite explicit regarding potential risks; however, potential benefits often are not discussed. The ICH E6 *Guideline for Good Clinical Practice* states that the IB should present information 'that enables a clinician, or potential investigator, to understand it and make his/her own unbiased risk–benefit assessment of the appropriateness of the proposed trial.' Often the background provided in the study protocol does not convey any of the benefits that might be expected to the individual or society through the development of the drug or device. The sponsor has the best insight as to the potential benefits and should include their thinking on these. Regulations require that the available information allow an 'unbiased risk–benefit assessment.' While omission of any assessment by the sponsor of benefits versus risks will permit an unbiased assessment, it may also result in an assessment that is not fully informed. The IRB makes the final determination on what risks are reasonable in relation to possible benefits, and is free to ignore the assessment of the sponsor.

Selection of subjects is equitable

The purpose of equitable subject selection is to ensure that the risks of research are spread out over the groups of individuals who are expected to benefit from the findings – the principle of justice described in the Belmont Report. Both the sponsor and local investigator need to be involved in meeting this goal. The local IRB will scrutinize eligibility criteria and recruitment methods as part of fulfilling this requirement, but can only influence recruitment at the institutional level. Sponsors can help by providing information about other sites involved in multicenter trials to show their efforts in distributing risks.

Informed consent will be sought

Merely providing an informed consent template is insufficient. As recently published articles point out, informed consent is a process; there is an over-reliance on the consent form itself; and methods for assessing participants' understanding of the risks, benefits, and their responsibilities are largely inadequate.[37,38] Despite all the details given in the sponsor's protocol for study-related procedures, little is routinely provided to the research team concerning the sponsor's expectations for the timing and process of obtaining informed consent. Ultimately, the local IRB is responsible for ensuring that appropriate methods are used to obtain consent. Even so, sponsors can assist in meeting this important obligation to research participants.

Informed consent will be documented

Again, over-reliance on the consent document is frequently observed. Investigators need to document not only that consent was obtained, as evidenced by the signed consent form, but also that the process, timing, and circumstances surrounding consent are documented in the medical record. The record should reflect any questions asked by the participant, how they were answered, and the methods used by the investigator to determine the participants' comprehension of each of the informed consent elements. Sponsors can take an active role in achieving this goal through investigator training and by providing forms or checklists to assist investigators in documenting the consent process.

Where appropriate, adequate provisions for data monitoring to ensure subject safety

As with other sections of a sponsored research protocol, great detail is provided related to AEs and how they should be reported to the sponsor. Care is taken to clearly discriminate between what will be considered a side-effect of the drug from those events that will be attributed to the underlying disease. Reporting requirements for the local investigator are outlined, and study monitors make frequent site visits to assure that reports are accurate and submitted in a timely fashion. What is often missing, but is of major importance to the IRB, is a discussion of how these reports will be handled once they are received by the sponsor. This is especially true for multicenter trials, where AEs may find their way to the site investigator and eventually to the IRB weeks or months after they have occurred. IRB members understand that instant access to AEs or unanticipated problems is unrealistic; but they would like some assurances that a process is being followed that will assist them in protecting research participant enrolled at their institution. This process is usually omitted from the clinical trial protocol. Lacking any information, the IRB is likely to assume that there is no plan to look at adverse and unanticipated events in a timely manner. This raises questions that the sponsor must answer, resulting in delays in starting the study. The process for handling these occurrences should be described in some detail. It is useful for the sponsor to include rules that site investigators can employ to determine whether a study participant should be removed from the trial. Similarly, a schedule for assessing all reported events and disseminating this information to investigators and IRBs will allay some concerns.

As discussed by Silverman, not every trial will require a Data Safety Monitoring Board (DSMB).[39] At the same time, a protocol mentioning that a DSMB will be constituted is of little value to the IRB. It is more important for the sponsor to provide a timeframe for the constitution of the DSMB and to share the plan developed by the board for interim analyses, stopping rules, and other patient safety issues. Timely submissions of DSMB reports to the IRB provide evidence that the sponsor and DSMB members are taking participant safety seriously. Unfortunately, some reports come to the IRB merely stating that the DSMB has met and decided that the trial should continue. This information is useless to the IRB. DSMBs should provide some assessment of the total number of study participants enrolled, the rate of study enrollment, the frequency of study violations and deviations, and an acknowledgement that AEs were reviewed, in addition to the decision to continue the study.

Where appropriate, adequate provisions to protect subject privacy and confidentiality

One of the underlying premises of medical research is the hope that the results will be generalizable, and offer society improved methods for the identification, understanding, treatment, and prevention of disease. To achieve this goal, health information from hundreds or thousands of individuals is combined, and distilled to provide innovative therapies. Researchers and sponsors have a responsibility to protect the health information of an individual. Inadvertent disclosures of health information potentially can affect the individual's ability to obtain a job or health insurance, or could otherwise stigmatize the individual in the community. In the USA, HIPAA regulations require that individuals be told how their health information will be used, for how long it will be made available, and who will have access to it. Since its implementation, investigators have identified HIPAA disclosure as another barrier to research recruitment for all kinds of research.[40,41] Furthermore, sponsors and investigators may need to make changes to the research plan in order to remain compliant with the rule.[42]

Two other issues that IRBs deal with regularly relate to HIV testing and screening for drugs of abuse. Laws related to HIV testing vary according to jurisdiction. Some states require pre- and post-test counseling and may require the use of a separate consent form. Sponsors have an understandable interest in making sure that participants enrolled in a trial are not using drugs of abuse. Not only might illegal drug use confuse the results of the study, but these participants may, at least in theory, expose the sponsor to additional study costs and liability. Since recreational drug use is illegal in most countries, collecting and documenting this illegal activity may expose the individual to prosecution and legal sanctions. In order to protect study participants, IRBs may require that the sponsor obtain a certificate of confidentiality.

Adequate safeguards to protect the rights and welfare of vulnerable subjects
Children, prisoners, pregnant women, the handicapped, and mentally impaired individuals are widely considered as vulnerable to exploitation in research. Special protections are given to these populations through 45 CFR Part 46 Subparts B, C, and D and to children in FDA-regulated research through 21 CFR Part 50 Subpart C. The ICH E6 *Guideline for Good Clinical Practice* expands the definition of vulnerable groups by including those who have a subordinate role in a hierarchical structure, such as students, employees, or members of the armed forces. Many of the potential problems involving vulnerable subjects can be dealt with through modifications of the eligibility criteria. When this cannot be done, the process of informed consent will fall under closer scrutiny. Consent procedures for vulnerable populations are fully addressed in Chapter 3.

Continuing review

DHHS, FDA, and ICH guidelines each require that the IRB 'should conduct continuing review of each ongoing trial at intervals appropriate to the degree of risk to human subjects, but at least once per year.' At the time of first approval, the IRB should determine how frequently the research should be reviewed for reapproval. The one-year interval is commonly applied to most research; however, early-phase drug or device studies may need to be resubmitted at three- or six-month intervals. Some investigator-initiated research or research using innovative therapies where risks are unknown may need to be reported to the IRB on a case-by-case basis. Continuing reviews address a wide range of issues including the number of participants enrolled and their demographics, AE reporting, the need for changes to the informed consent document, and a literature review to show that the research question being addressed is still important.[43] IRBs are at some disadvantage when multicenter trials are subjected to continuing review in that the committee usually does not have access to the totality of information available to the sponsor. Generally, their review will be based on the participants recruited at their site, which may or may not reflect the experience in the entire trial. Some sponsors facilitate the review process by providing local investigators with regular updates regarding enrollment and summaries of AEs. Despite the importance of the continuing review process, IRBs are frequently cited for failing to provide adequate continuing review of research.[44]

Final thoughts

Investigators and sponsors often experience frustration in dealing with local IRBs. Although some IRBs appear to have the mission of blocking clinical research, this is rarely the case. Sponsors, investigators, and IRB members each work to meet regulatory mandates and 'follow the rules.' Unfortunately, the rules are not always very specific and sometimes seem to come from different games. The sponsors' chances for success are improved by selecting investigators who have established relationships with their local IRB and understand the information that is needed to assure a timely and thorough review.

References

1. Fitzgerald MH, Phillips PA. Centralized and non-centralized ethics review: a five nation study. *Account Res* 2006; 13(1): 47–74.
2. Wainwright P, Saunders J. What are local issues? The problem of the local review of research. *J Med Ethics* 2004; 30(3): 313–317.
3. Angell E *et al.* Consistency in decision making by research ethics committees: a controlled comparison. *J Med Ethics* 2006; 32(11): 662–664.
4. Dyrbye LN *et al.* Medical education research and IRB review: an analysis and comparison of the IRB review process at six institutions. *Acad Med* 2007; 82(7): 654–660.
5. Gunsalus CK *et al.* The Illinois White Paper: improving the system for protecting human subjects: counteracting IRB 'mission creep'. *Qual Inq* 2007; 13(5): 617–649.
6. Meslin EM, Quaid KA. Ethical issues in the collection, storage, and research use of human biological materials. *J Lab Clin Med* 2004; 144(5): 229–234.

7. Jonathan K. Missing the forest: further thoughts on the ethics of bystander risk in medical research. *Camb Q Healthc Ethics* 2007; 16(4): 483–490.

8. Resnick DB, Sharp RR. Protecting third parties in human subjects research. [Cover story]. *IRB: Ethics & Human Research* 2006; 28(4): 1–7.

9. Candilis PJ *et al.* The need to understand IRB deliberations. *IRB: Ethics & Human Research* 2006; 28(1): 1–5.

10. Stair TO *et al.* Variation in institutional review board responses to a standard protocol for a multicenter clinical trial. *Acad Emerg Med* 2001; 8(6): 636–641.

11. Burman W *et al.* The effects of local review on informed consent documents from a multicenter clinical trials consortium. *Control Clin Trials* 2003; 24(3): 245–255.

12. Dilts DM, Sandler AB. Invisible barriers to clinical trials: the impact of structural, infra-structural, and procedural barriers to opening oncology clinical trials. *J Clin Oncol* 2006; 24(28): 4545–4552.

13. Nowak KS *et al.* Reforming the oversight of multi-site clinical research: a review of two possible solutions. *Accountability in Research: Policies & Quality Assurance* 2006; 13(1): 11–24.

14. Colt HG, Mulnard RA. Writing an application for a human subjects institutional review board. *Chest* 2006; 130(5): 1605–1607.

15. Kimmelman J. Ethics at Phase 0: clarifying the issues. *J Law Med Ethics* 2007; 35(4): 727–733.

16. Cohen A. Should we tolerate tolerability as an objective in early drug development? *Br J Clin Pharmacol* 2007; 64(3): 249–252.

17. Borer JS *et al.* Cardiovascular safety of drugs not intended for cardiovascular use: need for a new conceptual basis for assessment and approval. *Eur Heart J* 2007; 28(15): 1904–1909.

18. Nose Y. Institutional review board approval for clinical application of new medical devices rather than government agency. *Artif Organs* 2004; 28(12): 1057–1058.

19. Miller FG, Silverman HJ. The ethical relevance of the standard of care in the design of clinical trials. *Am J Respir Crit Care Med* 2004; 169(5): 562–564.

20. Freedman B, Glass KC. Placebo orthodoxy in clinical research II: ethical, legal, and regulatory myths. *J Law Med Ethics* 1996; 24(3): 252.

21. Amdur RJ, Biddle CJ. An algorithm for evaluating the ethics of a placebo-controlled trial. *Int J Cancer* 2001; 96(5): 261–269.

22. Miller FG. Ethical issues in surgical research. *Thorac Surg Clin* 2005; 15(4): 543–554.

23. Connolly SJMD *et al.* Pacemaker therapy for prevention of syncope in patients with recurrent severe vasovagal syncope: Second Vasovagal Pacemaker Study (VPS II): a randomized trial. *JAMA* 20037; 289(17): 2224–2229.

24. Christensen E. Methodology of superiority vs. equivalence trials and non-inferiority trials. *J Hepatol* 2007; 46(5): 947–954.

25. Halpern SD *et al.* The continuing unethical conduct of underpowered clinical trials. *JAMA* 2002; 288(3): 358–62.

26. Rosoff PM. Can underpowered clinical trials be justified? *IRB: Ethics & Human Research* 2004; 26(3): 16–19.

27. Koch A. Biostatistical methods for demonstrating efficacy in the regulatory setting. *Bundesgesundheitsblatt Gesundheitsforschung Gesundheitsschutz* 2005; 48(5): 572–579.

28. Freidlin B, Simon R. Adaptive signature design: an adaptive clinical trial design for generating and prospectively testing a gene expression signature for sensitive patients. *Clin Cancer Res* 2005; 11(21): 7872–7878.

29. Kelly PJ *et al.* An adaptive group sequential design for phase II/III clinical trials that select a single treatment from several. *J Biopharm Stat* 2005; 15(4): 641–658.

30. Zhang L, Rosenberger WF. Response-adaptive randomization for clinical trials with continuous outcomes. *Biometrics* 2006; 62(2): 562–569.

31. Mello MM *et al.* The rise of litigation in human subjects research. *Ann Intern Med* 2003; 139(1): 40–45.

32. Paasche-Ortow MK, Brancati FL. Assessment of medical school institutional review board policies regarding compensation of subjects for research-related injury. *Am J Med* 2005; 118(2): 175–180.

33. Shah S *et al*. Health law and ethics. How do institutional review boards apply the federal risk and benefit standards for pediatric research? *JAMA* 2004; 291(4): 476–482.

34. Sharp HM, Orr RD. When 'minimal risk' research yields clinically-significant data, maybe the risks aren't so minimal. *Am J Bioethics* 2004; 4(2): W32–W6.

35. Chuang-Stein CER, Pritchett Y. Measures for conducting comparative benefit:risk assessment. *Drug Inf J* 2008; 42(3): 223–233.

36. Garrison LP Jr *et al*. Assessing a structured, quantitative health outcomes approach to drug risk–benefit analysis. *Health Aff (Millwood)* 2007; 26(3): 684–695.

37. May T *et al*. Viewpoint: IRBs, hospital ethics committees, and the need for 'translational informed consent'. *Acad Med* 2007; 82(7): 670–674.

38. Sabik L *et al*. Informed consent: practices and views of investigators in a multinational clinical trial. *IRB: Ethics & Human Research* 2005; 27(5): 13–18.

39. Silverman H. Ethical issues during the conduct of clinical trials. *Proc Am Thorac Soc* 2007; 4(2): 180–184; discussion 4.

40. Ness RB. Influence of the HIPAA Privacy Rule on health research. *JAMA* 2007; 298(18): 2164–2170.

41. Dunlop AL *et al*. The impact of HIPAA authorization on willingness to participate in clinical research. *Ann Epidemiol* 2007; 17(11): 899–905.

42. De Wolf VA *et al*. Part II: HIPAA and disclosure risk issues. *IRB: Ethics & Human Research* 2006; 28(1): 6–11.

43. Gordon B, Prentice E. Continuing review of research involving human subjects: approach to the problem and remaining areas of concern. *IRB* 1997; 19(2): 8–11.

44. Bramstedt KA, Kassimatis K. A study of warning letters issued to institutional review boards by the United States Food and Drug Administration. *Clin Invest Med* 2004; 27(6): 316–323.

9

Pharmacovigilance

Stephen Klincewicz, Yuung Yuung Yap,

and Adrian Thomas

Introduction

Pharmacovigilance has been defined as 'the process and science of monitoring the safety of medicines and taking action to reduce risks and increase benefits from medicines.'[1] As a process, pharmacovigilance is influenced heavily by ethical, regulatory, and legal frameworks. As a science, it borrows heavily from the basic sciences of toxicology, pharmacology, and clinical medicine, as well as from the population-based disciplines of public health and epidemiology.

The data sources, analytic tools, and resources conscripted to assess a medicinal product's benefit–risk ratio depend on the stage of that product's life cycle. Typically, it is the time at which the product is first introduced in humans that the most relevant regulatory requirements of pharmacovigilance attach.

With the development of the International Conference on Harmonisation (ICH) initiative, there has been some attempt to develop harmonized scientific and technical guidelines related to the safety and efficacy of medicines.[2] Although the legal implementation of ICH guidelines varies in each jurisdiction, the initiative has been reasonably successful in setting international standards for pharmacovigilance in the Good Clinical Practice (GCP) environment. The *Guidance for Good Clinical Practice* (ICH E6)[3] sets the standards of GCP while the *Clinical Safety Data Management: Definitions and Standards for Expedited Reporting* (ICH E2A)[4] provides guidance on expedited safety reporting in clinical investigations.

In recent years, with the development and implementation of *Pharmacovigilance Planning* (ICH E2E),[5] there has also been a gradual transition from a focus on the reporting of adverse events toward a more comprehensive approach of integrating all source information about the product safety into a broader plan of proactive risk assessment and management.

Adverse events

Definition of adverse events

There are no universally accepted definitions of the terms 'adverse event' or 'adverse drug reaction.' While the use of the term 'side-effect' has generally been abandoned, the precise definition of these terms may vary between sources such as clinical pharmacology textbooks and country-specific laws and regulations. For GCP purposes, it is important that the appropriate definition be chosen since this may influence the evaluation and notification of such information to health authorities, investigators, and ethics committees. Although there are no universally accepted definitions, the terms 'adverse event' and 'adverse drug reaction' found in ICH E2A are generally well accepted. They are as follows:

Adverse Event (or Adverse Experience)

> Any untoward medical occurrence in a patient or clinical investigation subject administered a pharmaceutical product, which does not necessarily have to have a causal relationship with this treatment.[4]

An 'adverse event' can therefore be any unfavorable and unintended sign (including an abnormal laboratory finding, for example), symptom, or disease temporally associated with the use of a medicinal product, whether or not considered related to the medicinal product.

Adverse Drug Reaction (ADR)

> …all noxious and unintended responses to a medicinal product related to any dose should be considered adverse drug reactions.[4]

In the pre-approval setting, clinical experience with a new medicinal product or its new usages, particularly in terms of the therapeutic dose(s), may not be established. The phrase 'responses to a medicinal product' is defined in ICH as a causal relationship between a medicinal product and an adverse event. The causal relationship can be further defined as being at least a reasonable possibility that there is a relationship, i.e., the relationship cannot be ruled out. In the post-market setting, the well-accepted definition of an 'adverse drug reaction' for approved medicinal products is found in the WHO Technical Report 498 (1972) and reads as follows:

> A response to a drug which is noxious and unintended and which occurs at doses normally used in man for prophylaxis, diagnosis, or therapy of disease or for modification of physiological function.[6]

— serieusness
SCEu expeetedness.
└ causality

Classification of adverse events

The correct classification of adverse events is important because the classification will generally determine both the timeframe and format for reporting. Adverse events are typically classified according to the following three criteria.

Seriousness

'Seriousness' is a term assigned for regulatory purposes and not a term used in clinical context. A 'serious' adverse event (experience) or reaction comprises a subset of adverse events that either[4]

- results in death
- is life-threatening (The term 'life-threatening' in the definition of 'serious' refers to an event in which the patient was at risk of death at the time of the event; it does not refer to an event which hypothetically might have caused death if it were more severe.)
- requires inpatient hospitalization or prolongation of existing hospitalization
- results in persistent or significant disability/incapacity
- is a congenital anomaly/birth defect, or
- an important medical event.

Causality

The standard of causality is open to much discussion and debate and is not clearly articulated in the ICH guidance. In ICH E2A, the term 'reasonable possibility' is characterized by the phrase 'a causal relationship cannot be ruled out.'[4] However, in a later section that discusses the expediting of serious, unexpected adverse drug reactions, there is an additional explanation that 'the expression 'reasonable causal relationship' is meant to convey in general that there are facts (evidence) or arguments to suggest a causal relationship.'[4]

Expectedness

An individual unexpected adverse drug reaction is one that is inconsistent either in nature or in severity with those that have been described in the reference safety information for that particular product. For clinical investigations, this reference safety information is generally the Investigator's Brochure (IB).[3]

Reportable adverse event

In determining whether an adverse event should be reported, it must have the following four elements:[4]

- an identifiable patient
- an identifiable reporter

PRDAE

- a suspect drug
- an adverse event.

For regulatory purposes, initial reports containing the four elements should be submitted within the prescribed timelines. In clinical investigations, determination of the first three elements is relatively straightforward. It is more challenging when assessing the fourth element because the general definition of an adverse event is a very broad one. According to ICH E2A, an adverse event should be reported in an expedited fashion when it 'can be identified as serious and unexpected, and for which, in clinical investigation cases, there is a reasonable suspected causal relationship.'[4] In order to determine whether an adverse event is reportable and whether expedited reporting is appropriate, it is important to classify an adverse event appropriately according to criteria described above.

SUSARS

The first step is to determine whether the event is classified as 'a serious adverse event.' Issues related to causation or medical or scientific ability do not come into consideration at this stage. In practice this requires considerable medical and scientific judgment and, unfortunately, there are no gold standards for making such a determination. For example, certain important medical events may not be immediately life-threatening or result in death or hospitalization, but these should usually be considered as a 'serious adverse event' if the events jeopardize the patient or require intervention to prevent one of the other outcomes that would constitute a serious adverse event. Examples of such events are intensive treatment in an emergency room or at home for allergic bronchospasm; blood dyscrasias or convulsions that do not result in hospitalization; or development of drug dependency or drug abuse.[4]

In defining an adverse event, it is the temporal relationship with the administration of the product that is the cornerstone concept. In clinical investigation cases, there needs to be a reasonable causal relationship to the medicinal product. Causality does, however, play a role in nomenclature of an adverse drug reaction and is, in fact, the hallmark of this concept. Another problematic area is differentiating adverse events from outcomes. For example, a report of 'death' or 'hospitalization' without a specific cause might be considered a report of an outcome rather than an adverse event. While ICH E2A specifically includes these outcomes in its minimum criteria for reportability, this more inclusive definition does not appear uniformly in other pharmacovigilance laws or regulations. These differences, while subtle, are again important in GCP since the relevant characterization of emerging safety profile of the medicinal product will be dependent upon the correct recognition and attribution of an adverse event to a medicinal product.

Reporting guidelines and timeline

Pharmacovigilance in the clinical trial setting consists primarily of a systematic classification, triage, prioritization, and communication of the adverse events that are recorded as part of the trial protocol. The requirement for expedited reporting may vary according to jurisdiction. In many jurisdictions, only certain serious adverse events (e.g., serious adverse events that are suspected of having a causal relation to a medicinal product or as serious unlabeled adverse events) will require expedited reporting to health authorities. There are no standardized global reporting requirements for adverse event reporting from clinical trials. However, there are several general principles that apply to assessment and reporting from clinical trials. These principles are implicit in ICH E2A, although even these have been adopted with modification in those jurisdictions that are part of or who have recognized the ICH initiatives.

Reporting to health authorities

Within the GCP environment, there are several key recipients of safety information. General concepts of the ICH E2A and ICH E6 have been formalized into laws and regulations in various jurisdictions. In the USA, sponsors have the obligations to report adverse events arising from clinical trials according to the provisions set out in 21 CFR 312.32 (IND Regulation).[7] Sponsors of clinical trials in the European Community (EC) must report adverse event according to Directive 2001/20/EC (EU Regulation) and its related guidelines such as *Detailed guidance on the collection, verification and presentation of adverse reaction reports arising from clinical trials on medical products for human use* (April 2006 Guidance).[8,9] However, exact content, timing, format, and recipient listing varies from jurisdiction to jurisdiction and may be complex. Therefore, it is imperative to review local laws to determine the exact reporting requirements in each of the jurisdictions.

Reporting of safety information to health authorities is a requirement of sponsors and there may be some additional requirements to notify ethics committees and Institutional Review Boards (IRBs) as well as study subjects. For the sponsor, reporting timelines to the health authorities begin when the four elements of an adverse event, discussed above, are present. In general, reporting from the clinical trial is based on the factors of seriousness, expectedness, and causality as described earlier in the chapter. A subset of the adverse events classified as Serious Unexpected Adverse Drug Reactions (SUSARs) and that result in death or are considered life-threatening are reported in the most restrictive timeframe of 7 calendar days (by phone or by fax) and all other serious, unexpected adverse drug reactions are reported in 15 days. The 7-day report is an additional reporting requirement and does not supplant the need to submit these fatal and life-threatening serious, unexpected, related adverse drug experiences as a 15-day written report as well.

ICH has successfully harmonized the expedited reporting scheme for clinical trials in the EU and USA. Sponsors are required to report to the health authorities:

- 7-day reports (serious, unexpected, and related events that are fatal or life-threatening must be initially notified to the health authorities by phone or fax in addition to the subsequent written 15-day reports); and
- 15-day reports (for the serious and unexpected and causally related adverse events that are neither life-threatening nor fatal).

All other serious adverse drug reactions and, in some cases, serious adverse events are reported on a periodic basis (typically yearly). In many jurisdictions, an annual report of either an individual study or related clinical studies must be submitted along with any final study reports (when available) that summarize all the adverse events and/or adverse reactions.

Besides the harmonized expedited reporting scheme, it is important to point out that some spontaneous reports and other safety issues may also qualify for expedited reporting in some jurisdictions and thus sponsors should carefully review the additional requirements, which are summarized below.

Medicinal product undergoing evaluation

In many jurisdictions, when a medicinal product dossier is undergoing evaluation by a health authority for possible approval, the applicant has an additional reporting responsibility. Applicants are required to report all safety information relevant to understanding the safety profile of that medicinal product.

If the medicinal product is approved in certain jurisdictions, spontaneous reports that occur within these jurisdictions must be reported to the health authorities in the USA and EC where the medicinal products are undergoing evaluation. This would be true regardless of whether the dosage, formulation, or indication were to be different. In general, individual spontaneous case safety reports do not generally require a causality assessment and thus would likely need to be submitted regardless of a company causality assessment. The applicability of this general rule in a particular jurisdiction, however, should be verified since there may be differences in how to report spontaneous cases to a medicinal product dossier undergoing evaluation. In the USA, prior to the receipt of a New Drug Application (NDA), all source adverse event reporting to an Investigational New Drug Application (IND) is required under 21 CFR Section 312.32 until the medicinal product is approved. After approval, only those adverse events that emanate from that particular IND need to be reported.

Additional reporting requirements

ICH

An increased frequency and/or severity of 'expected' adverse drug reactions might also be sufficient to reconsider the safety profile of that medicinal product. The additional responsibility of reporting clinically significant increases in rates of occurrence of serious adverse events is discussed in ICH E2A.[4] Thus, this can be considered a two-step evaluative process. Unfortunately, there are no formulaic mechanisms for determining this reporting requirement. The first step would be to determine whether there is an increased rate of adverse event occurrence. If there were an increased rate of the occurrence, then the second step would be to perform a scientific evaluation to determine whether or not this increased rate was clinically meaningful.

Under ICH E2A, in addition to spontaneous reports, reports from the scientific literature, information from pre-clinical data on carcinogenicity and mutagenicity that is relevant to human safety, and safety conclusions reached from epidemiological studies are all candidates for reporting as well.[7] It specifically imposes a requirement to send, as expedited reports, an increased occurrence of a known adverse drug reaction that is 'clinically important.'[4] However, details that describe when such increased frequencies are considered 'clinically meaningful' are not described in the guidance and hence considerable judgment is required.

United States

The IND Regulation requires sponsors to promptly review 'all information relevant to the safety of the drug obtained or otherwise received by the sponsor from any source, foreign or domestic, including information obtained from any clinical or epidemiologic investigations, animal investigations, commercial marketing experience, reports in the scientific literature, and unpublished scientific papers as well as reports from foreign regulatory authorities that have not already been previously reported to the agency by the sponsor.'[7]

In addition to any adverse event that is serious, unexpected, and associated with the use of a medicinal product, the IND Regulation also imposes upon the sponsor an obligation to report, as a 15-calendar-day expedited report, 'any finding from tests in laboratory animals that suggest a significant risk for human subjects including reports of mutagenicity, teratogenicity, or carcinogenicity.'[7] Again, there are no specific details or guidance to assist in the determination of when animal study results can be extrapolated to make a determination of a 'significant risk' to humans.

European Community

The basic principles and timeframe for reporting SUSARs are outlined in the EU Regulation and these are consistent with ICH E2A.[9] Although there is a certain level of harmonization, there are also several additional expedited reporting requirements imposed upon sponsors conducting clinical trials in the EC.

The EU Regulation provides that the following safety issues qualify for expedited reported when they are such that they 'might materially alter the current benefit–risk assessment of an investigational medicinal product or that would be sufficient to consider changes in the investigational medicinal product administration or in the overall conduct of the trial.' For instance:[9]

- single case reports of an expected serious adverse reactions with an unexpected outcome (e.g., a fatal outcome)
- an increase in the rate of occurrence of an expected serious adverse reaction, which is judged to be clinically important
- post-study SUSARs that occur after the patient has completed a clinical trial and are reported by the investigator to the sponsor
- a new event relating to the conduct of the trial or the development of the investigational medicinal product likely to affect the safety of the subjects, such as:
  - a serious adverse event which could be associated with the trial procedures and which could modify the conduct of the trial
  - a significant hazard to the subject population such as lack of efficacy of an investigational medicinal product used for the treatment of a life-threatening disease
  - a major safety finding from a newly completed animal study (such as carcinogenicity)
- recommendations of the data monitoring committee, if and where relevant for the safety of the subject.

It is the nature of the EC legal system that each individual Member State must enact the provisions in the EU Regulation into its local laws. During implementation of these requirements, there may be local interpretation and nuances. Thus, it is advisable to review the individual Member State's local laws in order to ascertain the details.

Reporting to investigators and ethics committees

1/ Health Authorities.
2/ Investigators
3/ ethics committees.

In addition to obligations in reporting to health authorities, sponsors may have an obligation to provide adverse event information to investigators participating in a clinical trial program as well as to ethics committees. While the rationale for this requirement is not specifically stated, these requirements would appear to be consistent with the need to continuously inform those responsible for the oversight of subject safety with evolving safety information in a timely manner. This would include updating the informed consent form to include the new safety information and providing the opportunity to subjects to reconsider their participation in the study.

While ICH provides a framework for meeting this obligation, compliance with health authority requirements is complex and demands a thorough review of the regulatory requirements in each jurisdiction where the trial may be conducted. Globally, this obligation stems from Section 5.17.1 of ICH E6:[3]

> The sponsor should expedite the reporting to all concerned investigator(s)/ institutions(s), to the IRB(s)/IEC(s), where required, and to the regulatory authority(ies) of all adverse drug reactions (ADRs) that are both serious and unexpected.

ICH E6 also sets the standards on information to report to investigators and ethics committees, but the timeframe or formats for such reporting obligations are provided in ICH E2A.[3,4]

United States

The IND Regulation is silent in many areas relating to submitting adverse event reports to investigators and ethics committees. It is clear in the IND Regulation that sponsors must send all written expedited reports to all participating investigators within the 15-calendar-day period.[7]

However, there is no specific requirement detailing sponsor's obligation in other areas such as:

- sending the initial 7-day phone/fax notification to investigators
- notifying IRBs or ethics committees
- the timeframe or format for the submission of follow-up information. (It is simply stated that: 'Follow-up information to a safety report shall be submitted as soon as the relevant information is available.')[7]

Interestingly, the IND Regulation permits a certain flexibility. For example, the FDA or the sponsor can propose a different format and timeframe for reporting.[7] Thus, with appropriate prior approval, sponsors have the opportunity to develop specialized adverse event reporting procedures and timeframes that may be more appropriate to the goals of the study when they can be used without compromising subject safety.

European Community

The EU Regulation provides a differential reporting obligation to ethics committees and to investigators. This is a complex situation and the individual guidance should be reviewed carefully to ensure that appropriate procedures are in place to meet these reporting obligations. Under Section 5.1.5 of the April 2006 Guidance, fatal or life-threatening SUSARs, must be reported to health authorities and ethics committees in concerned member states within 7 days with subsequent written follow-up within 8 additional calendar days.[9]

When the trial is blinded, unblinding must generally occur to allow reporting to the health authorities and ethics committees.[9] The reporting requirement would depend on whether the comparator medicinal product is used in the trial as an investigational medicinal product. Where authorized medicinal product is used as a comparator, the adverse reaction must be reported if the adverse reaction is unexpected when assessed against its label. The sponsor must report to the health authority and the ethics committee of the concerned Member States all SUSARs associated with a comparator product in the concerned clinical trial even if this product is authorized.[9] Interestingly, in addition to reporting to health authorities and ethics committees, there is also a recommendation that the sponsor should transmit SUSARs to the marketing authorization holder of the approved comparator and inform them of the previous notification to the health authority.

If the comparator is a placebo, the events associated with placebo do not usually satisfy the criteria for a serious adverse drug reaction. However, if after unblinding the SUSAR is assessed to be associated with placebo, the events must be reported. Other SUSARS and events that are discussed above must be reported within the 15-day calendar period to the ethics committees as well as health authorities.

There are also other special considerations. For example, EC Member States may require that individual case safety reports that are sent to ethics committees be limited to those concerning individual subjects who have been recruited in that Member State.[9] This is akin to an 'opt-out' provision and presumably was intended to reduce the paperwork burden of individual case safety reports to investigators.

The EU Regulation would also appear to allow a lot of flexibility in reporting SUSARS to investigators.[9] There is only a general requirement to inform all investigators about 'findings that could adversely affect the safety of study subjects.' The sponsor is given discretion about the timing of this and allows for an aggregated line listing of reports that should be accompanied by a concise summary of the evolving safety profile. However, this listing should contain all SUSARS when the information is blinded so as to prevent notification of the investigators of the actual medicinal product that was administered.

Summarizing of adverse event information

ICH E2A contains a specific reporting responsibility on summarizing information obtained by a review of fatal or life-threatening serious unexpected adverse drug reactions.[4] This report must include an assessment of the importance and implication of the findings, including relevant previous experience with the same or similar medicinal products. There is no specific format for this additional analysis. Under this section of ICH E2A, expedited reports must be sent to 'regulators or other official parties requesting them.'[4] However, the specific requirement to send these analyses to investigators and ethics committees is not specifically addressed. Thus, local laws, regulations, ICH E6 and company policies should be evaluated in making the decision about how to report these to investigators, ethics committees, and IRBs.

In the USA, there is a more restrictive requirement that incorporates a requirement for a 'similar events analysis':

> In each written IND safety report, the sponsor shall identify all safety reports previously filed with the IND concerning a similar adverse experience, and shall analyse the significance of the adverse experience in light of the previous, similar reports.[7]

The format for this is not specified and the ability to prepare a comprehensive and meaningful analysis within that timeframe can be expected to be challenging. There would appear to be a wide discretion in the selection of report sources and types (i.e., clinical study cases, literature, spontaneous sources).

Signal detection

In general, there is very little published material about the procedures or formal process of signal detection in the GCP environment. In the broadest sense, a signal according to the World Health Organization (WHO) is 'reported information on a possible causal relationship between an adverse event and a drug which has not been previously detected.'[10] This can certainly be interpreted as including any new information about 'known' adverse drug reactions with respect to frequency of occurrence, severity of the adverse drug reactions, and new risk factors such as age, sex, underlying preexisting medical conditions, and concomitant drug usage.

The ICH guidelines do not provide specific details or suggestions about how to conduct 'signaling' on data that is acquired and synthesized during the drug development program. Therefore, the planning, development and implementation of any 'signaling program' must be performance-based. The goal of the signaling program should be the best possible understanding of the safety profile of the drug and not the adoption of any single methodological approach to the evaluation of clinical trial data.

Signal detection in clinical trials

Considering the amount of recent interest in monitoring safety during the conduct of clinical trials, there is relatively scant information available in the scientific published literature about safety signaling activities during clinical trials. There is, however, an excellent review of critical issues and practical recommendations in a publication by Council for International Organizations of Medical Sciences (CIOMS) entitled *Management of Safety Information from Clinical Trials: Report of CIOMS Working Group VI.*[11] While there is no universally accepted definition of a 'signal,' an excellent operational definition is as follows:

> A signal is simply an alert from any available source that a drug may be associated with a previously unrecognised hazard or that a known hazard may be quantitatively (e.g., more frequent) or qualitatively (e.g., more serious) different from existing expectations.[12]

In the clinical trials setting, there are multiple sources of information that might be relevant to the safety of enrolled subjects as well as to future beneficiaries of the eventually approved medicinal product. With respect to data from the clinical trial program itself, there are potentially two sources of signals.

The first comes from individual subject adverse drug experience reporting. This is largely data collected from clinical or laboratory investigations of specific subjects. For a new medicinal product, it is often one of these sentinel observations of adverse drug reactions that can prompt further detailed evaluation of potential safety issues. Adverse event investigations can be similar for both investigational and marketed products and include issues such as medication errors.[13] The second source of such data emanates from aggregate analysis of the information from clinical trials and will be typically, but not always, be represented by a disproportionate incidence rate in one arm of the treatment groups or among specific subpopulations. These two potential sources of information are relatively well characterized in the existing reporting regulations.[7]

In order to analyze this data, sponsors may apply the statistical methods described in ICH guidance on *Statistical Principles for Clinical Trials* (ICH E9) for evaluation of adverse events from clinical trials.[14] Similar requirements for reporting of sentinel individual case safety reports (i.e., those that are serious, unexpected, and causally related) appear in ICH E2A and for reporting of conclusions from an analysis of aggregate safety information in the form of either a similar-events analysis or increased-frequency analysis.[4]

Tools and techniques

Because of the relatively small number of subjects enrolled in a clinical trial program, the number of techniques used to evaluate safety data is relatively limited. In the USA, a comprehensive draft *Guidance or Industry: Premarketing Risk Assessment* discusses, in some detail, some recommendations about the types of analyses that can be performed as part of the risk assessment during the clinical development program.[15]

As mentioned earlier, many of the tools used to evaluate the data generated from the trial program itself will be statistical in nature and have been discussed above with respect to ICH E9. There has been increasing use of other statistical methodologies to look at the disproportionate representation of certain adverse event–drug pairs in post-marketing pharmacovigilance databases. A guideline on the use of some of these techniques has been published in the EC.[16] However, there has been very little published data on the use of these types of methods with clinical trial databases because these tend to be smaller in nature, have a very limited number of patients, and have a very small number of medicinal products included in the trial database.

Pharmacovigilance planning

With the development of ICH E2E, there is an important advance in creating a nexus between the pre-marketing risk assessment of a drug and the post-marketing pharmacovigilance milieu. There are four key principles described in this guideline that form the foundation of a solid proactive pharmacovigilance program:[5]

- planning of pharmacovigilance activities throughout the product life cycle
- science-based approach to risk documentation
- effective collaboration between regulators and industry
- applicability of the pharmacovigilance activities across the ICH regions.

The guidance provides for the development of a safety specification, which is, in essence, a concise summary of what is known about the product's safety as well as a critical appraisal of any missing data that would contribute to a more definitive knowledge of the medicinal product's safety profile. This systematic approach to pharmacovigilance planning will undoubtedly begin at an earlier stage of the product's life cycle and, by introducing a structure to the collection and analysis of safety information, should enhance pharmacovigilance during the pre-marketing stage.

The concept of pharmacovigilance planning is welcome, but its implementation in the various jurisdiction is yet to be determined.

Databases

Sponsor's database

During the early phases of drug development, it is almost certain that information about the safety and efficacy of a product will be contained only in the sponsor's database. As this will be a key source of data for the ongoing evaluation of safety data, particular care should be taken in coding adverse events, developing clear criteria for coding diagnoses (either as indications or for adverse events), and assuring that the data is accurate and complete.

Regulatory database

There may be occasions, however, when information about similar products or therapeutic classes of similar drugs might be useful. There appears to be a growing trend on the part of health authorities to increase the amount of information available to the general public in the absence of a specific request. The regulatory databases contain various amounts and details about adverse drug events that have been reported to health authorities. This information is often available for access via the internet and is thus available beyond the borders of a particular country. Whether or not this information will eventually prove to be of utility in a clinical trial program remains to be seen. However, the occurrence of a particular adverse drug reaction in a product with a similar structure or pharmacological characteristic may have some evidential value in the evaluation of a safety issue during drug development. Examples of such publicly available databases include Health Canada's Vigilance online database,[17] the FDA's AERS database,[18] the MHRA Anonymized Single Patient Reports (which is available to the Pharmaceutical Industry),[19] and the Drug Analysis Prints (available online at http://www.mhra.gov.uk/Safetyinformation/index.htm).

Epidemiologic databases

The eminent epidemiologist Sam Shapiro distinguishes between clinical medicine, which he states focuses on 'the cross-sectional or longitudinal evaluation of individual patients,' and epidemiology, which focuses on 'populations and usually over much longer time spans than clinical pharmacology.'[20]

While pre-marketing pharmacovigilance typically focuses on the generation of data from the clinical trial program, post-marketing pharmacovigilance focuses on information collected during actual use of the drug. While the spontaneous reporting system is a large contributor to the safety information, there has been a consistent trend toward increasing use of pharmacoepidemiologic data to augment this data source.[21] The source of epidemiologic data can include structured data collection systems from individual practitioner's offices such as the General Practice Research Database (GPRD)[22] or electronic medical records or administrative claims databases.[23] However, these research databases collect information almost exclusively on marketed products and hence their use for the evaluation of investigational medicinal product safety is almost non-existent except for any incidental information from subjects receiving them during a clinical trial or a very small number of patients who may receive them as part of a compassionate use scheme.

The GPRD describes itself as the world's largest longitudinal health care database and has been the source of many epidemiologic studies in areas of safety, drug utilization patterns, and information about the natural history of disease states and health outcomes and economics.[24] As it is focused on real-world observational data of selected general practitioners in the UK, it would be of limited or no direct value for information about a product prior to marketing. The GPRD can, though, provide substantial information about background disease rates and conditions that might be classified as adverse drug reactions in the clinical trial.

With an increasing emphasis on pharmacovigilance planning, the use of pharmacoepidemiologic research databases may play a larger role prior to marketing of the drug and may provide important information about background disease incidence rates, drug utilization, compliance patterns, and safety profiles of comparator drugs.

The use of disease-specific or drug-specific registries may also play a larger role in extending the observational period of subjects formerly enrolled in a clinical trial program.[25]

Conclusion

In preparing to develop a clinical trial program that meets global regulatory reporting requirements, it is necessary to understand the fundamental principles that drive regulatory reporting. In many of the jurisdictions, the reporting begins with understanding the definition of an adverse drug reaction, progresses in many cases to identifying a subset of these that require expedited reporting – typically based on a seriousness criteria coupled with either a geographic restriction based on the location (i.e., within the jurisdiction or outside of the jurisdiction), and, often, a final restriction based on information content (e.g., was the type of adverse drug reaction observed already notified to the stakeholders in the trial process [e.g., investigator, subjects, ethics committees]). As mentioned above, an understanding of these basic principles will then facilitate a more detailed evaluation of any local regulatory requirements.

Global pharmacovigilance harmonization is not yet a reality and, indeed, is not likely to occur in the future given the differences in health care systems in different jurisdictions. What is clear and probably more important in the future state is the integration of the life-cycle risk management process as a part of overall pharmacovigilance planning. This will now occur early in the development process.

As can be seen in ICH E2E, the focus will likely be less on determining specific reportability criteria and more on determining and quantifying the information to secure both the medicinal product's initial registration and its continued, future availability in the marketplace. Such information will likely not be safety information alone but will eventually be a combination of safety, efficacy, and effectiveness. This may include reviewing data from other databases such as electronic medical records or administrative claims databases. With this evolution, pharmacovigilance information will thus be only one component of the product's overall value to society.

References

1. European Commission [Online] (December 5, 2007). *Strategy to Better Protect Public Health by Strengthening and Rationalising European Pharmacovigilance*. Available from: http://ec.europa.eu/enterprise/pharmaceuticals/pharmacovigilance/docs/public-consultation_12-2007.pdf (accessed February 9, 2009).
2. Rockbold FW. Industry perspectives on ICH guidelines. *Stat Med* 2002; 21: 2947–2957.
3. International Conference on Harmonisation [Online] (June 2006). *Guidance for Industry: Good Clinical Practice, Consolidated Guidance*, ICH-E6. Available from: http://www.ich.org/LOB/media/MEDIA482.pdf (accessed December 14, 2008).
4. International Conference on Harmonisation [Online] (October 1994). *Guidance for Industry: Clinical Safety Data Management: Definitions and Standards for Expediting Reporting*, ICH E2A. Available from: http://www.ich.org/LOB/media/MEDIA436.pdf (accessed November 16, 2009).
5. International Conference on Harmonisation [Online] (November 2004). *Guidance for Industry: Pharmacovigilance Planning*, ICH E2E. Available from: http://www.ich.org/LOB/media/MEDIA1195.pdf (accessed November 16, 2009).
6. World Health Organization[Online] (1972). World Health Organization Technical Report Series no. 498. *International Drug Monitoring: The Role of National Centres*. Available from: http://www.who-umc.org/graphics/9277.pdf (accessed February 9, 2009).
7. Food & Drug Administration [Online] (April 2009). *Investigational New Drug Application, Title 21 Code of Federal Regulations Part 312*. Available from: http://www.accessdata.fda.gov/scripts/cdrh/cfdocs/cfcfr/CFRSearch.cfm?CFRPart=312&showFR=1 (accessed November 16, 2009).
8. European Commission [Online] (2001). *Directive 2001/20/EC*. Available from: http://ec.europa.eu/enterprise/pharmaceuticals/eudralex/vol-1/dir_2001_20/dir_2001_20_en.pdf (accessed January 26, 2009).
9. European Commission [Online] (April 2006). *Detailed Guidance on the Collection, Verification and Presentation of Adverse Reaction Reports Arising from Clinical Trials on Medical Products for Human Use*. Available from: http://ec.europa.eu/enterprise/pharmaceuticals/eudralex/vol-10/21_susar_rev2_2006_04_11.pdf (accessed February 9, 2009).
10. Edward IR, Biriell C. Harmonisation in pharmacovigilance. *Drug Saf* 1994; 10: 93–102.
11. World Health Organization. *Management of Safety Information from Clinical Trials: Report of CIOMS working Group VI*. Geneva: World Health Organization, 2005.
12. Waller PC, Lee EH. Responding to drug safety issues. *Pharmacoepidemiol Drug Saf* 1999; 8: 535–552.
13. Toft B. *External Inquiry into the Adverse Incident That Occurred at Queen's Medical Centre, Nottingham, 4th January 2001*. London: United Kingdom Department of Health, April 19, 2001.
14. International Conference on Harmonisation (ICH). *Guidance for Industry: Statistical Principles for Clinical Trials*, ICH E9. Geneva: ICH, 1998.

15. Food & Drug Administration (FDA). *Guidance for Industry: Premarketing Risk Assessment*. Washington, DC: FDA, March 2005.
16. European Medicines Agency (EMEA). *Guideline on the Use of Statistical Signal Detection Methods in the Eudravigilance Data Analysis System*. EMEA/106464/2006. London: EMEA, November 16, 2006.
17. Health Canada [Online] (February 19, 2008). *Canada Vigilance Online Database*. Available from: http://www.hc-sc.gc.ca/dhp-mps/medeff/databasdon/search-recherche-eng.php (accessed January 19, 2009).
18. Food & Drug Administration[Online] (August 7, 2002). *Adverse Event Reporting System (AERS)*. Available from: http://www.fda.gov/cder/aers/default.htm (accessed January 19, 2009).
19. Medicines and Healthcare products Regulatory Agency [Online] (May 14, 2009). *Anonymised Single Patient Reports*. Available from: http://www.mhra.gov.uk/ Safetyinformation/Reportingsafetyproblems/Medicines/ Reportingsuspectedadversedrugreactions/InformationforthePharmaceuticalIndustry/ AnonymisedSinglePatientReports/index.htm (accessed January 22, 2010).
20. Shapiro S. Looking to the 21st century: have we learned from our mistakes or are we doomed to compound them? *Pharmacoepidemiol Drug Saf* 2004; 13: 257–265.
21. Graham DJ *et al.* Spontaneous reporting – USA. In: Mann RD, Andrews E, eds. *Pharmacovigilance*. Chichester: Wiley, 2002.
22. Wood L. General Practice Research Database in the UK. In: Mann RD, Andrews E, eds. *Pharmacovigilance*. Chichester: Wiley, 2002.
23. Platt R *et al.* Pharmacovigilance in the HMO research network. In: Mann RD, Andrews E, eds. *Pharmacovigilance*. Chichester: Wiley, 2002.
24. Medicines and Healthcare products Regulatory Agency [Online] (1987). *The General Practice Research Database*. Available from: http://www.gprd.com/home/default.asp (accessed February 9, 2009).
25. Council for International Organizations of Medical Sciences (CIOMS). *Current Challenges in Pharmacovigilance Report of CIOMS Working Group V*, Geneva: CIOMS, 2001.

10

Clinical trial registration and reporting

Barbara Godlew, Shawn Pelletier, and Maureen Strange

Introduction and history

November 4, 2008 marked the twentieth anniversary of the Health Omnibus Programs Extension (HOPE) Act, which made the first attempts at making clinical trial information publicly accessible in the USA.[1] Under pressure from the public sector most affected by the rapidly spreading acquired immune deficiency syndrome (AIDS), Congress passed the 1988 HOPE Act, creating regulation and funding for AIDS drug research and development. The HOPE Act also provided for the AIDS Clinical Trials Information Service (ACTIS) database, which gave patients and others public access to information regarding ongoing and completed clinical trials.[2]

In the context of this chapter, the term 'clinical trial disclosure' has a dual meaning: clinical trial registration and disclosure of clinical trial results. The disclosure of clinical information can take many forms including, but not limited to, scientific/medical congress abstracts, medical journal articles, oral presentations at scientific meetings, clinical trial registry entries, and clinical trial results records. Clinical trial registration to a registry is the public and prospective disclosure of clinical trial protocol information at the initiation of a clinical trial to a publicly accessible internet-based database. Clinical trial results disclosure is the public and retrospective release of clinical trial results to a publicly accessible internet-based database. Disclosing clinical trial information allows patients, their families, and health care providers to make educated decisions about appropriate medical care. Additionally, it provides a 'checks and balances' system for publicly disclosed trial objectives for comparison to those published in medical journal articles or other publications.

Nearly 10 years after the HOPE Act in 1997, the Food and Drug Administration Modernization Act (FDAMA) widened public access to clinical trial information. FDAMA, Section 113, required the National Library of Medicine (NLM) to develop a publicly available internet-based registry that would encompass information for all clinical trials for serious and life-threatening conditions or diseases.[3] On February 29, 2000 the NLM released the first version of ClinicalTrials.gov, which was populated with more than 4000 records primarily from National Institutes of Health-conducted trials.[4,5,6] The difficulty in establishing a government-sanctioned list that defined serious and life-threatening diseases and conditions coupled with differences between commercial, research, and governmental organizations, and concerns from the pharmaceutical industry over releasing commercially sensitive information before a new drug received FDA approval deterred registration of trials to ClinicalTrials.gov. Indeed, a government-sponsored status report on FDAMA Section 113 found that only 35% of eligible trials for serious and life-threatening conditions or diseases were actually registered.[7]

In October 2002, the Pharmaceutical Research and Manufacturers of America (PhRMA) issued the *Principles on Conduct of Clinical Trials and Communication of Clinical Trial Results*,[8] which started the voluntary effort for pharmaceutical companies to disclose clinical trial results in 2004. The PhRMA Principles state the communication of clinical trial results should be 'timely communication of meaningful results of controlled clinical trials of marketed products or investigational products that are approved for marketing, regardless of outcome.' A short time later, the *Joint Position on the Disclosure of Clinical Trial Information via Clinical Trial Registries and Databases* was developed through a cooperative effort with the European Federation of Pharmaceutical Industries and Associations (EFPIA), the International Federation of Pharmaceutical Manufacturers Associations (IFPMA) and the Japan Pharmaceutical Manufacturers Associations (JPMA) and PhRMA, which called for a global approach to clinical trial registries and disclosure of results information.[9]

In 2004, clinical trial disclosure became controversial when the International Committee of Medical Journal Editors (ICMJE) addressed the issue of inconsistent reporting of trials and trial results, which affected virtually all stakeholders involved in the conduct of clinical trials: the pharmaceutical industry, medical and scientific academia, government agencies, legal entities, regulatory authorities, and so on. The ICMJE simultaneously published an editorial in their respective journals that they would no longer publish manuscripts resulting from Phase 2–4 interventional clinical trials not prospectively registered to a free and publicly accessible internet-based registry prior to the enrollment of the first participant.[10] Phase 4 trials involve marketed products and may be interventional or observational in nature, but are most frequently observational clinical trials, which differ substantially

Box 10.1

Interventional clinical trials are those in which an investigator assigns healthy volunteers or patients, based on a protocol, to receive specific diagnostic, therapeutic, or other types of interventions. Study teams follow the progress of the participants and assess the biomedical and/or health outcomes.

Observational clinical trials are non-interventional trials that observe lifestyle choices, assess quality of life of specific diseases, and have a predetermined study population in which investigators do not assign protocol-designated interventions, but prescribe care according to the participants' needs. Sometimes, these trials do not involve participants (i.e., retrospective database meta-analyses).

from interventional or controlled trials (see Box 10.1). The ICMJE required the registration of interventional trials but not of observational trials.

Additionally, the ICMJE required inclusion of a strict dataset of 20 items, some of which the pharmaceutical industry and academia claimed were proprietary and commercially sensitive. A second ICMJE editorial was published in 2005 to clarify the requirements and to acknowledge cases in which registering certain types of trials (i.e., Phase 1 exploratory trials whose prespecified goal investigates the disease's biology or whose preliminary findings direct further research) might slow innovation[11] by publicly displaying proprietary information. At the same time, while initially excluding Phase 1 trials,[12] the World Health Organization (WHO) called for the registration of all clinical trials,[13] albeit with different sets of criteria for the registrant (i.e., the sponsor) and the register (i.e., entity that holds a registry and/or results database). Variable criteria may lead to confusion and could threaten the registrants' and registers' credibility with the public through the disclosure of potentially differing information. For example, the WHO criteria call for the registration of Phase 1 trials where the Food and Drug Administration Amendments Act (FDAAA) includes only Phase 2 to 4. As such, without knowing the detailed criteria, researchers, journalists, and others may develop a mistaken impression that the registrant or register is withholding certain information. In 2008, ClinicalTrials.gov was populated with more than 53 000 trials with locations in more than 150 countries from all sectors of clinical research.[14] In 2010, ClinicalTrials.gov was populated with >88 000 trials in 172 countries.[14] In addition to the ClinicialTrials.gov website, many other websites worldwide contain clinical trial disclosure information.

To this point, the clinical research industry focused primarily on providing prospective clinical trial protocol information. In 2005, the state government of Maine, USA, passed a law requiring pharmaceutical manufacturers to post clinical trial data for prescription drugs marketed to consumers in Maine.[15] Maine requires the posting of clinical trial data (registration and results) on a publicly accessible database. Likewise, US federal law (FDAAA) followed suit in 2007 and has expanded disclosure requirements to include clinical trial results. Other countries, including but not limited to France, Italy, and China, have added or will add trial results to their existing clinical trials registry. Details regarding clinical trial registration and results disclosure, legislative requirements, and implications for future clinical development follow.

Clinical trial registration

Clinical trial registration exists for a number of reasons as illustrated in Figure 10.1. Clinical trial registries are different from patient registries, and distinguishing between the two can be confusing. Clinical trial registration provides information about protocol design and investigational products in controlled

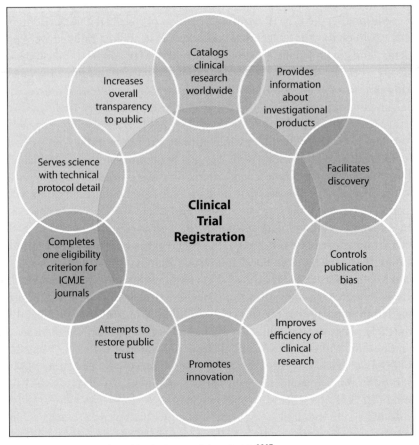

Figure 10.1   Reasons for public disclosure of clinical trials.[16,17]

> ### Box 10.2
>
> ### What is a patient registry?
>
> - Database that collects data on real world patient experiences
> - Allows scientists to evaluate care in broad populations
> - Provides useful information regarding use, safety, and effectiveness of treatments when clinical trials are not feasible (i.e., pregnancy, specific disease states, rare diseases)
>
> ### Areas of focus in patient registries
>
> - Natural history of a disease
> - Clinical and cost-effectiveness
> - Monitoring safety
> - Quality of care measurements

environments or under controlled conditions. Patient registries (see Box 10.2), typically used after the product receives health authority approval, are databases that collect data on diverse populations receiving treatment (i.e., real world patient experiences in broad populations).

As previously mentioned, FDAMA 113 created a clinical trial central repository, ClinicalTrials.gov, aimed to provide information about clinical trials for patients with serious or life-threatening diseases or conditions. Major elements such as brief title, brief summary, and eligibility criteria are all written such that patients can easily understand the information. The data elements required are listed in Table 10.1.

Many stakeholders outside of the pharmaceutical industry believed that the registration of trials for serious or life-threatening diseases and conditions was limiting and that more should be disclosed about other types of clinical trials. Pressure from key stakeholders, including the ICMJE (for 'clinically directive' trials[16]), the WHO for 'all clinical trials as a scientific, ethical and moral responsibility'[17], Maine (marketed products sold in the state) as well as updated federal legislation (for Phase 2–4 adding to FDAMA requirements), increased the scope of disclosure. An example of the meaningfulness of stakeholder pressure is that of the ICMJE 2004 editorial declaring registration of clinical trials as a condition of publication increasing the number of trials registered: from May through October 2005, the number of trials registered to ClinicalTrials.gov from the National Institutes of Health (NIH) and other federal agencies, the pharmaceutical/biotechnology/medical device industry, academia, foundations, and other organizations increased 73%[18] (see Figure 10.2). In 2007, the

Table 10.1 Food and Drug Administration Modernization Act (FDAMA) and FDA Amendments Act (FDAAA) data element requirements

Category	FDAMA data element	FDAAA data element
Descriptive information	• Brief title (in lay language) • Brief summary (in lay language) • Study design/study phase/study type • Condition or disease • Intervention	• Brief title, intended for the lay public[a] • Brief summary, intended for the lay public • Primary purpose • Study design[a] • For an applicable drug clinical trial, the study phase • Study type • Primary disease or condition being studied or focus of study[a] • Intervention name and type[a] • Study start date[a] • Expected completion date • Target number of subjects[a] • Outcomes, including primary and secondary outcome measures[a]
Recruitment information	• Study status information • Overall study status (e.g., recruiting, no longer recruiting) • Individual site status • Eligibility criteria/gender/age	• Eligibility criteria[a] • Gender • Age limits • Whether trial accepts healthy volunteers • Overall recruitment status[a] • Individual site status • If drug not approved under section 505 of federal Food, Drug, and Cosmetic Act or licensed under section 351 of this act, specify whether or not there is expanded access to the drug under section 561 of federal Food, Drug, and Cosmetic Act for those who do not qualify for enrollment in the clinical trial and how to obtain information about such access

Table 10.1 *(continued)*		
Location and contact information	• Location of trial • Contact information (includes an option to list a central contact person for all trial sites)	• Sponsor[a] • Responsible party, by official title[a] • Facility name and facility contact information (including the city, state, and ZIP code for each clinical trial location, or toll-free number through which such location information may be accessed)
Administrative information	• Unique protocol ID number • Study sponsor • Verification date	• Unique protocol identification number[a] • Other protocol identification numbers, if any[a] • Food and Drug Administration IND/IDE protocol number and record verification date

[a] Denotes an ICMJE element. ICMJE elements (20 fields) also include trial registration date, funding sources, secondary sponsors, official scientific title of the study, and research ethics review. Responsible party equates to responsible contact person and research contact person as listed in ICMJE 20 elements. Primary and key secondary outcomes are listed separately in ICMJE elements. Study type as defined by ICMJE is equivalent to study design in FDAAA. Research ethics review replaced with countries of recruitment in 2006.

ICMJE, following a plan to assess the impact of their requirement to register trials, published a follow-up editorial expanding their scope of trials to include Phase 1 beginning mid 2008.[19]

As with the trial types, the data elements vary depending on the organization or legislative body. The ICMJE, WHO, and country requirements/laws do settle on common themes for the data elements required for registration at trial initiation. For example, all agree on: (1) administrative data such as a unique trial number, study sponsor(s), names of organizations providing funding; (2) protocol-specific information such as official title, intervention(s), condition being studied, study type, primary and secondary outcome measures, and eligibility criteria; and (3) enrollment information such as study location, recruitment status, and contact information of the study facility and sponsor. However, variation exists in the level of detail required depending on where the study is conducted or where the study site is located. For example, global privacy laws play a role and may act as a barrier to listing investigator information, name, and contact number on a public website. The timeline for registering a clinical trial is also variable between organizations and legislative bodies such as the WHO and ICMJE. For

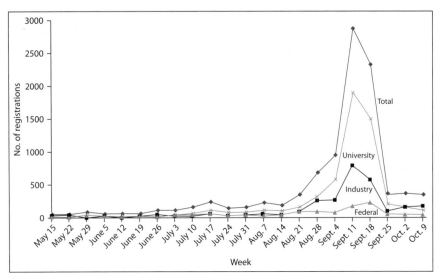

Figure 10.2 Response to ICMJE mandate.[18] (Copyright 2005 Massachusetts Medical Society. All rights reserved. Used by permission.)

example, the WHO and ICMJE support registration before the enrollment of the first participant in a clinical trial, while US legislation supports registration within 21 days of (i.e., no later than 21 days after) the first participant/patient visit.

Registries have proliferated globally in response to local laws or requirements. Often, individual countries require that records are displayed in the local language. Table 10.2 provides a short, non-exhaustive list of international clinical trial registries. Many of the individual countries and regions as well as regulatory agencies also established sets of registration criteria for data elements. The many registries and their individual requirements may create difficulty in cataloging clinical trials worldwide as duplication of the same trial in different registers will very likely occur. Both the WHO search portal[17] and the IFPMA search portal[20] can produce listings of clinical trials from virtually all known registries. In addition to duplication, the cost of creating and maintaining a clinical trial registry is substantial as the daily operations and technical expertise and infrastructure support must adapt as technological advances evolve.

In the USA, state and federal regulations are in place for the registration of clinical trials at initiation. The fundamental principles for registration of trials are consistent across state and federal law. Legislation drives compliance and, in effect, levels the highly competitive pharmaceutical playing field for all stakeholders who sponsor and conduct clinical trials through trial type and data content.

Table 10.2 International registries		
Registry	**Country**	**Website**
ANZCTR	Australia, New Zealand	http://www.anzctr.org.au/
ChiCTR	China	http://www.chictr.org/Default. aspx
ISRCTN	United Kingdom	http://isrctn.org/
NTR	The Netherlands	http://www.trialregister.nl/ trialreg/index.asp
Répertoire des essais cliniques de médicaments	France	https://icrepec.afssaps.fr/Public/ index.php
SANCTR	South Africa	http://www.sanctr.gov.za/
Sperimentazioni Clinica dei Medicinali	Italy	http://oss-sper-clin. agenziafarmaco.it/cgi-bin/ ossc_index_pub?FILE=cerca_ct

Clinical trial results databases

Regulators and stakeholders worldwide agree on the need to disclose results from interventional or controlled clinical trials. These trials generate great interest for the scientific community, regulators, and the general public. Clinical trial result disclosure can be done through scientific/medical congress abstracts, peer-reviewed medical journal articles, and oral presentations at scientific meetings. A Clinical Study Report (CSR) synopsis or peer-reviewed medical journal articles are acceptable methods for sharing results with the public.

Although the Maine law requires a specific way to share results, the law conflicts with the US federal legislation and other policies. A particular challenge that organizations and researchers share is the risk of 'prepublication' of clinical trial results. Some scientific and medical journal editors require that results are 'embargoed' or kept constrained prior to the journal's acceptance and publication. This can cause difficulty in recognizing that peer-reviewed publications are acceptable disclosure of clinical trial results. Quite commonly, the review process of a manuscript may take as much as 1 to 2 years. Consequently, trial results are often posted before a decision is made on the acceptance or rejection of a manuscript once a drug, biologic, or device is FDA-approved for marketing. As a result, some journals may reject manuscripts whose results have been posted in compliance with the law.

As companies voluntarily disclosed clinical trial results prior to the enactment of federal legislation, variability in the types of trials that were disclosed emerged as did the venues on which the information was publicly available. Some organizations disclosed results only for marketed products of controlled clinical trials; others disclosed results for investigational products still under development, in addition to their marketed products. Some organizations created their own website to post results, while others used the PhRMA-sponsored website (ClinicalStudyResults.org). The inconsistency of what was disclosed and where it was published resulted primarily from individual organizational policy. Additionally, individual interpretations of trial phase definitions, along with minor variations of the report template used to display results added to the mix. In general, however, clinical trial results are publicly disclosed one year after the last participant/patient visit has occurred.

Another 'disconnect' in trial results disclosure is the lack of a one-to-one match between the registration of trials and the reporting of results. Because trial registration began with FDAMA and trial results disclosure began with PhRMA, trial results postings do not always have a 'mate' in a registry and vice versa. This is due to a variety of reasons such as the ICMJE requirements for publication and organizations practicing due diligence through disclosing results from trials completed prior to the PhRMA recommended timeframe of October 1, 2002. Another reason for the disconnect is mismatched requirements imposed by non-binding organizations such as the WHO and ICMJE and binding legislation such as FDAAA. For example, the WHO and ICMJE call for registration of all interventional clinical trials, but US federal legislation requires registration and results disclosure of clinical trial information for Phase 2–4 trials.

As previously noted, Phase 4 clinical trials are conducted after a product receives health authority approval and may be either interventional or observational. Observational 'real-world' data (i.e., epidemiology, treatment adherence, treatment outcomes, etc.) often supplements findings from interventional clinical trials and provides valuable insight about a product's use in a large population. As a result, publication of the findings of observational studies is valuable not only to the product's sponsor but to patients and health care providers. However, until recently, neither non-binding organizations nor binding legislation require the public disclosure of observational trial protocol or results information. Therefore, many researchers and sponsors did not register or disclose results from observational trials, while a small number of companies did, depending on their individual company policies. Maine now requires the registration of observational trials, while federal legislation does not.

More countries now require disclosure of results and the criteria and timeframe associated with it differ depending upon the country. This variability increases the need for uniform global requirements to promote accurate, consistent, and efficient disclosure processes. Despite the worldwide effort to increase the level of transparency in clinical research, inherent flaws exist between what is registered and what is disclosed after analyzing the data and finalizing the report. For example, clinical trial registration information is written for the public in lay language, while the disclosure of results is written for scientists and physicians, is more complex, and often includes statistical tables. As a result, the manner in which results are displayed and the terminology is used may be challenging for the public. The issue of what is useful information to the public is widely debated. Some stakeholders want more information such as adverse events (i.e., side-effects) experienced during the trial or a list of protocol deviations. While this information is valuable to investigators and health care providers, it may add to the information overload inexperienced users sometimes face (newly diagnosed patients, family members, etc.). Explaining trial results in a scientifically factual and objective manner, while remaining non-technical and understandable to the public, without being misleading or promotional according to FDA definitions, remains a challenge.

As the transparency initiative that began in the 1980s continues to move forward, disclosure of clinical trial information will continue to evolve. Both binding and non-binding organizations shape policies involving key clinical data disclosure and may, perhaps, someday change the manner in which clinical trials are developed and conducted.

Legislation and regulatory requirements

The FDA Amendments Act of 2007 (FDAAA) was signed into law on September 27, 2007 and requires registration of controlled clinical investigations for drug and device trials no later than 21 days after enrollment of the first participant in a clinical trial (see Box 10.3).

FDAAA also expanded the data elements in the ClinicalTrials.gov database. Data elements of FDAMA and FDAAA are compared in Table 10.1.

A subset of legacy data in the register required updating to the FDAAA data elements. Provisions in the legislation require updates to recruitment status of registered clinical trials throughout the trial life cycle within 30 days of the actual status change. Key features of FDAAA are the inclusion of registration for device trials, the inclusion of academia and other entities as responsible parties, and expansion of the required data elements. In addition, FDAAA creates the opportunity for ClinicalTrials.gov to drive the technology for system development and formatting advances in reporting of trial results.

Within one year of enactment (September 27, 2008), FDAAA required the NIH to establish a database that includes basic information of applicable

Box 10.3 *(Taken from United States Law)*

Applicable Drug Clinical Trial

A *controlled clinical investigation*, other than a Phase 1 clinical investigation, of a drug subject to section 505 of the Federal Food, Drug, and Cosmetic Act or to section 351 of this Act.

Applicable Device Clinical Trial

A prospective clinical study of health outcomes comparing an intervention with a device subject to section 510(k), 515, or 520(m) of the Federal Food, Drug, and Cosmetic Act against a control in human subjects (other than a small clinical trial to determine the feasibility of a device, or a clinical trial to test prototype devices where the primary outcome measure relates to feasibility and not to health outcomes).

Controlled Clinical Investigation

Clinical investigation means any *experiment* in which a drug is administered or dispensed to, or used involving, one or more human subjects. For the purposes of this part, *an experiment* is any use of a drug except for the use of a marketed drug in the course of medical practice.

clinical trial results for pharmaceutical products approved for at least one use. The NIH initially populated the results database from existing ClinicalTrials.gov registration records. The results database must include (1) a table of participant demographic data and baseline characteristics, (2) primary and secondary outcome measures with a table of values for each outcome measure for each arm of the trial (including results of statistical significance tests), (3) a point of contact, and (4) affirmation or denial of an agreement restricting principal investigators from discussing or publishing trial results after completion. Within 3 years after enactment (September 27, 2010), FDAAA requires the NIH to expand the clinical trial registry and results database further, for example, the possible inclusion of results for investigational products. Sponsors must assure certification of compliance to the registration and result reporting sections of FDAAA as part of the FDA's drug approval process.

Clinical trial disclosure implications for future therapeutic development

While clinical trial disclosure requires careful thought and engaged collaboration among various stakeholders, several unexpected complexities arose as a

Table 10.3 Clinical trial disclosure opportunities and risks

Opportunities

Issue	Rationale
Ensures patient access to new therapies	<ul><li>ClinicalTrials.gov originally designed for patients with AIDS, other serious/life-threatening diseases</li><li>>88 000 trials in >172 countries</li><li>May enhance/save lives</li><li>May increase trial enrollment</li><li>Gives patients, providers information→informed choices</li></ul>
Access to non-significant results	<ul><li>Non-significant (i.e., negative) trials ≠ bad trials</li><li>Drives innovation</li><li>Avoids prescribing of wrong drug to wrong patient</li></ul>
Reduce unnecessary duplicate trials	<ul><li>Fewer patients at risk</li><li>↓ cost to stressed health care system</li><li>↓ research/development cost</li><li>>88 000 trials in ClinicalTrials.gov = overlap</li></ul>
Drive compliance to business processes in global organizations	<ul><li>Internal processes must address inconsistencies in electronic clinical trial management systems</li><li>↑ accountability of trial count/status to corporate senior management and to health authorities</li><li>↓ duplicative trials within organization (often between company affiliates)</li><li>↑ tracking of clinical trial milestones</li></ul>
Create innovative trial designs by reviewing registered trials	<ul><li>Encourages new designs within drug class; 'cross pollination' of designs across classes</li></ul>
Potential for better outcome measures	<ul><li>Better, cleaner protocols→better outcome measures</li></ul>
Prescribing to appropriate populations	<ul><li>Overuse or overprescribing may not occur</li><li>Health authorities may not pull drug from market due to negative effects from use in unintended or incorrect populations</li></ul>
Public perception	<ul><li>May help offset public perception of pharmaceutical industry from 'profiteers' to 'providers'</li></ul>

Table 10.3 *(continued)*	
Risks	
Release of previously deemed proprietary information	● Unique study design variables, new molecular entities, new use of approved drugs exposed
Provide information on compounds in development	● Shortens competitor's time in designing study protocols
Race to marketplace	● Sharing proprietary information ↓ return on investment ● New Drug Application and Biologic License Application filing date can be estimated based on number of Phase 3 trials in registry
Unintended liability	● Lay public may misinterpret results/terminology ● Most physicians are not researchers, may be uncomfortable with interpreting research materials ● Potential misinterpretation without full safety/efficacy data or risk–benefit analysis
Fight for grants and 'publish or perish'	Academia protective of research
Privacy concerns	European Union; others have strict privacy laws concerning identifying information posted on internet

result of the ICMJE call for registration. Some of these complexities, both opportunities and risks, are addressed in Table 10.3. Based on these opportunities and risks, clinical trial design and management may evolve at the later stages in the development life cycle (e.g., Phase 3) to encompass more novel designs and more efficient business processes.

Summary

While many agree, in principle, that clinical trial registration and result reporting are beneficial, what remains challenging is the manner in which one discloses the data. The audience is wide and diverse: patient, study participants, health care providers, academia, clinical researchers, journal editors, legislators, and many others. Each of these groups brings with it particular and differing needs of the registered data elements and the result summaries as well. For example, the request to simplify the data yet retain its scientific and technical nature adds to the complexity of disclosure issues.

Looking forward, additional guidance and legislation on the disclosure of clinical trial information is likely. The increase in global requirements for clinical trial disclosure raises the need for uniform requirements to promote accurate, consistent, and efficient disclosure processes. The challenge for all stakeholders worldwide involved will be in providing the right balance of information to ensure that patients, study participants, and the public are well served and not under-served.

References

1. Health Omnibus Programs Extension of 1988, Pub. L. No. 100–607, 102 Stat. 3048 (November 4, 1988).
2. Katz DG *et al.* The AIDS clinical trials information service (ACTIS): a decade of providing clinical trials information. *Public Health Rep* 2002; 117(2): 123–130.
3. Food and Drug Administration Modernization Act of 1997, Pub. L. No. 115, 111 Stat. 2296 (November 21, 1997).
4. Food and Drug Administration [Online] (March 22, 2000). *Guidance for Industry: Information Program on Clinical Trials for Serious or Life-Threatening Diseases: Draft Guidance.* US Department of Health and Human Services, Food and Drug Admin- istration, Center for Drug Evaluation and Research (CDER), Center for Biologics Evaluation and Research (CBER).
5. National Institutes of Health. *ClinicalTrials.gov* [homepage]. Bethesda (MD): National Institutes of Health. Available from: http://www.clinicaltrials.gov (accessed April 24, 2008).
6. McCray AT, Ide NC. Design and implementation of a national clinical trials registry. *J Am Med Inform Assoc* 2000; 3(7): 313–323.
7. Toigo T (2005). *FDAMA Section 113: Status Report on Implementation.* [Online]. Washington: US Department of Health and Human Services (US). Available from: http://www.fda.gov/oashi/clinicaltrials/section113/113report/default.htm (accessed April 30, 2008).
8. Pharmaceutical Research and Manufacturers of America (PhRMA). *Public Disclosure of Clinical Trial Results. Principles on Conduct of Clinical Trials and Communication of Clinical Trial Results.* Washington, DC: PhRMA, 2002; 19–23.
9. International Federation of Pharmaceutical Manufacturers and Associations (IFPMA) [Online] (September 2005). *Joint Position on the Disclosure of Clinical Trial Information via Clinical Trial Registries and Databases.* Geneva: IFPMA. Available from http://ifpma.org (accessed April 30, 2008).
10. De Angelis C *et al.* Clinical trial registration: a statement from the International Committee of Medical Journal Editors. *N Engl J Med* 2004; 351(12): 1250–1251.
11. De Angelis *et al.* Is this clinical trial fully registered? A statement from the International Committee of Medical Journal Editors. *N Engl J Med* 2005; 352(23): 2436–2438.
12. Dickersin K. Report to the World Health Organization (WHO) on a plan for international registration of controlled trials: draft. February 29, 2004.
13. Chan AW (October 26, 2006). Global opportunities and challenges for trial registration: update from the WHO registry platform. Presentation at XIV Cochrane Colloquium, Dublin, Ireland. Available from: http://www.cochrane.org/resources/videos/Pembroke_Plenary4_15.30_Chan.pdf (accessed April 30, 2008).
14. National Institutes of Health. *ClinicalTrials.gov* [homepage]. Bethesda (MD): National Institutes of Health. Available from: http://www.clinicaltrials.gov (accessed April 20, 2010).
15. Food and Drug Administration Amendments Act of 2007, Pub. L. No. 110-85 Stat. 823, (September 27, 2007).
16. DeAngelis C, Drazen JM, Frizelle FA *et al.* Is this clinical trial fully registered? A statement from the international committee of medical journal editors. *N Engl J Med* 2005; 352(23): 2436–2438.
17. WHO International Clinical Trial Registry Platform [Online] *Frequently Asked Questions: Which Trials Should Be Registered?* Available from: http://www.who.int/ictrp/faq/en/index.html (accessed April 24, 2008).

18. Zarin DA *et al.* Trial registration at ClinicalTrials.gov between May and October. *N Engl J Med* 2005; 353(26): 2779–2787.

19. Laine C *et al.* Clinical trial registration: looking back and moving ahead. *Ann Intern Med* 2007; 147: 275–277.

20. International Federation of Pharmaceutical Manufacturers and Associations (IFPMA) [Online] *Clinical Trials Portal* [home page]. Geneva: IFPMA. Available from: http://clinicaltrials.ifpma.org/no_cache/en/myportal/index.htm (accessed April 8, 2008).

11

Quality assurance

Peter Smith

Introduction

As stated in other chapters of this book, Good Clinical Practice (GCP) principles focus on protection of human subject rights and ensure that the data generated by the clinical trial are both valid and accurate. This chapter will discuss quality assurance (QA) and auditing concepts as related to GCP. Overall responsibility for the quality of the clinical study lies with the sponsor. According to International Conference on Harmonisation (ICH) E6 GCP guidelines:[1]

- The sponsor is responsible for implementing and maintaining quality assurance and quality control systems with written Standard Operating Procedures (SOPs) to ensure that trials are conducted and data are generated, documented (recorded), and reported in compliance with the protocol, GCP, and the applicable regulatory requirement(s).
- The sponsor is responsible for securing agreement from all involved parties to ensure direct access to all trial-related sites, source data/ documents, and reports for the purpose of monitoring and auditing by the sponsor, and inspection by domestic and foreign regulatory authorities.
- Quality control should be applied to each stage of data handling to ensure that all data are reliable and have been processed correctly.
- Agreements, made by the sponsor with the investigator/institution and any other parties involved with the clinical trial, should be in writing, as part of the protocol or in a separate agreement.

A comprehensive quality system is critical to ensuring that a study is conducted in compliance with GCP. Through the use of written SOPs, as well as a robust training system, the sponsor should implement a quality control system to ensure that the trial is conducted, and the data are generated, recorded, and reported in compliance with the protocol, GCP, and local regulatory requirements. It is important that quality control is applied at all steps of the research process.[1]

Sponsors typically employ a Clinical Quality Assurance (CQA) unit; the major remit of the group is to oversee quality and compliance of the clinical development plan utilizing various types of audits as the measuring tool.

Audits are not just limited to sponsor-directed audits. The clinical trial investigator and the sponsor should be aware that there are several external entities that have the right to inspect any trial-related aspects.[1] The investigator/institution should permit monitoring and auditing by the sponsor, as well as inspection by the appropriate regulatory authority or authorities). Some examples of different types of audits include: Institutional Review Board (IRB)-directed audits to examine the ethical conduct of the trial, regulatory oversight routine inspections that may be directed at high-enrolling clinical sites, and regulatory oversight 'for-cause' inspections that result from a reported concern related to the clinical trial.

The execution of audits as well as follow-up on the progress of critical corrective action are key steps to ensure that audits are adding value to clinical development and that the sponsor is in compliance with regulatory requirements.[2] This portion of the book will describe quality systems, explain how QA is integral to GCP, and explain the study-specific auditing process. Although system audits are an important aspect of a research QA function, this chapter will focus only on the audits of clinical trial processes and procedures.

Defining quality

To begin this chapter, quality must be defined and understood. Quality can be defined as the total set of characteristics of a product or service that affect the ability to satisfy the stated or implied needs of the customer. Therefore, a quality system is defined by the organizational structure, responsibilities, procedures, process, and resources for implementing the management of quality. The quality system is a set of checks and balances that helps to ensure the quality of the data and to ensure that the study was conducted according to the standards of GCP. Quality systems include the aspects of QA and quality control (QC).

Quality assurance is the systematic and independent examination of all clinical trial-related activities and documentation. These actions are established to ensure that the data generated, documented, and reported during the trial are in compliance with GCP and applicable regulatory requirements.[1]

Quality control is the operational techniques and activities undertaken within the QA system to verify that the requirements for quality of the clinical trial activities have been fulfilled.[1] QC is data driven and done in real-time. It is performed at the local level and is specific to a particular aspect of the business. ICH GCP dictates that a system of both QA and QC is implemented and maintained by the sponsor.

Quality assurance is the cornerstone of success in GCP. The need for QA in studies is increasing as the landscape of clinical research is changing. There are a greater number of studies being conducted at a greater number of investigator sites. The globalization of clinical research into countries without previous experience with GCP has created a need for stronger QA programs in clinical trials. The addition of electronic record keeping has only heightened this need. Sponsor organizations must strive to build quality into trials from the beginning, assuring quality throughout the conduct and establishment of an infrastructure that is committed to continuous improvement as a part of the sponsor organization as well as the investigator organization.[3]

Quality assurance is considered a critical sponsor responsibility and the QA of both the sponsor and investigator site are considered part of this expectation. The QA program should function independently of the rest of the organization in order to remove any inappropriate influence over the outcome of auditing.

Auditing: purpose of auditing

An audit is an evaluation of a person, organization, system, process, project, or product. Audits are performed to understand the validity and reliability of information, and to assess a system's internal control. The goal of an audit is to express an opinion on the entity under evaluation based on work done on a test basis. Due to practical constraints, an audit seeks to provide only reasonable assurance that the statements are free from material error.

Audits are defined in the ICH GCP guideline glossary as

> a systematic and independent examination of trial related activities and documents to determine whether the evaluated trial related activities were conducted, and the data were recorded, analyzed and accurately reported according to the protocol, sponsor's standard operating procedures (SOPs), Good Clinical Practice (GCP), and applicable regulatory requirement(s).[1]

Audits are the fundamental instrument used by the QA function to gather information and data so that an independent set of recommendations can be made to management. The most important of these issues would be those describing significant non-compliance with the regulatory requirements and the clinical protocol that potentially have a direct effect on subject safety. In these cases, management would be expected to act swiftly in mitigating or minimizing the identified risk through an implementation of corrective actions.

Other issues that would be noted in an audit may include minor areas of non-compliance that, if left uncorrected, could result in systematic and serious compliance problems. Management would also be well served by consideration of the recommendations in relation to the efficiency of the organizations under their supervision. This last type of recommendation is particularly applicable in smaller organizations where an independent assessment serves to identify better ways to perform certain critical functions such as the development of clinical trial documents.

Clinical Study Protocol and Clinical Study Report (CSR) development typically employ complicated systems where multiple disciplines have to coordinate information, ideas, and analyses into a single concise document. The independent assessment of the development process may uncover inefficiencies that may lead to future non-compliance. As an example, a lack of version control over draft documents may not be a compliance issue. However, if multiple versions of a document are being reviewed by different parties simultaneously, there is a good chance that the resulting document will be incomplete and contain inaccuracies. This process inefficiency would lead to non-compliance.

Audits, therefore, should be performed in as structured a manner as possible. In this way, all of the objectives should be met. A structure for any audit can be described in an SOP and would generally include the following sections:

- Study Title (if there is a study that is the subject of the audit)
- Audit Objective
- Audit Preparation
- Audit Process
- Audit Reporting and Corrective Action.

The audit types that are the subject of the audit plan include:

- Clinical Investigator Audit
- Sponsor Audit
- Vendor or Contractor Audit
- Document Audit (Protocol, Clinical Study Report, Investigator's Brochure)
- Data Base Audit
- Pharmacy Audit (Investigational Medicinal Product Accountability)
- IRB/Independent Ethics Committee (IEC) Audits.

The audit plan

The audit plan is the fundamental planning tool for CQA oversight. Typically, upon receipt of an audit assignment, the lead auditor responsible for all phases of that audit will prepare a one- to two-page document that will define the purpose and scope of the audit. The plan is developed through an evaluation of the overall project and the project objectives and serves as a link between the preparatory stage and the execution of the audit.[4] Prospective audit plans should be finalized with the approval of management. The coordination of the audit activities with the needs of management is critical to ensure that management stay informed regarding all relevant quality issues within a research and development program.

The priorities for the project are based on the regulatory objectives. Those objectives dictate the studies that will be most important to the program. This amounts to a risk-based approach that should be implemented in order to help manage the audit program and should be implemented for all CQA audit programs.[2]

The priorities should be based on each study objective in relation to the plan for the submission of the application for marketing approval for the product. Those studies that are pivotal to the marketing application should be the primary focus of the audit plan. The details of each study are needed to define the audits to be performed. In addition, any contract organizations that will be involved in the studies should be identified and the role that they are to play should be defined. On the basis of the studies supported and the role, audits are proposed within the plan.

The plan begins with the studies that will be considered pivotal to the marketing application. The study designs and objectives are outlined. This is a crucial step in planning because this criterion will define the audit activities necessary for proper oversight. For example, a randomized, blinded trial will require that the statistical programming be included in the oversight program. This is particularly true if the program is generated by an independent statistician or a contract organization.

For each study, the following criteria should be identified:

- studies planned (late phase)
- contractors to be included (roles defined)
- number of subjects
- number of clinical sites.

Based on these criteria, the numbers of clinical sites, the timing of the audits and the specific investigator sites to be visited are determined. The clinical site audits performed in the early stages of the study are performed to evaluate the enrollment procedures for the study. Any issues with initial investigational material shipment, subject enrollment, subject consent, and data collection procedures can be identified and resolved prior to subject enrollment increasing.

Clinical site audits are typically performed toward the end of enrollment to detect data management issues. In addition, it is these visits where the most important investigators or high-enrolling investigators are visited and evaluated in relation to a potential regulatory authority inspection.

Contract organizations are typically visited during the qualification process. The role of QA must be very clear during these visits. There is a distinct difference between evaluating an organization for capabilities and evaluating it against compliance requirements. The capability assessment should be performed by the sponsor project team and only after organizations are listed as capable should a quality assessment be performed. The quality assessment is one part of the overall assessment of an organization and cannot be the sole criterion for choosing the appropriate vendor.

Document audits are performed to ensure compliance of those document with the applicable regulatory requirements and to ensure that the documents are consistent and accurate in the representation of information, whether that be study conduct (protocol) or data presentations (Investigator's Brochure, CSR).

Conduct of the audit

Before the audits begin, the QA department prepares an annual auditing plan with input from the rest of the organization. It also plans for the need to perform 'for-cause' audits. When a decision is made to audit a specific organization or study, an audit plan is developed. The specific sites are notified of the intended audit with a general overview of the audit plan. The audit may be conducted by an individual or by a group of individuals. Usually, the auditor is identified as one having experience with the particular processes being audited. Prior to the audit, the auditor will review key documents relative to the audit including, but not limited to: study protocol, study plan, SOPs specific to the organization, and the organizational chart for the site being audited.

The audit will begin with a meeting of the auditing team and representatives from the site being audited. During the audit, the auditor will tour the facilities, talk to key individuals in delivering the business, and review documents relative to the purpose of the audit. At the conclusion of the audit, the auditor will present a summary of findings and the site will have an opportunity to respond to any outstanding issues. Within a specified period, the auditor will release an audit report to both the site as well as the sponsor department requesting the audit.

The site will then respond to the audit with a corrective action plan. The corrective action plan is then reviewed and agreed to by the sponsor. An audit certificate is then issued. It is quite common that on subsequent audits corrective actions will be assessed to ensure that the problem has not continued.

Types of audit

There are several types of audits that are related to GCP, many of which will not be discussed in this chapter. This chapter will focus mainly on clinical investigator audits, vendor audits, and audits of clinical trial documentation.

Clinical investigator audits

The clinical investigator site audit may be considered the centerpiece of a clinical quality audit program. These audits are performed to assess an investigator's regulatory compliance and clinical data quality (including adherence to the protocol).[2] The reasons why this audit is so fundamental to the audit program are as follows.

1. The clinical data that are collected, particularly at investigator sites that are participating in a pivotal clinical trial, are critical to the safety and efficacy evaluation for that study and more importantly, for the marketing application.

2. The data quality that is audited for quality consists of data that are collected and managed by processes that are not specifically controlled by the sponsor. It is true that there is sponsor oversight, but the data standards utilized are potentially owned by the principal investigator (PI).

3. The investigational sites that are considered important for a marketing application may, in all likelihood, be visited and inspected by a representative of a health authority. A sponsor audit of these investigators will help ensure that the expectations of the health authority representatives will be or have been met.

4. The clinical investigator site is the point of subject exposure to investigational material and is the point where subject risk is most apparent. Oversight of the conduct of the study at this location is fundamental to the evaluation of subject safety.

While it is clear that investigators participating in pivotal Phase III studies are the most critical, it has been argued that it may also be important to include Phase II studies as part of an audit program.[5] Phase II studies may become pivotal and in most cases are important to decision making in order to advance the clinical development program.

The objective of the clinical investigator audit is to determine that the clinical investigator site is conducting the study in compliance with the regulatory requirements, clinical trial protocol, appropriate guidances, and sponsor standards.[6] It is important to determine whether the PI is ultimately responsible for all activities related to study conduct. A second objective is to determine that the site is prepared to successfully host a regulatory authority inspection. The most effective and efficient preparation for an inspection is performed before a study starts,[7] but it is equally important to prepare investigational sites when it is apparent which sites may be selected for a regulatory inspection. A third objective may be to investigate a specific issue or set of issues identified in a previous audit or monitoring visit. This type of audit is often referred to as a 'for-cause' audit.

While evaluating the conduct of the study at the clinical investigator site, it is also important to evaluate the monitoring practices that were employed by the sponsor or the sponsor agent. The audit process begins with a review of the clinical protocol, protocol amendments, and current Investigator's Brochure (IB). This review should result in a sufficient understanding of the following:

- proposed treatment
- subject enrollment criteria
- study procedures
- study end points
- safety event report criteria.

Monitoring reports, shipping documents, and relevant contracts or agreements may be included in the pre-audit review to ensure that there is a complete understanding of the expectations and evaluation of the site by the clinical group.

The obligations of investigators and sponsors are described in the regulatory requirements and guidances. Refer to Chapter 4 for a description of the responsibilities of an investigator and Chapter 5 for the responsibilities of a sponsor.

The review is performed with the sponsor and investigator guidances and requirements as a basis. The auditor uses these tools to develop a protocol-specific audit worksheet. The worksheet provides structure to the audit and allows for an organized, complete audit of the clinical investigational site.

A typical study-specific checklist is adapted from a general worksheet. When an audit is planned for a study site, the general worksheet is adapted for that study and that particular site. This development process makes it easier to create a study-specific checklist that is also consistent with the guidances and regulatory requirements. It is a very powerful instrument to be used during the audit.

Next, it is necessary to schedule the audit with the clinical investigator. Upon initial inspection, the expectation would be that the site should be open to an audit at any time. In fact, because the primary objective of an investigator and the site staff is subject safety, the schedule must be flexible. The site staff is given a degree of latitude in the actual schedule for the visit. It is critical for key site study personnel such as the PI and the study coordinator to be present during the audit. The responsible clinical study monitor should be available to assist the auditor(s).[2] The objective of the audit must be clearly stated to the site and its staff. The form of this contact is typically both personal (phone is best, e-mail should be used only as a refinement) and then as a written, signed correspondence. The signed correspondence describes the schedule of the visit in detail. The dates of the visit are reiterated and the agenda is presented. With expectations clearly defined, the audit has the best chance of successful completion.

The audit begins with formal introductions and then a confirmation of the audit agenda. Using the prepared audit worksheet, the auditor evaluates the following:

- PI oversight
- informed consent administration
- completeness and adequacy of essential regulatory documents
- adequacy of the facility, including:
  - all necessary equipment to perform necessary procedures
  - subject visit areas
  - investigational material storage
  - case record and subject file storage
- reporting capabilities
- investigational material accountability
- case report data (review against subject source record files)
- adverse event reporting
- IRB/IEC communication
- sponsor monitoring oversight.

All items listed above are important to the conduct of the study at the site. The most critical of these is the evaluation of PI oversight. The experience and diligence of the PI are critical because they allow for the adequate and compliant conduct of the study at the site.

The results of the audit should determine that the PI is the person ultimately responsible for the conduct of the study at the study site, which includes oversight of the study staff. There may be other staff, including subinvestigators who perform a bulk of the work on the trial; however, delegation of the tasks for the study needs to be clearly documented to ensure that the PI has retained overall control of the trial. An observation of poor communication with the PI puts the safety of the study subjects at risk and may be followed by a multiple and often serious deficiencies of GCP. Safety reporting is critical because it demonstrates and results in optimization of the safe treatment of study subjects during the study.

The staff resources must also be evaluated. According to Ronald L. Koller, Investigator, Los Angeles District, US Food and Drug Administration: 'Not having the appropriate resources at a clinical site presents a problem. Doing more with less is one of the problems.' The observation of insufficient staff could potentially lead to the observation of compliance issues at the site.[8]

Adverse event reporting to the responsible IRB or IEC ensures safe treatment of study subjects through independent review. The report to the sponsor allows for the evaluation of individual events against reported experiences for the entire study. This is particularly important in a multi-center trial. Risks identified through trend analysis can be mitigated where possible, resulting in optimally safe treatment of the subjects.

Finally, the evaluation of the sponsor oversight is critical because the communication between sponsor and site is necessary for the investigator to successfully implement the protocol procedures. The sponsor obligations for the reporting of significant safety events can only be accomplished through a careful review of the subject case records against the completed Case Report Forms (CRFs) where the data have been captured.

The remainder of the audit items are evaluated through an organized review of the documents at the site. It is important to verify that the sponsor is closely monitoring investigational material accountability. The receipt, disposition, use, and return of product must be documented for all administrations of the Investigational Medicinal Product (IMP). Deficiencies noted in this process demonstrate a lack of control over the sponsor's primary investment in the drug program. More importantly, there is the potential that deficiencies in IMP accountability may confound the analysis of the study. Response to the IMP dose cannot be measured if there is no verification of the dose that was actually administered.

When the audit visit is completed, a verbal report is made to the PI and the site staff. The objective of the verbal report is to discuss and clarify any issues noted during the audit. The role of the auditor is not to make recommendations directly to the site staff. This is part of the monitoring function. In order to maintain the necessary independence, the official report must be made to sponsor management, who then authorizes corrective actions through the monitor and the monitoring process.

The written report is generated on the basis of the audit process, the audit observations, and the discussion with the PI. It is sometimes helpful to make recommendations to the clinical study monitor and management. The responsible monitor then receives the written report and implements the agreed and necessary corrective actions at the site.

It is usually helpful for the auditor to follow up on the recommendations for corrective action to ensure timely implementation. There are times, however, when resources are limited and the number of observed issues precludes complete follow-up. In this case, it is necessary for the responsibility to be shifted to the clinical monitoring function. In these cases, it would be advisable to follow up only on issues that directly affect subject safety or the primary end point to be analyzed.

The QA effort can provide invaluable support of these key objectives. A critical take-home message about clinical site audits is that the QA is a supporting function only and must remain independent and objective.

Vendor audits

In addition to the clinical site audit, any vendors collaborating with the sponsor on the clinical trial have the potential for audit as well. The objective of the vendor audit is to evaluate a contract vendor for participation in a trial or to evaluate the performance with respect to the conduct of a trial. This audit, if performed to evaluate for participation in the trial, will assess compatibility with sponsor systems, assessing the vendor for both flexibility and specificity of performance. It will also determine whether the vendor personnel are appropriately experienced, trained, and qualified and provide an understanding of the vendor capabilities in relation to the scope of services and activity requested.

The first objective involves the evaluation of a vendor to participate in a study. There are critical aspects to the type of audit.

1   There must be a proposed, but not executed, scope of work or a contract in place. The description of the proposed scope of work determines what capabilities must be assessed.
2   Assurance that the contract has not been executed is necessary in case significant compliance issues are noted. The qualification becomes invalid if the vendor has already been contractually obligated to fulfill the roles defined for the study.

The prequalification audit would be performed prior to placement of a contract, and it is a theoretical assessment of compliance, evaluating the potential for capabilities should they be contracted. The compliance audit is different in that it evaluates the scope of work covered by a contract and assesses the effectiveness of the vendor.

The audit preparation follows the same general process as the clinical investigator audit. A general worksheet or checklist is developed that is adapted from the requirements, standards, and the proposed scope of work. The categories typically identified in the worksheet and evaluated during the visit are:

1   organization and personnel
2   employee training
3   facility design
4   facility operations
5   physical security
6   disaster recovery.

For a qualification assessment, the objectives are defined as the qualification of the capabilities and quality systems related to study-defined obligations. The obligations to be transferred are adapted from the proposed scope of work. The audit is conducted adhering to the checklist with a focus on the management oversight of the facility.

The audit process begins with an evaluation of management oversight. Each item reviewed should be considered against management control. For example, when evaluating the organization and personnel, it is typical to review the job descriptions for those employees. An important question is whether the job descriptions are signed by management. This signature demonstrates that management is overseeing the organization with respect to the qualifications of employees hired. Control over these job descriptions would then lead to control over the training program to be employed in support of those job functions described.

An important metric is management involvement in the review of SOPs. Management signatures on SOPs illustrate that management participates in the functions throughout the facility. Management oversight in the implementation of policies and standards is important to the qualification of any establishment, particularly when considered against the typical model defined by the regulatory requirements. Management is responsible and is ultimately in the position to oversee the policies and, more importantly, to effect any necessary corrective actions when noted.

Another important consideration during the qualification of a contractor is the facility design. For a contractor such as an analytical laboratory or an IMP distributor, the design must be consistent with the obligations intended to be fulfilled. Much thought should be given to these considerations. As the facility is assessed during a tour, equipment to be utilized and the system for maintenance and calibrating is evaluated. An auditor should remember to assess how the facility staff addresses problems identified and how management supports the staff. Most studies, especially those that are pivotal will involve multiple testing procedures and complicated study designs. Only a strong, experienced management structure will be able to accomplish the goals for the study while addressing the contingencies encountered during that study.

Finally, consideration should be give to facility disaster recovery because the regulatory requirement and standards dictate that data and records need to be retained for periods well after the work is completed. More importantly, sponsors depend on the data being available in spite of unanticipated problems. Technology is available and current industry standards dictate a significant back-up and recovery system that includes both the physical and electronic environments. The typical disasters that must be accounted for include power outages due to severe weather as well as more significant natural disasters. For some facilities that located are in high-risk areas such as hurricane zones, the disaster recovery must include provisions for transfer or 'mirroring' of the data at remote sites.

The vendor audit is conducted where the study has been awarded and work is under way with respect to the scope of work and the signed contract. The objective of the audit in this case is to evaluate that the vendor is performing as expected (according to the regulatory requirements, standards, and contractual agreements that are in place). The contractual agreements will usually describe a study protocol that is either being supported or conducted completely by the vendor.

Appendix 2 in Vendor Technical agreement -

The checklist is adapted to include the provisions of the scope of work and the protocol to be supported. The sample checklist should have the questions necessary for the requirements and standards. Once the checklist has been adapted, the typical audit process is implemented.

The emphasis of this audit, as opposed to the qualification audit, is on the collected data or the output for the study. Careful consideration should be given to the data handling conventions. All data should be handled so that there is a standard and obvious audit trail. This audit trail includes the person making the original observation along with the date of the observation. Any data changes to a paper document must be made so as not to obscure the original entry. These changes should also identify the person making the change, the date of the change, and the reason that the change has been made. The vendor must have a written procedure that describes the data handling process in detail.

The audit report for the vendor audit is determined by the original objective of the audit. If the audit objective was to qualify a vendor for participation in a study prior to the contract being signed, then the report should be written in a manner that describes the capabilities, the level of compliance, and the robustness of the quality system employed at that facility. It is important to describe the level of management oversight and participation. This assessment is integral to the development of a successful partnership.

An organization with strong management will react quickly when contingencies arise during a study (and they always will). The type of contingency may be related to the conduct of the clinical trial, resource allocation during the trial, or enrollment of suitable subjects. Weak management will, through a lack of understanding or attention, very often fail to implement the actions needed to complete a successful trial. Remember that the contract organization being assessed is not only performing for the one or two days that they are under assessment, but they will have to perform for the entire length of the proposed participation. The assessment should absolutely consider the risk that is being accepted when an agreement is signed with that contractor.

Document audits

The conduct of any clinical trial is represented by the documentation that is generated as a result of the conduct and completion of the study. In turn, the quality of the documentation must reflect the quality of the processes and procedures used to create these documents. An important function of QA is the oversight of the various documents that are generated during conduct of clinical research. Those documents include, but are not limited to, the clinical protocol, the IB, and the CSR.

The checklist or worksheet is developed for each document type on the basis of the regulatory requirements and organizational standards. The regulatory requirements for documents are generally loose, resulting in a greater dependence on the organizational standards and SOPs. The objective of the audits is to ensure that the information and data presented are complete, organized, internally consistent, and compliant with format standards.

Because the regulatory review of these documents is crucial to the approval of any marketing application, a secondary objective of the audit is to determine the reviewability of the document. This increases the chances that documents within applications will be received favorably. In the case of CSRs, a favorable review often leads to an approved marketing application.

Clinical Study Protocol

The clinical protocol is the document that is at the center of the conduct of a clinical trial. It should describe in detail how the study is performed and then should be available to all study personnel for reference during the trial.[9] For this reason, completeness, consistency, and compliance with regulatory requirements and standards are crucial. The objective of the protocol audit is to ensure that the document is complete and consistent while meeting the applicable regulatory requirements and the appropriate sponsor standards.

The US regulatory requirements for the content of a clinical study protocol are defined in 21 CFR 312.23.[10] Each protocol will include the specific information necessary to conduct that study. There is no regulatory requirement for the format of a protocol, although there is a generally accepted standard that appears in ICH E6 Guidance. If an organization does not follow this format, it is important that the audit ensure that all sections and topics are included in the modified protocol format.

The checklist must be prepared using a combination of the regulatory requirements, guidances, and organizational standards. While the format of the protocol is always important, the most crucial aspect is the consistency of the study objectives to the description of the study population, study end points, study drug administration, and analysis. While the checklist can help to identify that all of the sections are present, only an in-depth review of the protocol itself can determine internal consistency and completeness.

It is understood that an evaluation of this type may be a challenge to an auditor who does not have the extensive clinical trial experience of a medical monitor, but the audit is valuable nonetheless. It may also be true that a review of the protocol from a different perspective may result in the identification some basic and very important inconsistencies.

It is rare that an auditor is asked to sign or approve a clinical protocol. Given that the role of an audit is supportive of the actual development of the protocol, a signature may be considered inappropriate.

Investigator's Brochure

According to ICH E6:

> The Investigator's Brochure (IB) is a compilation of the clinical and non-clinical data on the investigational product(s) that are relevant to the study of the product(s) in human subjects. Its purpose is to provide the investigators and others involved in the trial with the information to facilitate their understanding of the rationale for, and their compliance with, many key features of the protocol, such as the dose, dose frequency/interval, methods of administration, and safety monitoring procedures. The IB also provides insight to support the clinical management of the study subjects during the course of the clinical trial.[1]

An IB is unique in that it is a living, ever-developing document. As each subject in a research program is exposed to therapy and new adverse events appear, the events are incorporated into the brochure. The audit of this document then should include both the current information along with the system that is in place to ensure that the document is continually updated.

The US regulatory requirements for the content of the IB are described in 21 CFR 312.23.[10] The general information to be included is the chemistry, pharmacology, and toxicity data along with any risks that are known to be associated with the use of the product. There is no required format, but the generally recognized standard for the format of the IB appears in the ICH E6 Guidance.[1]

The objective of this audit is to

- determine the completeness and accuracy of the brochure
- ensure that it is clear and consistent so that the PIs may use the brochure effectively to manage the study subjects
- evaluate the system in place to update the brochure such that it ensures timely, efficient, and complete revision of the document.

The checklist is generated from the standard for format and content that is applicable. The review for internal consistency of the data includes the evaluation of statements made against the data tables. Also, the tabular data is reviewed against any available subject listings. This may be a challenge since the summary safety data appearing in the brochure may be derived from multiple studies. These integrated summaries can be assessed by reviewing the programs used in their generation. Any statistical programs, particularly those involving integrated summaries, should include specific requirements for all programs and then a validation or peer review to ensure that the programs have met those requirements.

The audit report should include any errors noted in the data review, a description of any inconsistencies in the presentation of the data, and finally a description of any inefficiencies in the management or update of the document that may result in an incomplete or inaccurate brochure.

Clinical Study Report

'One of the most critical of the documents submitted as part of the Common Technical Document, masterpiece of a marketing authorization application, is the CSR, which represents the integrated full report of efficacy and safety data for an individual study of a therapeutic or diagnostic agent.'[11] The purpose of the CSR, then, is to present data that is 'complete, free from ambiguity, well organized, and easy to review',[12] presenting final outcomes of the study in a way that is scientifically sound and objective. On the other hand, we know that the overall goal of every research and development program is to gain marketing approval for the new drug. To this point, the CSR is the main instrument to support that the data and analyses presented sufficiently demonstrate that the investigational drug used as proposed is safe and effective.

Very often these two goals diverge. In order to optimally demonstrate that the study supports the safety and efficacy of a drug, it becomes necessary to represent the data in a way that is not completely objective. This is perfectly acceptable as long as the data or the data representations are not false or misleading. The role of the CSR audit is to determine whether the CSR has met all applicable standards and regulatory requirements and does not represent the data in a way that is false or misleading.

The US requirements for a CSR are defined in 21 CFR 314 and are very general. There are no requirements for the format of a CSR. The generally accepted format is described in the ICH Guidance E3 *Structure and Content of Clinical Study Reports*. This guidance is very comprehensive and serves as the model for all CSRs. In some cases there may be deviations based on the specific characteristics of a study. These format standards should be pre-defined with a consistent process for development of the CSR in place. This would go a long way in ensuring high quality within the document.

The objective of the audit is to determine that the CSR is in compliance with all applicable regulatory requirements and appropriate standards; also, to ensure that the report is consistent, accurate, and adequate when evaluated against the objectives of the study as defined in the study protocol and related amendments.

The preparation for a CSR audit is first to determine what format standard was used. It is important that a pre-defined process and format be examined. This standard should be used in preparation for the CSR audit plan as well as the checklist to be used to ensure that all of the applicable sections of the CSR have been included.

Since the volume of data in a CSR is typically large, a complete check of the data would in turn require extraordinary resources. Some form of sampling is required.[11] However, in every study there are certain items that must be correct. These are the critical data defined as 'any data in which a single non-conforming item would render the report unsuitable.'[13]

The audit plan for a CSR must include a description of how the internal consistency and accuracy of the document are to be evaluated as well as what, if any, sampling will be employed. The internal consistency is evaluated through a review of the statements and claims made regarding the data. Then, the consistency of the statements is checked against the tables and figures appearing in the report. Lastly, the data appearing in the tables and figures are audited against the individual subject listings appearing in the report appendices. It is here that the sampling can be best utilized. One of many sampling designs is referenced at the end of this chapter.[13]

The audit of the tables and listings against the raw data may also be performed outside of the CSR audit process as a data base audit. The timing of this audit would be prior to the finalization of the tables, listings, and figures so that the programming steps for the CSR would not have to be duplicated unnecessarily.

For pivotal trial reports, it is necessary to compare all data appearing in the individual data listings with the actual CRF data that was used to populate the data base. The data samples should be chosen giving priority to the most important data points such as primary efficacy parameters and significant safety events. Other data must also be included to ensure that there is not a systematic error in the database itself. Under normal circumstances, a database is not approved until it has undergone significant QC review. This fact should allow for a high degree of confidence that the database is acceptable.

It may also be appropriate to evaluate the process for statistical analysis and programming. This task can be complicated. In some cases, if the statistics are simple (e.g., mean or standard deviation), it may be possible to perform confirmatory calculations. In other cases (e.g., comparative statistical analysis or correlations), this may be impossible. In those cases, the auditor evaluates the process for the development and validation of the programs. There should be documentation in place to demonstrate that all programs have been peer-reviewed or quality control checked.

Once the data have been audited for adequacy, accuracy, and consistency, the statements and claims made in the report are reviewed for appropriateness and consistency with the study objectives. The auditor must ensure that all statements made have a basis in the data analysis and representations made in the report. A second, but equally important, consideration is that the data should be presented clearly and unambiguously. Statements made that do not have a clear basis in the data represented should be reported to the author.

The audit findings related to the data must be reported. Keep in mind that if sampling was used, findings in the data may represent potential systematic errors in the data. The complete corrective action for a noted observation should include correcting a specific data value and correcting a systematic error affecting many data points. For example, if two or three sample means are noted as incorrect in a chemistry summary data table, it could mean that there was a systematic problem with the application program. In this case rather than correcting the two or three discrepant values, the entire program would have to be checked and re-generated.

The CSR is the final and most important representation of the clinical trial work performed. It is intended to support that a drug is safe and efficacious and worthy of marketing approval. An independent evaluation of this document for adequacy, accuracy, and internal consistency can be critical to the successful review of the report and, eventually, marketing approval for the drug.

Summary

QA   Quality assurance is the systematic and independent examination of clinical trial-related activities and documentation. These actions are established to ensure that, in conjunction with management oversight and QC procedures, the trial is performed and the data generated, documented, and reported are in compliance with GCP and applicable regulatory requirements. Although QA is considered a critical sponsor responsibility, QA of both the sponsor obligations and investigator site are considered part of this expectation.

Audits are the fundamental instrument used by the QA function to gather information and data so that an independent set of recommendations can be made to management. The most important of these would relate to observations of significant non-compliance with the regulatory requirements and the clinical protocol that might have a direct effect on subject safety.

A QA department prepares an annual auditing plan with input from the entire research organization. It also plans for the need to perform 'for-cause' audits where necessary.

The specific activities related to QA are typically described in an audit plan. Prospective audit plans should be finalized with the approval of management. The coordination of the audit activities with the needs of management is critical to ensure that management stays informed regarding all relevant quality issues within a research and development program.

A comprehensive audit program typically includes investigational site audits, vendor audits, and document audits. Each of these audits is conducted with the specific objective of informing management or responsible individuals of corrective actions that are necessary. It is also important that any critical compliance or patient safety issues be identified and corrected as quickly and completely as possible.

A comprehensive, independent QA system that includes evaluations of investigational sites, vendors, and documents generated by a research organization is an invaluable tool for management of a research function. The system supports management in ensuring that processes, procedures, and documents generated from the research and development program meet the organization standards and applicable industry requirements.

References

1. International Conference on Harmonisation (ICH). *Guidance for Industry: Good Clinical Practice, Consolidated Guidance*, ICH-E6. Geneva: ICH, 1996.
2. Li H *et al*. Developing and implementing a comprehensive clinical QA audit program. *Qual Assur J* 2007; 11: 128–137.
3. Lepay DA (2001). *GCP, Quality Assurance, and FDA* [Online]. Available from: www. fda.gov/oc/gcp/slideshows/lepay2001/SQAWeb.ppt (accessed February 5, 2009).
4. Russell JP, ed. *The Quality Audit Handbook*, 2nd edn. Milwaukee: ASQ Quality Press, 2000.
5. Winchell T. Clinical quality assurance: auditing of Phase II clinical trials. *Qual Assur J* 2003; 7: 155–156.
6. Valania M. Quality control and assurance in clinical research. *Applied Clinical Trials Online* March 2006. Available from: URL:http://appliedclinicaltrialsonline.findpharma. com/appliedclinicaltrials/CRO%2FSponsor+Articles/Quality-Control-and-Assurance-in-Clinical-Research/ArticleStandard/Article/detail/310811 (accessed May 6, 2009).
7. Winchell T. New day: CQA. *Qual Assur J* 2003; 7: 86–89.
8. Koller R. FDA inspector perspectives: GCPs and inspections of clinical investigators and sponsors. *SoCRA Source* May 2004: 11–16.
9. Fortwengel G. *Clinical Study Protocol: Guide for Clinical Trial Staff*. Basel: Karger, 2004: 25–30.
10. Food & Drug Administration [Online] (April 2009). *Investigational New Drug Application, Title 21 Code of Federal Regulations Part 312*. Available from: http:// www.accessdata.fda.gov/scripts/cdrh/cfdocs/cfcfr/CFRSearch.cfm? CFRPart=312&showFR=1 (accessed January 22, 2010).
11. Alfaro VI *et al*. Abbreviated clinical study reports with investigational medicinal products for human use: current guidelines and recommendations. *Croat Med J* 2007 Dec; 48(6): 871–877.
12. International Conference on Harmonisation (ICH). *Guideline for Industry: Structure and Content of Clinical Study Reports*, ICH-E3. Geneva: ICH, July 1996.
13. Townshend IJ, Bissell AF. Sampling for clinical report auditing author(s). *The Statistician* 1987; 36(5) Special Issue: Industry, Quality and Statistics: 531–539.

12

Future implications of Good Clinical Practice

Thomas Jacobsen

There are many challenges that will affect Good Clinical Practice (GCP) as we progress through the twenty-first century and new science and technology evolves. Some of the major challenges of the future of GCP center on the globalization of clinical research, genomics research, gene transfer research, stem cell research, and the implementation of nanotechnology. An outline of these issues, along with some possible solutions is presented in this chapter.

Globalization of clinical research

Industry is clearly moving toward globalization of clinical research and drug development. Clinical trials are conducted around the world and sponsors seek marketing approval in many countries. International harmonization helps to bring consistency to clinical research, regardless of location of the research. For example, there has been much discussion of clinical trials in Europe in terms of a research support program and how the European Union (EU) will face the challenge of genetic studies. One of the main objectives of the EU was to develop improved patient-oriented strategies for the prevention and management of disease and for healthy living and aging. The research concentrates on translating the new knowledge created by genomics and other fields of basic research into applications that will improve both clinical practice and public health.[1]

There is a continuing search of research sites throughout the world to locate specific patient populations with a high incidence of a particular condition, genetic composition, or environmental conditions. A major issue that researchers confront is the study and development of global ethical practices. International harmonization makes it possible for research to be conducted all over the world while maintaining merit and meaning.

Clinical trial research is highly competitive and invested sponsors must be prepared to be flexible and have choices other than their initial locations. Increasing regulatory demand to include additional patient data as well as the competitive nature of clinical development has led industry to a more global outlook for clinical trials. The major drug development regions of the world (North America, Europe, and Japan) account for a large proportion of research, but markets such as those in Asia, Latin America, and Africa are emerging as viable locations and vital options for clinical trials run by pharmaceutical and biotech companies.[2] The emerging regions are favorable because of large, growing populations that have an unmet need for treatment and as well as being affected by diseases of interest.

Sponsors might perform research in certain regions because they believe that clinical development may provide health care professionals with experience in using their product in a particular region where a given disease may be prevalent. Some sponsors also carry out post-marketing clinical trials in these countries in order to gain a better understanding of characteristics of pharmacokinetics, pharmacodynamics, and the safety profile of this specific population exposed to the medicine.[3]

The globalization of clinical trials is inevitable. In many cases, such as Latin America, the market is already fairly mature and is able to provide monetary incentives for companies to operate in those locations. There are considerable benefits that sponsors can gain from operating in these regions, given the enormous expense of drug development and the competition they face in bringing a drug successfully to market.[2]

The competition to expand research into emerging regions is growing, but there remains one difficult question to answer: How best to involve subjects in clinical trials without seeming to exploit subjects? Legal, regulatory, and clinical research settings may not be as clearly defined in these regions as in established markets; therefore, the same standards as used in developed countries should be employed in emerging regions (i.e., International Conference on Harmonisation GCP Guidelines). Oversight is the responsibility of the sponsor conducting the trial to ensure proper care of patients enrolled in their study even if there is a lack of binding international guidelines.

In more established markets, there have been a number of instances in which patient participation in clinical trials has been identified as contributing to advances in medical research and treatments, even when taking into account the commercial gains for the sponsors involved. When integrating emerging regions into global clinical programs, pharmaceutical companies should insure that they can bring similar demonstrable benefits to local communities.[2]

The trend of increasing international clinical trials activity for the pharmaceutical sector is not surprising, but it does raise several issues concerning potential patients. In more established markets, the regulatory, ethical, and clinical research environments are fairly well defined; therefore, companies have and often rely on previous experience to help them adapt to developing changes in these regions. In direct contrast, emerging region environments are less clear-cut and guidelines acceptable elsewhere may not apply. Some regions may want the autonomy to establish their own rules as they see fit. Furthermore, when outlining the commercial benefits of operating in emerging markets and recruiting patients rapidly from large populations, extreme care must be taken in how these actions could be perceived. When publicized from a purely commercial standpoint, the objectives of clinical trials in emerging markets could provide an inaccurate perception that ethical standards will not be maintained. All members of the clinical trial team have a duty to care for patients involved in trials globally and commercial objectives should not interfere with this responsibility.[2]

Genomics

There is often confusion between the terms pharmacogenomics and pharmacogenetics. Pharmacogenomics is the study of the whole genome and of the entirety of expressed and non-expressed genes, while pharmacogenetics describes the presence of individual properties as a consequence of having inherited them.[4] The terms may be similar, but they are not interchangeable. Currently, many clinical studies have a pharmacokinetic aspect to them; however, it is pharmacogenomics that will potentially make the greatest impact on the future of the conduct of clinical trials. The former will help in the clinical setting to find the best medicine for patients, the latter in the setting of pharmaceutical research and development to find the best drug candidate from a given series of compounds under evaluation for a particular disease state.

A fundamental understanding of the nature of genetic predispositions to disease, pathology, and of drug action at the molecular level is essential for the future progress of health care. Pharmacogenomics will not directly pertain to finding the right medicine for the patient but will focus on finding the right medicine for the disease. Defining a genetic pattern assists in defining a particular disease risk, leading to intervention by the use of preemptive therapy. For example, if one is able to screen children for certain types of malignancies, the opportunity arises to prevent this process and intervene in the development of the disease, thus sparing the morbidity and mortality associated with the malignancy.

Over the next 25 years, the information and subsequent drug molecules created from our knowledge of genetics, including the Human Genome Project, will become a part of conventional medical practice and play an increasing role in the diagnosis and prognosis of a patient's health. Both the

USA and the EU are comparable in their involvement in gene therapy. This is demonstrated by a substantial increase in the number of clinical trials, the number of sponsors who organize trials, and the amount of funding being put forth for such trials. The question remains: How will this impact the way trials involving genetic material are conducted?

Genetic research in drug development involves special considerations and disclosures, which are related to and addressed in the informed consent (IC) process described in Chapter 3 and Chapter 8. These disclosures are of practical importance in the context of available options and strategies for incorporating genetic objectives into clinical studies, and are of ethical importance in terms of implications of genetic data to be derived from such studies, including potential risks for genetic discrimination.

In multinational drug trials and registration efforts, IC policies may be inconsistent among Institutional Review Boards (IRBs) or Independent Ethics Committees (IECs), and in some cases IRB/IEC requirements may be contradictory between different countries. This creates a unique opportunity to reflect upon the ethical, legal, and social challenges associated with personalized genomics.

The Pharmacogenetics Working Group (PWG) is a voluntary association of pharmaceutical companies who attempt to help address the issues described above. The main objective of PWG is to assist researchers, IRBs/IECs, and regulatory agencies about how to ensure protection of human subjects involved in pharmacogenetic research.[4]

At the point of initial IC, the research participant provides his or her autonomy-based consent to sequencing or examination of his or her genome. Ethically, investigators should discuss the implications for family members and encourage participants to include close genetic relatives in the IC process. The risks associated with participation in genetic research can be minimized by utilizing professional integrity, maintaining confidentiality, implementing data protection security measures, and full disclosure to the patient and family members affected.[5]

Practically speaking, the crucial issue is not only the sensitive nature of the information, but ultimately how and to what extent the information is used. With regard to the release of data, there is an emerging ethical consensus to protect not only individuals but families as well. Privacy becomes more difficult to manage because of the distribution of information to the patients and family members. As the risks to relatives increase, the ethical obligation toward them intensifies. Again, full disclosure to family members is crucial, and the permissibility of unauthorized disclosure will depend on the clinical relevance of the information and the potential to alleviate known health risks.

The proper use of medical information should adhere to a set of principles that reflect both justice and equality. It will be critically important that the research community endorses guidelines that support the beneficial and legitimate use of data in the patients' interest while simultaneously protecting the individual.

Gene transfer

Eighteen-year-old Jesse Gelsinger, a participant in the experimental gene therapy trial for ornithine transcarbamylase deficiency, died on Friday, September 17, 1999, four days after being injected with a high-dose viral vector and therapeutic gene at the University of Pennsylvania.[6] Findings suggest that the experimental drug used in the trial – a modified cold virus, or vector, incorporating a potentially corrective gene for Mr. Gelsinger's genetic disease – initiated an unusual immune-system response that led to multiple organ failure and death. He was the first person known to have died as a result of gene therapy.

Gene transfer represents a relatively new possibility for the treatment of rare genetic disorders and common multifactorial diseases by changing the expression of a person's genes. Typically, gene transfer involves using a vector such as a virus to deliver a therapeutic gene to the appropriate target cells. The technique, still in its infancy and not yet available outside of clinical trials, was originally envisioned as a treatment of monogenic disorders, but the majority of trials now focus on the treatment of cancer, infectious diseases, and vascular disease. New tools, such as genomics, RNA interference, chromosomal insulators, and other techniques in their infancy may one day provide new therapeutic options.

Human gene transfer raises several important ethical issues, in particular the potential use of genetic therapies for genetic enhancement and the impact of germline gene transfer on future generations. Recent developments in gene transfer have lead to questions regarding potential risks and ethics. The risks associated with gene transfer are twofold: one sort resides in its conceptual features and the second in its methodological features. These risks are summarized in Table 12.1.[7]

Future ethics committees face formidable challenges in weighing the risk versus benefit for these trials and the oversight of risk disclosure during the IC process. The complexity of risk from gene transfer strongly influences against the practice of using only local ethics committees to review trials.[8] In areas that do not mandate a central review, committees should consider submitting the protocol to a review body such as the Recombinant DNA Advisory Committee (RAC), where expertise in this area is abundant.[7] Hazards associated with gene transfer studies have been validated by clinical experience and investigators should fully disclose that previous human gene transfer trials have involved unforeseen consequences.

Table 12.1 Potential risk associated with gene transfer[7]	
Conceptual features	**Methodological features**
• Use of active ingredients rather than chemicals where vectors are capable of proliferating • Use of genetic material that directly affects gene expression • Ability to function simultaneously as a delivery device via the vector and as a pharmacological agent via the transgene • Stable gene modification that has risks with long latencies that can lead to toxicities over time • Inducing immunity against typical therapies, leading to immune over-reaction	• Small number of animal models for predicting vector safety • Use of a wide variability of human response to vectors • Possibility of non-linear dose–response curves with transfer gene vectors

Gene transfer clinical trials have a unique oversight process that is conducted by the National Institutes of Health (NIH) through the RAC and the NIH Guidelines for Research Involving Recombinant DNA Molecules and by the Food and Drug Administration (FDA) through regulation (including scientific review, regulatory research, testing, and compliance activities, including inspection and education). FDA regulations apply to all clinical gene transfer research, while NIH governs gene transfer research that is supported with NIH funds or that is conducted at or sponsored by institutions that receive funding for recombinant DNA research. As part of ongoing efforts to ensure patient protection in gene therapy trials, the FDA and the NIH have initiatives in place to strengthen the safeguards for individuals enrolled in clinical studies for gene therapy. These two new initiatives – the Gene Therapy Clinical Trial Monitoring Plan and the Gene Transfer Safety Symposia – complement and advance current patient protections. These initiatives include improved clinical trial monitoring (performed by a third party) and reporting as well as providing critical forums (educational symposia) for the sharing and analysis of medical/scientific data from gene transfer research.[9]

Stem cell research

In addition to genomics, another area of large impact on future drug development is the advent of stem cell research. After the first successful bone marrow transplants in the 1960s, subsequent advances in immunosuppressive and antibiotic therapy have made hematopoietic progenitor cell transplantation an established treatment for a wide variety of genetic and malignant diseases.[10]

The use of human embryonic stem cells (hESCs) is one of the most controversial and hotly debated topics in medical science today. The debate revolves around the ethics of two techniques used to manipulate human embryos. The most common argument is that both techniques involve the destruction of human life. In addition, national regulation and oversight of stem cell transplantation are either inefficient or non-existent in many countries. Current practices of stem cell transplantation raise questions that need to be jointly addressed by clinicians, scientists, health regulators, and ethicists, as well as representatives of civil society, in particular those who are donors and/or recipients.[11]

As a class of therapeutic agents, stem-cell-based products meet the definition of several different types of regulated products: biologic products, drugs, devices, xenotransplantation products and human cells, tissues, and cellular and tissue-based products. The last category – human cells, tissues, and cellular and tissue-based products – is defined as articles containing or consisting of human cells or tissues that are intended for implantation, transplantation, infusion, or transfer into a human recipient. By definition, any therapies that are considered to be stem-cell-based products fall into this category and thus are subject to the regulations that govern these products.[10]

A diversity of opinion exists among researchers about the feasibility of initiating pilot clinical studies using human stem cells. Some researchers are of the opinion that, within the next five years, it is reasonable to expect that human stem cells will be used in transplantation settings to replace dead or dying cells within organs, such as the failing heart, or that genetically modified human stem cells will be created for delivery of therapeutic genes. Others argue that a good deal of additional information about the basic biology of human stem cells needs to be accumulated before the therapeutic potential in humans can be assessed.[10,11]

Clinical studies involving the transplantation of blood-restoring, or hematopoietic, stem cells have been performed for a number of years. Reconstituting the blood and immune systems through stem cell transplantation is an established practice for treating hematological malignancies such as leukemia and lymphoma. Transplantation of hematopoietic stem cells resident in the bone marrow or isolated from cord blood or circulating peripheral blood is used to counter the destruction of certain bone marrow cells caused by high-intensity chemotherapeutic regimens that are used to treat various solid tumors. Moreover, clinical trials are being conducted to assess the safety and efficacy of hematopoietic stem cell transplantation for treating various autoimmune conditions including multiple sclerosis, lupus, and rheumatoid arthritis.

The purpose of genetic testing is to establish whether the human stem cells in question are suitable for use in the context of a particular clinical situation. For example, embryos derived from a donor with a family history of cardiovascular disease may not be best suited for the derivation of cardiac muscle cells intended to repair damaged heart tissue. Similarly, the use of molecular genetic analysis could detect a mutation in the gene for alpha-synuclein. This gene is known to be responsible for the rare occurrence of early-onset Parkinson disease. Detection of such a genetic abnormality in neuronal progenitor cells derived from an established embryonic germ cell line could block the use of those cells as a treatment for a number of neuro-degenerative conditions, including Parkinson disease.

Although precedents exist for the clinical use of human stem cells, there is considerable reluctance to proceed with clinical trials involving human stem cells derived from embryonic and fetal sources. This hesitancy extends to adult human stem cells of non-hematopoietic origin, even though, by contrast, their plasticity is generally considered to be lower than that of their embryo- and fetus-derived counterparts. For human stem cells to advance to the stage of clinical investigation, a virtual safety net composed of a core set of safeguards is required.

Safety assurance begins with adequate and careful donor screening, regardless of human stem cell origin. Routine testing should be performed to prevent the inadvertent transmission of infectious diseases. Additionally, pedigree assessment and molecular genetic testing should be considered. This is arguably the case when human stem cells intended for transplantation are derived from an allogeneic donor – that is, someone other than the recipient – especially if the cells are obtained from a master cell bank that has been established using human embryonic stem or human embryonic germ cells. Other additional safety measures include: using standardized practices for establishing cultured human stem cell lines; using mouse embryonic fibroblast feeder cells to keep the embryonic cells in a proliferating, undifferentiated condition; identifying the cells that make up a human stem cell population; and transplanting human stem cells into animals to demonstrate that the therapy does what it is supposed to do ('proof of concept') and to assess toxicity.

Nanotechnology

Another area that will impact the future of good clinical practice is the advent of novel drug delivery. New delivery systems may be able to target specific sites in the body where the drug needs to be delivered to increase clinical benefit and decrease toxicities. Some of these items include pump devices, new sustained-release mechanisms, and the use of nanotechnology. How these novel delivery systems are implemented in clinical trials will be as important as the drug being delivered.

Most of today's drugs are delivered by various routes: orally, intramuscularly, intravenously, subcutaneously, ocularly, transdermally, buccally, rectally, vaginally, or by inhalation. These are not always the most efficient routes of administration for a particular therapy. New biologic drugs such as proteins and nucleic acids will require novel delivery technologies that minimize side-effects and lead to better compliance.[12,13] Similarly, the success of DNA and RNA therapies depends on such innovative drug delivery techniques.[14] Market forces drive the need for new, effective drug delivery methods.[15] In many cases the success of a drug is dependent on the delivery method. This exemplified by the presence of more than 300 companies based in the USA in the industry of developing drug delivery systems.[16,17] The delivery and targeting of pharmaceutical and therapeutic agents is the forefront of nanomedicine. Nanomedicine involves the identification of precise targets related to specific clinical conditions and choice of the appropriate nanocarriers to achieve the acquired responses while minimizing side-effects.[18] Nanomedicine is a large area and includes nanoparticles, nanomachines, nanofibers, polymeric nanoconstructs, and nanoscale microfabrication-based devices.[18]

While possessing awesome potential, nanotechnology has inherent dangers. Care must be taken to seriously examine its potential consequences. Granted, nanotechnology may never become as powerful and prolific as envisioned by its scientists, but as with any potential, near-horizon technology, the exercise of formulating solutions to potential ethical issues before the technology is irreversibly adopted by society should be performed. Examining the ethics of developing nanotechnology and creating policies that will aid in its development will eliminate or at least minimize its damaging effects on society.[19]

Currently, the nanotechnology research agenda is primarily controlled by the government and applies to a diversity of fields. It is impossible to synchronize everyone's principles. It has not yet been decided who should create and enforce policies regarding clinical trials. This is true not only for the USA but for other countries as well; therefore, the institution of national policies and guidelines would be of great benefit in bringing such technologies to fruition. Full informed consent prior to the participation of human subjects in any scientific research is essential and is codified by the Declaration of Helsinki. Refer to Chapter 3 for more information about the IC process. In relation to the goals and risks of a particular nanotechnology study, it is the IRB that ultimately makes this decision. Those who currently serve on IRBs may not be readily conversant with or knowledgeable about this particular area.

In 1996, the FDA started the Nanotechnology Task Force, which has made various recommendations to address regulatory challenges presented by products that use nanotechnology, especially regarding products not subject to pre-market authorization requirements, taking into account the evolving state of the science in this area. The goal of the FDA is to assist in

Table 12.2 Recommendations of the Nanotechnology Task Force[20]

- Requesting data and other information about effects of nanoscale materials on safety and, as appropriate, effectiveness of products
- Providing guidance to manufacturers about when the use of nanoscale ingredients may require submission of additional data
- Changing the product's regulatory status or pathway, or merit taking additional or special steps to address potential safety or product quality issues
- Seeking public input on the adequacy of the FDA's policies and procedures for products that combine drugs, biological products, and/or devices containing nanoscale materials to serve multiple uses, such as both a diagnostic and a therapeutic intended use
- Encouraging manufacturers to communicate with the agency early in the development process for products using nanoscale materials, particularly with regard to such highly integrated combination products

the development of a transparent, consistent, and predictable regulatory pathway for such products. Recommendations made by the task force are summarized in Table 12.2.[20]

The very nature of nanoscale materials – their dynamic quality as the size of nanoscale features changes, for example, and their potential for diverse applications – may permit the development of highly integrated combinations of drugs, biological products, and/or devices, having multiple types of uses, such as combined diagnostic and therapeutic intended uses. There is enormous potential for nanotechnology, and further research in this arena involves those with authority to anticipate detrimental scenarios and alleviate potential harms. This can be accomplished by combining GCPs with creative approaches to integrate this into this new technology.

Conclusion

In conclusion, the future GCPs in clinical research presents challenges and opportunities for both researchers and research participants. The need for collaborative, evidenced-based efforts that produce simpler and better research guidance than what is currently in place is evident. Genomics is an important new area in the understanding of disease process and drug action, offering opportunities to stratify patients to achieve the best treatment outcomes. With regard to gene transfer, a tremendous amount of genomic data can be found, but there is very little appreciation of its function or significance. In addition, the risks are poorly understood, and it is the responsibility of researchers to characterize the risks while attending to the complex ethical challenges of conducting these types of studies. In order to realize the potential of stem-cell research, the current ethical debate needs to produce acceptable policy while ensuring patient safety. Ethical guidelines and policy need to be developed for nanotechnology research in order to develop nanotechnology safely while still reaping its promised benefits.

It is clear that more work is needed in this complex arena of GCP, not only in the novel areas outlined in this chapter but also in the areas related to ethics, policy making, and globalized adoption. In order to move forward, there needs to be consistency in legal, ethical, and medical requirements and regulation of GCP around the globe.

References

1. O'Donnell P (2002). *Europe Looks at Trials in Future Research* [Online]. Available from: http://www.appliedclinicaltrialsonline.findpharma.com/appliedclinicaltrials/EU/Europe-Looks-at-Trials-in-Future-Research/ArticleStandard/Article/detail/89348 (accessed February 21, 2008).
2. Kermani F, Lovell-Hoare C (2005). *Global Clinical Studies: With Great Power Comes Great Responsibility* [Online]. Available from: http://www.contractpharma.com/articles/2005/04/global-clinical-studies (accessed February 21, 2008).
3. Hynes CL *et al.* (2000). *Issues of Concern in Clinical Development: The Growing Size of the Clinical Dossier* [Online]. Available from: http://www.cmr.org (accessed March 18, 2008).
4. Anderson DC *et al.* Elements of informed consent for pharmacogenetic research: perspective of the pharmacogenetics work group. *Pharmacogenet J* 2002; 2: 284–292.
5. McGuire AL *et al.* Research ethics and the challenge of whole-genome sequencing. *Nat Rev Genet* 2008; 9(2): 152–156.
6. Stolberg SG. The biotech death of Jesse Gelsinger. *N Y Times Mag* 1999 Nov 28: 136–140, 149–150.
7. Kimmelman J. Protection at the cutting edge: the case for central review of human gene transfer research. *CMAJ* 2003; 3: 477–488.
8. Kimmelman J. Recent developments in gene transfer: risks and ethics. *BMJ* 2005; 330: 79–82.
9. Food & Drug Administration, US Department of Health and Human Services [Online]. (March 7, 2000). *New Initiative to Protect Participants in Gene Therapy Trials* Available from: http://www.fda.gov/bbs/topics/NEWS/NEW00717.html (accessed April 23, 2008).
10. Thomas ED. Landmarks in the development of haematopoietic cell transplantation. *World J Surg* 2000; 24: 815–818.
11. Schulz-Baldes A *et al.* International perspectives on ethics and regulation of human cell and tissue transplantation. *Bull World Health Org* 2007; 85(12): 941–948.
12. Kefalides PT. New methods for drug delivery. *Ann Intern Med* 1998; 128: 1053–1055.
13. Bradbury J. Beyond pills and jabs. *Lancet* 2003; 362: 1984–1985.
14. El-Aneed A. An overview of the current delivery systems in cancer gene therapy. *J Control Release* 2004; 94: 1–14.
15. Henry CM. New wrinkles in drug delivery. *Chem Eng News* 2004; 82: 37–42.
16. Hughes GA. Nanostructure-mediated drug delivery. *Nanomedicine* 2005; 1(1): 22–30.
17. D'Aquino R. Good drug therapy: it's not just the molecule – it's the delivery. *CEP Mag* 2004; 100: 15S–17S.
18. Moghimi S *et al.* Nanomedicine: current status and future prospects. *FASEB J* 2005; 19: 311–330.
19. Chen A (2002). *The Ethics of Nanotechnology* [Online]. Available from: http://ethicsweb.ca/nanotechnology (accessed April 24, 2008).
20. von Escenbach AC (2007). *Nanotechnology: A Report of the U.S. Food and Drug Administration Nanotechnology Task Force* [Online]. 2007. Available from: http://www.fda.gov/ScienceResearch/SpecialTopics/Nanotechnology/NanotechnologyTaskForceReport2007/default.htm (accessed February 17, 2010).

Appendix 1

The Nuremberg Code

Reprinted from *Trials of War Criminals before the Nuremberg Military Tribunals* under Control Council Law No. 10, Vol. 2. Washington, D.C.: U.S. Government Printing Office, 1949, pp. 181–182. Available from: http://ohsr.od.nih.gov/guidelines/nuremberg.html.

1   The voluntary consent of the human subject is absolutely essential. This means that the person involved should have legal capacity to give consent; should be so situated as to be able to exercise free power of choice, without the intervention of any element of force, fraud, deceit, duress, over-reaching, or other ulterior form of constraint or coercion; and should have sufficient knowledge and comprehension of the elements of the subject matter involved as to enable him to make an understanding and enlightened decision. This latter element requires that before the acceptance of an affirmative decision by the experimental subject there should be made known to him the nature, duration, and purpose of the experiment; the method and means by which it is to be conducted; all inconveniences and hazards reasonable to be expected; and the effects upon his health or person which may possibly come from his participation in the experiment.

2   The duty and responsibility for ascertaining the quality of the consent rests upon each individual who initiates, directs or engages in the experiment. It is a personal duty and responsibility which may not be delegated to another with impunity.

3   The experiment should be such as to yield fruitful results for the good of society, unprocurable by other methods or means of study, and not random and unnecessary in nature.

4   The experiment should be so designed and based on the results of animal experimentation and a knowledge of the natural history of the disease or other problem under study that the anticipated results will justify the performance of the experiment.

5   The experiment should be so conducted as to avoid all unnecessary physical and mental suffering and injury.

6   No experiment should be conducted where there is an a priori reason to believe that death or disabling injury will occur; except, perhaps, in those experiments where the experimental physicians also serve as subjects.

7   The degree of risk to be taken should never exceed that determined by the humanitarian importance of the problem to be solved by the experiment.

8   Proper preparations should be made and adequate facilities provided to protect the experimental subject against even remote possibilities of injury, disability, or death.

9   The experiment should be conducted only by scientifically qualified persons. The highest degree of skill and care should be required through all stages of the experiment of those who conduct or engage in the experiment.

10   During the course of the experiment the human subject should be at liberty to bring the experiment to an end if he has reached the physical or mental state where continuation of the experiment seems to him to be impossible.

11   During the course of the experiment the scientist in charge must be prepared to terminate the experiment at any stage, if he has probable cause to believe, in the exercise of the good faith, superior skill and careful judgment required of him that a continuation of the experiment is likely to result in injury, disability, or death to the experimental subject.

Appendix 2

World Medical Association Declaration of Helsinki: Ethical Principles for Medical Research Involving Human Subjects

World Medical Association 59th WMA General Assembly, Seoul, October 2008.

Available from: http://www.wma.net/en/30publications/10policies/b3/index.html.

A. Introduction

1   The World Medical Association (WMA) has developed the Declaration of Helsinki as a statement of ethical principles for medical research involving human subjects, including research on identifiable human material and data.

   The Declaration is intended to be read as a whole and each of its constituent paragraphs should not be applied without consideration of all other relevant paragraphs.

2   Although the Declaration is addressed primarily to physicians, the WMA encourages other participants in medical research involving human subjects to adopt these principles.

3   It is the duty of the physician to promote and safeguard the health of patients, including those who are involved in medical research. The physician's knowledge and conscience are dedicated to the fulfilment of this duty.

4   The Declaration of Geneva of the WMA binds the physician with the words, 'The health of my patient will be my first consideration,' and the International Code of Medical Ethics declares that, 'A physician shall act in the patient's best interest when providing medical care.'

5   Medical progress is based on research that ultimately must include studies involving human subjects. Populations that are underrepresented in medical research should be provided appropriate access to participation in research.

6   In medical research involving human subjects, the well-being of the individual research subject must take precedence over all other interests.

7   The primary purpose of medical research involving human subjects is to understand the causes, development and effects of diseases and improve preventive, diagnostic and therapeutic interventions (methods, procedures and treatments). Even the best current interventions must be evaluated continually through research for their safety, effectiveness, efficiency, accessibility and quality.

8   In medical practice and in medical research, most interventions involve risks and burdens.

9   Medical research is subject to ethical standards that promote respect for all human subjects and protect their health and rights. Some research populations are particularly vulnerable and need special protection. These include those who cannot give or refuse consent for themselves and those who may be vulnerable to coercion or undue influence.

10   Physicians should consider the ethical, legal and regulatory norms and standards for research involving human subjects in their own countries as well as applicable international norms and standards. No national or international ethical, legal or regulatory requirement should reduce or eliminate any of the protections for research subjects set forth in this Declaration.

B. Basic Principles for All Medical Research

11   It is the duty of physicians who participate in medical research to protect the life, health, dignity, integrity, right to self-determination, privacy, and confidentiality of personal information of research subjects.

12   Medical research involving human subjects must conform to generally accepted scientific principles, be based on a thorough knowledge of the scientific literature, other relevant sources of information, and adequate laboratory and, as appropriate, animal experimentation. The welfare of animals used for research must be respected.

13   Appropriate caution must be exercised in the conduct of medical research that may harm the environment.

14   The design and performance of each research study involving human subjects must be clearly described in a research protocol. The protocol should contain a statement of the ethical considerations involved and should indicate how the principles in this Declaration have been addressed. The protocol should include information regarding funding,

sponsors, institutional affiliations, other potential conflicts of interest, incentives for subjects and provisions for treating and/or compensating subjects who are harmed as a consequence of participation in the research study. The protocol should describe arrangements for post-study access by study subjects to interventions identified as beneficial in the study or access to other appropriate care or benefits.

15 The research protocol must be submitted for consideration, comment, guidance and approval to a research ethics committee before the study begins. This committee must be independent of the researcher, the sponsor and any other undue influence. It must take into consideration the laws and regulations of the country or countries in which the research is to be performed as well as applicable international norms and standards but these must not be allowed to reduce or eliminate any of the protections for research subjects set forth in this Declaration. The committee must have the right to monitor ongoing studies. The researcher must provide monitoring information to the committee, especially information about any serious adverse events. No change to the protocol may be made without consideration and approval by the committee.

16 Medical research involving human subjects must be conducted only by individuals with the appropriate scientific training and qualifications. Research on patients or healthy volunteers requires the supervision of a competent and appropriately qualified physician or other health care professional. The responsibility for the protection of research subjects must always rest with the physician or other health care professional and never the research subjects, even though they have given consent.

17 Medical research involving a disadvantaged or vulnerable population or community is only justified if the research is responsive to the health needs and priorities of this population or community and if there is a reasonable likelihood that this population or community stands to benefit from the results of the research.

18 Every medical research study involving human subjects must be preceded by careful assessment of predictable risks and burdens to the individuals and communities involved in the research in comparison with foreseeable benefits to them and to other individuals or communities affected by the condition under investigation.

19 Every clinical trial must be registered in a publicly accessible database before recruitment of the first subject.

20 Physicians may not participate in a research study involving human subjects unless they are confident that the risks involved have been adequately assessed and can be satisfactorily managed. Physicians must immediately stop a study when the risks are found to outweigh the

potential benefits or when there is conclusive proof of positive and beneficial results.

21 Medical research involving human subjects may only be conducted if the importance of the objective outweighs the inherent risks and burdens to the research subjects.

22 Participation by competent individuals as subjects in medical research must be voluntary. Although it may be appropriate to consult family members or community leaders, no competent individual may be enrolled in a research study unless he or she freely agrees.

23 Every precaution must be taken to protect the privacy of research subjects and the confidentiality of their personal information and to minimize the impact of the study on their physical, mental and social integrity.

24 In medical research involving competent human subjects, each potential subject must be adequately informed of the aims, methods, sources of funding, any possible conflicts of interest, institutional affiliations of the researcher, the anticipated benefits and potential risks of the study and the discomfort it may entail, and any other relevant aspects of the study. The potential subject must be informed of the right to refuse to participate in the study or to withdraw consent to participate at any time without reprisal. Special attention should be given to the specific information needs of individual potential subjects as well as to the methods used to deliver the information. After ensuring that the potential subject has understood the information, the physician or another appropriately qualified individual must then seek the potential subject's freely-given informed consent, preferably in writing. If the consent cannot be expressed in writing, the non-written consent must be formally documented and witnessed.

25 For medical research using identifiable human material or data, physicians must normally seek consent for the collection, analysis, storage and/or reuse. There may be situations where consent would be impossible or impractical to obtain for such research or would pose a threat to the validity of the research. In such situations the research may be done only after consideration and approval of a research ethics committee.

26 When seeking informed consent for participation in a research study the physician should be particularly cautious if the potential subject is in a dependent relationship with the physician or may consent under duress. In such situations the informed consent should be sought by an appropriately qualified individual who is completely independent of this relationship.

27 For a potential research subject who is incompetent, the physician must seek informed consent from the legally authorized representative. These

individuals must not be included in a research study that has no likelihood of benefit for them unless it is intended to promote the health of the population represented by the potential subject, the research cannot instead be performed with competent persons, and the research entails only minimal risk and minimal burden.

28 When a potential research subject who is deemed incompetent is able to give assent to decisions about participation in research, the physician must seek that assent in addition to the consent of the legally authorized representative. The potential subject's dissent should be respected.

29 Research involving subjects who are physically or mentally incapable of giving consent, for example, unconscious patients, may be done only if the physical or mental condition that prevents giving informed consent is a necessary characteristic of the research population. In such circumstances the physician should seek informed consent from the legally authorized representative. If no such representative is available and if the research cannot be delayed, the study may proceed without informed consent provided that the specific reasons for involving subjects with a condition that renders them unable to give informed consent have been stated in the research protocol and the study has been approved by a research ethics committee. Consent to remain in the research should be obtained as soon as possible from the subject or a legally authorized representative.

30 Authors, editors and publishers all have ethical obligations with regard to the publication of the results of research. Authors have a duty to make publicly available the results of their research on human subjects and are accountable for the completeness and accuracy of their reports. They should adhere to accepted guidelines for ethical reporting. Negative and inconclusive as well as positive results should be published or otherwise made publicly available. Sources of funding, institutional affiliations and conflicts of interest should be declared in the publication. Reports of research not in accordance with the principles of this Declaration should not be accepted for publication.

C. Additional Principles for Medical Research Combined with Medical Care

31 The physician may combine medical research with medical care only to the extent that the research is justified by its potential preventive, diagnostic or therapeutic value and if the physician has good reason to believe that participation in the research study will not adversely affect the health of the patients who serve as research subjects.

32   The benefits, risks, burdens and effectiveness of a new intervention must
      be tested against those of the best current proven intervention, except in
      the following circumstances:
      - The use of placebo, or no treatment, is acceptable in studies where
        no current proven intervention exists; or
      - Where for compelling and scientifically sound methodological
        reasons the use of placebo is necessary to determine the efficacy or
        safety of an intervention and the patients who receive placebo or no
        treatment will not be subject to any risk of serious or irreversible
        harm. Extreme care must be taken to avoid abuse of this option.

33   At the conclusion of the study, patients entered into the study are
      entitled to be informed about the outcome of the study and to share any
      benefits that result from it, for example, access to interventions
      identified as beneficial in the study or to other appropriate care or
      benefits.

34   The physician must fully inform the patient which aspects of the care are
      related to the research. The refusal of a patient to participate in a study
      or the patient's decision to withdraw from the study must never interfere
      with the patient–physician relationship.

35   In the treatment of a patient, where proven interventions do not exist or
      have been ineffective, the physician, after seeking expert advice, with
      informed consent from the patient or a legally authorized
      representative, may use an unproven intervention if in the physician's
      judgement it offers hope of saving life, re-establishing health or
      alleviating suffering. Where possible, this intervention should be made
      the object of research, designed to evaluate its safety and efficacy. In all
      cases, new information should be recorded and, where appropriate,
      made publicly available.

Appendix 3

The Belmont Report: Ethical Principles and Guidelines for the Protection of Human Subjects of Research

The National Commission for the Protection of Human Subjects of Biomedical and Behavioral Research, April 18, 1979.
Available from: http://ohsr.od.nih.gov/guidelines/belmont.html.

Ethical Principles & Guidelines for Research Involving Human Subjects

Scientific research has produced substantial social benefits. It has also posed some troubling ethical questions. Public attention was drawn to these questions by reported abuses of human subjects in biomedical experiments, especially during the Second World War. During the Nuremberg War Crime Trials, the Nuremberg code was drafted as a set of standards for judging physicians and scientists who had conducted biomedical experiments on concentration camp prisoners. This code became the prototype of many later codes intended to assure that research involving human subjects would be carried out in an ethical manner.

The codes consist of rules, some general, others specific, that guide the investigators or the reviewers of research in their work. Such rules often are inadequate to cover complex situations; at times they come into conflict, and they are frequently difficult to interpret or apply. Broader ethical principles will provide a basis on which specific rules may be formulated, criticized and interpreted.

Three principles, or general prescriptive judgments, that are relevant to research involving human subjects are identified in this statement. Other principles may also be relevant. These three are comprehensive, however, and are stated at a level of generalization that should assist scientists, subjects, reviewers and interested citizens to understand the ethical issues inherent in research involving human subjects. These principles cannot always be applied so as to resolve beyond dispute particular ethical problems. The objective is to provide an analytical framework that will guide the resolution of ethical problems arising from research involving human subjects.

This statement consists of a distinction between research and practice, a discussion of the three basic ethical principles, and remarks about the application of these principles.

A. Boundaries Between Practice and Research

It is important to distinguish between biomedical and behavioral research, on the one hand, and the practice of accepted therapy on the other, in order to know what activities ought to undergo review for the protection of human subjects of research. The distinction between research and practice is blurred partly because both often occur together (as in research designed to evaluate a therapy) and partly because notable departures from standard practice are often called 'experimental' when the terms 'experimental' and 'research' are not carefully defined.

For the most part, the term 'practice' refers to interventions that are designed solely to enhance the well-being of an individual patient or client and that have a reasonable expectation of success. The purpose of medical or behavioral practice is to provide diagnosis, preventive treatment or therapy to particular individuals. By contrast, the term 'research' designates an activity designed to test an hypothesis, permit conclusions to be drawn, and thereby to develop or contribute to generalizable knowledge (expressed, for example, in theories, principles, and statements of relationships). Research is usually described in a formal protocol that sets forth an objective and a set of procedures designed to reach that objective.

When a clinician departs in a significant way from standard or accepted practice, the innovation does not, in and of itself, constitute research. The fact that a procedure is 'experimental,' in the sense of new, untested or different, does not automatically place it in the category of research. Radically new procedures of this description should, however, be made the object of formal research at an early stage in order to determine whether they are safe and effective. Thus, it is the responsibility of medical practice committees, for example, to insist that a major innovation be incorporated into a formal research project.

Research and practice may be carried on together when research is designed to evaluate the safety and efficacy of a therapy. This need not cause any confusion regarding whether or not the activity requires review; the general rule is that if there is any element of research in an activity, that activity should undergo review for the protection of human subjects.

B. Basic Ethical Principles

The expression 'basic ethical principles' refers to those general judgments that serve as a basic justification for the many particular ethical prescriptions and evaluations of human actions. Three basic principles, among those generally accepted in our cultural tradition, are particularly relevant to the ethics of research involving human subjects: the principles of respect of persons, beneficence and justice.

1. Respect for Persons

Respect for persons incorporates at least two ethical convictions: first, that individuals should be treated as autonomous agents, and second, that persons with diminished autonomy are entitled to protection. The principle of respect for persons thus divides into two separate moral requirements: the requirement to acknowledge autonomy and the requirement to protect those with diminished autonomy.

An autonomous person is an individual capable of deliberation about personal goals and of acting under the direction of such deliberation. To respect autonomy is to give weight to autonomous persons' considered opinions and choices while refraining from obstructing their actions unless they are clearly detrimental to others. To show lack of respect for an autonomous agent is to repudiate that person's considered judgments, to deny an individual the freedom to act on those considered judgments, or to withhold information necessary to make a considered judgment, when there are no compelling reasons to do so.

However, not every human being is capable of self-determination. The capacity for self-determination matures during an individual's life, and some individuals lose this capacity wholly or in part because of illness, mental disability, or circumstances that severely restrict liberty. Respect for the immature and the incapacitated may require protecting them as they mature or while they are incapacitated.

Some persons are in need of extensive protection, even to the point of excluding them from activities which may harm them; other persons require little protection beyond making sure they undertake activities freely and with awareness of possible adverse consequence. The extent of protection afforded should depend upon the risk of harm and the likelihood of benefit. The judgment that any individual lacks autonomy should be periodically reevaluated and will vary in different situations.

In most cases of research involving human subjects, respect for persons demands that subjects enter into the research voluntarily and with adequate information. In some situations, however, application of the principle is not obvious. The involvement of prisoners as subjects of research provides an instructive example. On the one hand, it would seem that the principle of respect for persons requires that prisoners not be deprived of the opportunity to volunteer for research. On the other hand, under prison conditions they may be subtly coerced or unduly influenced to engage in research activities for which they would not otherwise volunteer. Respect for persons would then dictate that prisoners be protected. Whether to allow prisoners to 'volunteer' or to 'protect' them presents a dilemma. Respecting persons, in most hard cases, is often a matter of balancing competing claims urged by the principle of respect itself.

2. Beneficence

Persons are treated in an ethical manner not only by respecting their decisions and protecting them from harm, but also by making efforts to secure their well-being. Such treatment falls under the principle of beneficence. The term 'beneficence' is often understood to cover acts of kindness or charity that go beyond strict obligation. In this document, beneficence is understood in a stronger sense, as an obligation. Two general rules have been formulated as complementary expressions of beneficent actions in this sense: (1) do not harm and (2) maximize possible benefits and minimize possible harms.

The Hippocratic maxim 'do no harm' has long been a fundamental principle of medical ethics. Claude Bernard extended it to the realm of research, saying that one should not injure one person regardless of the benefits that might come to others. However, even avoiding harm requires learning what is harmful; and, in the process of obtaining this information, persons may be exposed to risk of harm. Further, the Hippocratic Oath requires physicians to benefit their patients 'according to their best judgment.' Learning what will in fact benefit may require exposing persons to risk. The problem posed by these imperatives is to decide when it is justifiable to seek certain benefits despite the risks involved, and when the benefits should be foregone because of the risks.

The obligations of beneficence affect both individual investigators and society at large, because they extend both to particular research projects and to the entire enterprise of research. In the case of particular projects, investigators and members of their institutions are obliged to give forethought to the maximization of benefits and the reduction of risk that might occur from the research investigation. In the case of scientific research in general, members of the larger society are obliged to recognize the longer term benefits and risks that may result from the improvement of knowledge and from the development of novel medical, psychotherapeutic, and social procedures.

The principle of beneficence often occupies a well-defined justifying role in many areas of research involving human subjects. An example is found in research involving children. Effective ways of treating childhood diseases and fostering healthy development are benefits that serve to justify research involving children – even when individual research subjects are not direct beneficiaries. Research also makes it possible to avoid the harm that may result from the application of previously accepted routine practices that on closer investigation turn out to be dangerous. But the role of the principle of beneficence is not always so unambiguous. A difficult ethical problem remains, for example, about research that presents more than minimal risk without immediate prospect of direct benefit to the children involved. Some have argued that such research is inadmissible, while others have pointed out that this limit would rule out much research promising great benefit to children in the future. Here again, as with all hard cases, the different claims covered by the principle of beneficence may come into conflict and force difficult choices.

3. Justice

Who ought to receive the benefits of research and bear its burdens? This is a question of justice, in the sense of 'fairness in distribution' or 'what is deserved.' An injustice occurs when some benefit to which a person is entitled is denied without good reason or when some burden is imposed unduly. Another way of conceiving the principle of justice is that equals ought to be treated equally. However, this statement requires explication. Who is equal and who is unequal? What considerations justify departure from equal distribution? Almost all commentators allow that distinctions based on experience, age, deprivation, competence, merit and position do sometimes constitute criteria justifying differential treatment for certain purposes. It is necessary, then, to explain in what respects people should be treated equally. There are several widely accepted formulations of just ways to distribute burdens and benefits. Each formulation mentions some relevant property on the basis of which burdens and benefits should be distributed. These formulations are (1) to each person an equal share, (2) to each person according to individual need, (3) to each person according to individual effort, (4) to each person according to societal contribution, and (5) to each person according to merit.

Questions of justice have long been associated with social practices such as punishment, taxation and political representation. Until recently these questions have not generally been associated with scientific research. However, they are foreshadowed even in the earliest reflections on the ethics of research involving human subjects. For example, during the 19th and early 20th centuries the burdens of serving as research subjects fell largely upon poor ward patients, while the benefits of improved medical care flowed primarily to private patients. Subsequently, the exploitation of unwilling prisoners as research subjects in Nazi concentration camps was condemned as a particularly flagrant injustice. In this country, in the 1940's, the Tuskegee syphilis study used disadvantaged, rural black men to study the untreated course of a disease that is by no means confined to that population. These subjects were deprived of demonstrably effective treatment in order not to interrupt the project, long after such treatment became generally available.

Against this historical background, it can be seen how conceptions of justice are relevant to research involving human subjects. For example, the selection of research subjects needs to be scrutinized in order to determine whether some classes (e.g., welfare patients, particular racial and ethnic minorities, or persons confined to institutions) are being systematically selected simply because of their easy availability, their compromised position, or their manipulability, rather than for reasons directly related to the problem being studied. Finally, whenever research supported by public funds leads to the development of therapeutic devices and procedures, justice demands both that these not provide advantages only to those who can afford them and that such research should not unduly involve persons from groups unlikely to be among the beneficiaries of subsequent applications of the research.

C. Applications

Applications of the general principles to the conduct of research leads to consideration of the following requirements: informed consent, risk/benefit assessment, and the selection of subjects of research.

1. Informed Consent

Respect for persons requires that subjects, to the degree that they are capable, be given the opportunity to choose what shall or shall not happen to them. This opportunity is provided when adequate standards for informed consent are satisfied.

While the importance of informed consent is unquestioned, controversy prevails over the nature and possibility of an informed consent. Nonetheless, there is widespread agreement that the consent process can be analyzed as containing three elements: information, comprehension and voluntariness.

Information

Most codes of research establish specific items for disclosure intended to assure that subjects are given sufficient information. These items generally include: the research procedure, their purposes, risks and anticipated benefits, alternative procedures (where therapy is involved), and a statement offering the subject the opportunity to ask questions and to withdraw at any time from the research. Additional items have been proposed, including how subjects are selected, the person responsible for the research, etc.

However, a simple listing of items does not answer the question of what the standard should be for judging how much and what sort of information should be provided. One standard frequently invoked in medical practice, namely the information commonly provided by practitioners in the field or in the locale, is inadequate since research takes place precisely when a common understanding does not exist. Another standard, currently popular in malpractice law, requires the practitioner to reveal the information that reasonable persons would wish to know in order to make a decision regarding their care. This, too, seems insufficient since the research subject, being in essence a volunteer, may wish to know considerably more about risks gratuitously undertaken than do patients who deliver themselves into the hand of a clinician for needed care. It may be that a standard of 'the reasonable volunteer' should be proposed: the extent and nature of information should be such that persons, knowing that the procedure is neither necessary for their care nor perhaps fully understood, can decide whether they wish to participate in the furthering of knowledge. Even when some direct benefit to them is anticipated, the subjects should understand clearly the range of risk and the voluntary nature of participation.

A special problem of consent arises where informing subjects of some pertinent aspect of the research is likely to impair the validity of the research. In many cases, it is sufficient to indicate to subjects that they are being invited to participate in research of which some features will not be revealed until the research is concluded. In all cases of research involving incomplete disclosure, such research is justified only if it is clear that (1) incomplete disclosure is truly necessary to accomplish the goals of the research, (2) there are no undisclosed risks to subjects that are more than minimal, and (3) there is an adequate plan for debriefing subjects, when appropriate, and for dissemination of research results to them. Information about risks should never be withheld for the purpose of eliciting the cooperation of subjects, and truthful answers should always be given to direct questions about the research. Care should be taken to distinguish cases in which disclosure would destroy or invalidate the research from cases in which disclosure would simply inconvenience the investigator.

Comprehension

The manner and context in which information is conveyed is as important as the information itself. For example, presenting information in a disorganized and rapid fashion, allowing too little time for consideration or curtailing opportunities for questioning, all may adversely affect a subject's ability to make an informed choice.

Because the subject's ability to understand is a function of intelligence, rationality, maturity and language, it is necessary to adapt the presentation of the information to the subject's capacities. Investigators are responsible for ascertaining that the subject has comprehended the information. While there is always an obligation to ascertain that the information about risk to subjects is complete and adequately comprehended, when the risks are more serious, that obligation increases. On occasion, it may be suitable to give some oral or written tests of comprehension.

Special provision may need to be made when comprehension is severely limited – for example, by conditions of immaturity or mental disability. Each class of subjects that one might consider as incompetent (e.g., infants and young children, mentally disabled patients, the terminally ill and the comatose) should be considered on its own terms. Even for these persons, however, respect requires giving them the opportunity to choose to the extent they are able, whether or not to participate in research. The objections of these subjects to involvement should be honored, unless the research entails providing them a therapy unavailable elsewhere. Respect for persons also requires seeking the permission of other parties in order to protect the subjects from harm. Such persons are thus respected both by acknowledging their own wishes and by the use of third parties to protect them from harm.

The third parties chosen should be those who are most likely to understand the incompetent subject's situation and to act in that person's best interest. The person authorized to act on behalf of the subject should be given an opportunity to observe the research as it proceeds in order to be able to withdraw the subject from the research, if such action appears in the subject's best interest.

Voluntariness

An agreement to participate in research constitutes a valid consent only if voluntarily given. This element of informed consent requires conditions free of coercion and undue influence. Coercion occurs when an overt threat of harm is intentionally presented by one person to another in order to obtain compliance. Undue influence, by contrast, occurs through an offer of an excessive, unwarranted, inappropriate or improper reward or other overture in order to obtain compliance. Also, inducements that would ordinarily be acceptable may become undue influences if the subject is especially vulnerable.

Unjustifiable pressures usually occur when persons in positions of authority or commanding influence – especially where possible sanctions are involved – urge a course of action for a subject. A continuum of such influencing factors exists, however, and it is impossible to state precisely where justifiable persuasion ends and undue influence begins. But undue influence would include actions such as manipulating a person's choice through the controlling influence of a close relative and threatening to withdraw health services to which an individual would otherwise be entitled.

2. Assessment of Risks and Benefits

The assessment of risks and benefits requires a careful arrayal of relevant data, including, in some cases, alternative ways of obtaining the benefits sought in the research. Thus, the assessment presents both an opportunity and a responsibility to gather systematic and comprehensive information about proposed research. For the investigator, it is a means to examine whether the proposed research is properly designed. For a review committee, it is a method for determining whether the risks that will be presented to subjects are justified. For prospective subjects, the assessment will assist the determination whether or not to participate.

The Nature and Scope of Risks and Benefits

The requirement that research be justified on the basis of a favorable risk/benefit assessment bears a close relation to the principle of beneficence, just as the moral requirement that informed consent be obtained is derived primarily from the principle of respect for persons. The term 'risk' refers to a possibility that harm may occur. However, when expressions such as 'small risk' or 'high risk' are used, they usually refer (often ambiguously) both to the chance (probability) of experiencing a harm and the severity (magnitude) of the envisioned harm.

The term 'benefit' is used in the research context to refer to something of positive value related to health or welfare. Unlike, 'risk,' 'benefit' is not a term that expresses probabilities. Risk is properly contrasted to probability of benefits, and benefits are properly contrasted with harms rather than risks of harm. Accordingly, so-called risk/benefit assessments are concerned with the probabilities and magnitudes of possible harm and anticipated benefits. Many kinds of possible harms and benefits need to be taken into account. There are, for example, risks of psychological harm, physical harm, legal harm, social harm and economic harm and the corresponding benefits. While the most likely types of harms to research subjects are those of psychological or physical pain or injury, other possible kinds should not be overlooked.

Risks and benefits of research may affect the individual subjects, the families of the individual subjects, and society at large (or special groups of subjects in society). Previous codes and Federal regulations have required that risks to subjects be outweighed by the sum of both the anticipated benefit to the subject, if any, and the anticipated benefit to society in the form of knowledge to be gained from the research. In balancing these different elements, the risks and benefits affecting the immediate research subject will normally carry special weight. On the other hand, interests other than those of the subject may on some occasions be sufficient by themselves to justify the risks involved in the research, so long as the subjects' rights have been protected. Beneficence thus requires that we protect against risk of harm to subjects and also that we be concerned about the loss of the substantial benefits that might be gained from research.

The Systematic Assessment of Risks and Benefits

It is commonly said that benefits and risks must be 'balanced' and shown to be 'in a favorable ratio.' The metaphorical character of these terms draws attention to the difficulty of making precise judgments. Only on rare occasions will quantitative techniques be available for the scrutiny of research protocols. However, the idea of systematic, nonarbitrary analysis of risks and benefits should be emulated insofar as possible. This ideal requires those making decisions about the justifiability of research to be thorough in the accumulation and assessment of information about all aspects of the research, and to consider alternatives systematically. This procedure renders the assessment of research more rigorous and precise, while making communication between review board members and investigators less subject to misinterpretation, misinformation and conflicting judgments. Thus, there should first be a determination of the validity of the presuppositions of the research; then the nature, probability and magnitude of risk should be distinguished with as much clarity as possible. The method of ascertaining risks should be explicit, especially where there is no alternative to the use of such vague categories as small or slight risk. It should also be determined whether an investigator's estimates of the probability of harm or benefits are reasonable, as judged by known facts or other available studies.

Finally, assessment of the justifiability of research should reflect at least the following considerations: (i) Brutal or inhumane treatment of human subjects is never morally justified. (ii) Risks should be reduced to those necessary to achieve the research objective. It should be determined whether it is in fact necessary to use human subjects at all. Risk can perhaps never be entirely eliminated, but it can often be reduced by careful attention to alternative procedures. (iii) When research involves significant risk of serious impairment, review committees should be extraordinarily insistent on the justification of the risk (looking usually to the likelihood of benefit to the subject – or, in some rare cases, to the manifest voluntariness of the participation). (iv) When vulnerable populations are involved in research, the appropriateness of involving them should itself be demonstrated. A number of variables go into such judgments, including the nature and degree of risk, the condition of the particular population involved, and the nature and level of the anticipated benefits. (v) Relevant risks and benefits must be thoroughly arrayed in documents and procedures used in the informed consent process.

3. Selection of Subjects

Just as the principle of respect for persons finds expression in the requirements for consent, and the principle of beneficence in risk/benefit assessment, the principle of justice gives rise to moral requirements that there be fair procedures and outcomes in the selection of research subjects.

Justice is relevant to the selection of subjects of research at two levels: the social and the individual. Individual justice in the selection of subjects would require that researchers exhibit fairness: thus, they should not offer potentially beneficial research only to some patients who are in their favor or select only 'undesirable' persons for risky research. Social justice requires that distinction be drawn between classes of subjects that ought, and ought not, to participate in any particular kind of research, based on the ability of members of that class to bear burdens and on the appropriateness of placing further burdens on already burdened persons. Thus, it can be considered a matter of social justice that there is an order of preference in the selection of classes of subjects (e.g., adults before children) and that some classes of potential subjects (e.g., the institutionalized mentally infirm or prisoners) may be involved as research subjects, if at all, only on certain conditions.

Injustice may appear in the selection of subjects, even if individual subjects are selected fairly by investigators and treated fairly in the course of research. Thus injustice arises from social, racial, sexual and cultural biases institutionalized in society. Thus, even if individual researchers are treating their research subjects fairly, and even if IRBs are taking care to assure that subjects are selected fairly within a particular institution, unjust social patterns may nevertheless appear in the overall distribution of the burdens and benefits of research. Although individual institutions or investigators may not be able to resolve a problem that is pervasive in their social setting, they can consider distributive justice in selecting research subjects.

Some populations, especially institutionalized ones, are already burdened in many ways by their infirmities and environments. When research is proposed that involves risks and does not include a therapeutic component, other less burdened classes of persons should be called upon first to accept these risks of research, except where the research is directly related to the specific conditions of the class involved. Also, even though public funds for research may often flow in the same directions as public funds for health care, it seems unfair that populations dependent on public health care constitute a pool of preferred research subjects if more advantaged populations are likely to be the recipients of the benefits.

One special instance of injustice results from the involvement of vulnerable subjects. Certain groups, such as racial minorities, the economically disadvantaged, the very sick, and the institutionalized may continually be sought as research subjects, owing to their ready availability in settings where research is conducted. Given their dependent status and their frequently compromised capacity for free consent, they should be protected against the danger of being involved in research solely for administrative convenience, or because they are easy to manipulate as a result of their illness or socioeconomic condition.

Glossary

Adapted from International Conference on Harmonisation E6 Guideline for Good Clinical Practice (available from: http://www.ich.org/LOB/media/MEDIA482.pdf).

Adverse Drug Reaction (ADR)	In the pre-approval clinical experience with a new medicinal product or its new usages, particularly as the therapeutic dose(s) may not be established: all noxious and unintended responses to a medicinal product related to any dose should be considered adverse drug reactions. The phrase 'responses to a medicinal product' means that a causal relationship between a medicinal product and an adverse event is at least a reasonable possibility, i.e., the relationship cannot be ruled out. Regarding marketed medicinal products: a response to a drug which is noxious and unintended and which occurs at doses normally used in man for prophylaxis, diagnosis, or therapy of diseases or for modification of physiological function.
Adverse Event (AE)	Any untoward medical occurrence in a patient or clinical investigation subject administered a pharmaceutical product and which does not necessarily have a causal relationship with this treatment. An Adverse Event (AE) can therefore be any unfavorable and unintended sign (including an abnormal laboratory finding), symptom, or disease temporally associated with the use of a medicinal (investigational) product, whether or not related to the medicinal (investigational) product.

Approval (in relation to Institutional Review Boards)	The affirmative decision of the IRB that the clinical trial has been reviewed and may be conducted at the institution site within the constraints set forth by the IRB, the institution, Good Clinical Practice (GCP), and the applicable regulatory requirements.
Audit	A systematic and independent examination of trial-related activities and documents to determine whether the evaluated trial-related activities were conducted and the data were recorded, analyzed, and accurately reported according to the protocol, sponsor's Standard Operating Procedures (SOPs), Good Clinical Practice (GCP), and the applicable regulatory requirement(s).
Audit Certificate	A declaration of confirmation by the auditor that an audit has taken place.
Audit Report	A written evaluation by the sponsor's auditor of the results of the audit.
Audit Trail	Documentation that allows reconstruction of the course of events.
Blinding	A procedure in which one or more parties to the trial are kept unaware of the treatment assignment(s). Single-blinding usually refers to the subject(s) being unaware, and double-blinding usually refers to the subject(s), investigator(s), monitor, and, in some cases, data analyst(s) being unaware of the treatment assignment(s).
Case Report Form (CRF)	A printed, optical, or electronic document designed to record all of the protocol-required information to be reported to the sponsor on each trial subject.
Central Institutional Review Board (IRB) or Commercial IRB	An IRB that conducts reviews on behalf of all study sites that agree to participate in the centralized review process.
Clinical Trial/Study	Any investigation in human subjects intended to discover or verify the clinical, pharmacological and/or other pharmacodynamic effects of an investigational product(s), and/or to identify any

adverse reactions to an investigational product (s), and/or to study absorption, distribution, metabolism, and excretion of an investigational product(s) with the object of ascertaining its safety and/or efficacy. The terms clinical trial and clinical study are synonymous.

Clinical Trial/Study Report

A written description of a trial/study of any therapeutic, prophylactic, or diagnostic agent conducted in human subjects, in which the clinical and statistical description, presentations, and analyses are fully integrated into a single report.

Comparator (Product)

An investigational or marketed product (i.e., active control), or placebo, used as a reference in a clinical trial.

Compliance (in relation to clinical trials)

Adherence to all the trial-related requirements, Good Clinical Practice (GCP) requirements, and the applicable regulatory requirements.

Confidentiality

Prevention of disclosure, to other than authorized individuals, of a sponsor's proprietary information or of a subject's identity.

Contract

A written, dated, and signed agreement between two or more involved parties that sets out any arrangements on delegation and distribution of tasks and obligations and, if appropriate, on financial matters. The protocol may serve as the basis of a contract.

Coordinating Investigator

An investigator assigned the responsibility for the coordination of investigators at different centers participating in a multicentre trial.

Contract Research Organization (CRO)

A person or an organization (commercial, academic, or other) contracted by the sponsor to perform one or more of a sponsor's trial-related duties and functions.

Direct Access

Permission to examine, analyze, verify, and reproduce any records and reports that are important to evaluation of a clinical trial. Any party (e.g., domestic and foreign regulatory authorities, sponsor's monitors, and auditors) with direct access should take all reasonable precautions within the constraints of the applicable regulatory requirement(s) to maintain the confidentiality of subjects' identities and sponsor's proprietary information.

Documentation

All records, in any form (including, but not limited to, written, electronic, magnetic, and optical records, and scans, X-rays, and electrocardiograms) that describe or record the methods, conduct, and/or results of a trial, the factors affecting a trial, and the actions taken.

Equipoise

A state of genuine uncertainty on the part of the investigator regarding the comparative therapeutic merits of each arm in a clinical trial.

Essential Documents

Documents which individually and collectively permit evaluation of the conduct of a study and the quality of the data produced.

Good Clinical Practice (GCP)

A standard for the design, conduct, performance, monitoring, auditing, recording, analyses, and reporting of clinical trials that provides assurance that the data and reported results are credible and accurate, and that the rights, integrity, and confidentiality of trial subjects are protected.

Independent Data Monitoring Committee (IDMC) (Data and Safety Monitoring Board, Monitoring Committee, Data Monitoring Committee)

An independent data monitoring committee that may be established by the sponsor to assess at intervals the progress of a clinical trial, the safety data, and the critical efficacy end points, and to recommend to the sponsor whether to continue, modify, or stop a trial.

Impartial Witness

A person, who is independent of the trial, who cannot be unfairly influenced by people involved with the trial, who attends the informed consent process if the subject or the subject's legally acceptable representative cannot read, and who reads the informed consent form and any other written information supplied to the subject.

Independent Ethics Committee (IEC)

An independent body (a review board or a committee, institutional, regional, national, or

supranational), constituted of medical
professionals and non-medical members, whose
responsibility it is to ensure the protection of the
rights, safety and well-being of human subjects
involved in a trial and to provide public assurance
of that protection, by, among other things,
reviewing and approving/providing favorable
opinion on the trial protocol, the suitability of the
investigator(s), facilities, and the methods and
material to be used in obtaining and documenting
informed consent of the trial subjects.

The legal status, composition, function,
operations and regulatory requirements
pertaining to Independent Ethics Committees
may differ among countries, but should allow
the Independent Ethics Committee to act in
agreement with GCP as described in the
International Conference on Harmonisation E6
Good Clinical Practice Guideline.

Informed Consent
A process by which a subject voluntarily
confirms his or her willingness to participate in a
particular trial, after having been informed of all
aspects of the trial that are relevant to the
subject's decision to participate. Informed
consent is documented by means of a written,
signed, and dated informed consent form.

Informed Consent Form
A document explaining all relevant study
information to assist a study volunteer in
understanding the expectations and
requirements of participation in a clinical trial.
This document is presented to and signed by the
study subject prior to initiating study
procedures.

Inspection
The act by a regulatory authority or authorities
of conducting an official review of documents,
facilities, records, and any other resources that
are deemed by the authority(ies) to be related to
the clinical trial and that may be located at the
site of the trial, at the sponsor's and/or Contract
Research Organization's (CRO's) facilities, or at
other establishments deemed appropriate by the
regulatory authority(ies).

Institution (medical)

Any public or private entity or agency or medical or dental facility where clinical trials are conducted.

Institutional Review Board (IRB)

An independent body constituted of medical, scientific, and non-scientific members, whose responsibility is to ensure the protection of the rights, safety, and well-being of human subjects involved in a trial by, among other things, reviewing, approving, and providing continuing review of trial protocol and amendments and of the methods and material to be used in obtaining and documenting informed consent of the trial subjects.

Interim Clinical Trial/ Study Report

A report of intermediate results and their evaluation based on analyses performed during the course of a trial.

Investigational Product

A pharmaceutical form of an active ingredient or placebo being tested or used as a reference in a clinical trial, including a product with a marketing authorization when used or assembled (formulated or packaged) in a way different from the approved form, or when used for an unapproved indication, or when used to gain further information about an approved use.

Investigator

A person responsible for the conduct of the clinical trial at a trial site. If a trial is conducted by a team of individuals at a trial site, the investigator is the responsible leader of the team and is referred to as the Principal Investigator.

Investigator's Brochure

A compilation of the clinical and non-clinical data on the investigational product(s) that is relevant to the study of the investigational product(s) in human subjects.

Legally Acceptable Representative

An individual or juridical or other body authorized under applicable law to consent, on behalf of a prospective subject, to the subject's participation in the clinical trial.

Monitoring

The act of overseeing the progress of a clinical trial, and of ensuring that it is conducted, recorded, and reported in accordance with the protocol, Standard Operating Procedures (SOPs), Good Clinical Practice (GCP), and the applicable regulatory requirement(s).

Monitoring Report
A written report from the monitor to the sponsor after each site visit and/or other trial-related communication according to the sponsor's SOPs.

Multicenter Trial
A clinical trial conducted according to a single protocol but at more than one site, and therefore, carried out by more than one investigator.

Non-clinical/Pre-clinical Study
Biomedical studies not performed on human subjects.

Opinion (in relation to Independent Ethics Committee)
The judgment and/or the advice provided by an Independent Ethics Committee (IEC).

Protocol
A document that describes the objective(s), design, methodology, statistical considerations, and organization of a trial. The protocol usually also gives the background and rationale for the trial, but these could be provided in other protocol-referenced documents.

Protocol Amendment
A written description of a change(s) to or formal clarification of a protocol.

Quality Assurance (QA)
All those planned and systematic actions that are established to ensure that the trial is performed and the data are generated, documented (recorded), and reported in compliance with Good Clinical Practice (GCP) and the applicable regulatory requirement(s).

Quality Control (QC)
The operational techniques and activities undertaken within the quality assurance system to verify that the requirements for quality of the trial-related activities have been fulfilled.

Quorum
The number of people required to be present for decisions to be allowed to be made.

Randomization
The process of assigning trial subjects to treatment or control groups using an element of chance to determine the assignments in order to reduce bias.

Regulatory Authorities	Bodies having the power to regulate. Regulatory Authorities include the authorities that review submitted clinical data and those that conduct inspections. These bodies are sometimes referred to as 'competent authorities'.
Serious Adverse Event (SAE) or Serious Adverse Drug Reaction (Serious ADR)	Any untoward medical occurrence that at any dose: • results in death • is life-threatening • requires inpatient hospitalization or prolongation of existing hospitalization • results in persistent or significant disability/ incapacity, or • is a congenital anomaly/birth defect.
Source Data	All information in original records and certified copies of original records of clinical findings, observations, or other activities in a clinical trial necessary for the reconstruction and evaluation of the trial. Source data are contained in source documents (original records or certified copies).
Source Documents	Original documents, data, and records (e.g., hospital records, clinical and office charts, laboratory notes, memoranda, subjects' diaries or evaluation checklists, pharmacy dispensing records, recorded data from automated instruments, copies or transcriptions certified after verification as being accurate copies, microfiches, photographic negatives, microfilm or magnetic media, radiographs, subject files, and records kept at the pharmacy, at the laboratories, and at medico-technical departments involved in the clinical trial).
Sponsor	An individual, company, institution, or organization which takes responsibility for the initiation, management, and/or financing of a clinical trial.
Sponsor-Investigator	An individual who both initiates and conducts, alone or with others, a clinical trial, and under

whose immediate direction the investigational product is administered to, dispensed to, or used by a subject. The term does not include any person other than an individual (e.g., it does not include a corporation or an agency). The obligations of a sponsor-investigator include both those of a sponsor and those of an investigator.

Standard Operating Procedures (SOPs)
Detailed, written instructions to achieve uniformity of the performance of a specific function.

Subinvestigator
Any individual member of the clinical trial team designated and supervised by the investigator at a trial site to perform critical trial-related procedures and/or to make important trial-related decisions (e.g., associates, residents, research fellows).

Subject/Trial Subject
An individual who participates in a clinical trial, either as a recipient of the investigational product(s) or as a control.

Subject Identification Code
A unique identifier assigned by the investigator to each trial subject to protect the subject's identity and used in lieu of the subject's name when the investigator reports adverse events and/or other trial-related data.

Trial Site
The location(s) where trial-related activities are actually conducted.

Unexpected Adverse Drug Reaction
An adverse reaction, the nature or severity of which is not consistent with the applicable product information (e.g., Investigator's Brochure for an unapproved investigational product or package insert/summary of product characteristics for an approved product).

Vulnerable Subjects
Individuals whose willingness to volunteer in a clinical trial may be unduly influenced by the expectation, whether justified or not, of benefits associated with participation, or of a retaliatory response from senior members of a hierarchy in case of refusal to participate. Examples are members of a group with a hierarchical

structure, such as medical, pharmacy, dental, and nursing students, subordinate hospital and laboratory personnel, employees of the pharmaceutical industry, members of the armed forces, and persons kept in detention. Other vulnerable subjects include patients with incurable diseases, persons in nursing homes, unemployed or impoverished persons, patients in emergency situations, ethnic minority groups, homeless persons, nomads, refugees, minors, and those incapable of giving consent.

Well-being (of the trial subjects)   The physical and mental integrity of the subjects participating in a clinical trial.

Index

Center for Devices and Radiological Health 19
Center for Drug Evaluation and Research
  18, 19
development meetings 24
End-of-Phase II meetings 25
Food, Drug and Cosmetic Act, Title 21 18,
  19–27
Form 1571 (IND cover sheet) 20
gene transfer 208
informed consent 44, 45, 59
Institutional Review Boards 144
International Conference on
  Harmonisation 16
Investigational New Drug Application 19–27
meetings 24–27
nanotechnology 211
New Drug Application/Biologic License
  Application 19, 27
pre-IND meetings 25
pre-NDA meetings 26
Prescription Drug User Fee Act 18
Protection of Human Subjects 23
responsibilities 27
roles and responsibilities 27
Type A meetings 25
Type B meetings 25
Type C meetings 27
Food and Drug Administration Modernization
  Act (FDAMA) 168, 172, 176, 177
Food, Drug Cosmetic Act (FD&CA)
  informed consent 42
  Kefauver-Harris Amendments 42
Food, Drug and Cosmetic Act, Title 21 12,
  18, 19–27
"for-cause" audits 188, 189
form and process, informed consent 44–51
Freedman, Benjamin 104
full board reviews 140
functions, Institutional Review Boards 123–125
funding 6

Gelsinger, Jesse 207
General Practice Research Database
  (GPRD) 162
Gene Therapy Clinical Trial Monitoring
  Plan 208
genetic testing 209
gene transfer 208
Gene Transfer Safety Symposia 208
genomics 205–207
Germany see Nuremberg Code
Getz, Ken 50
globalization of clinical research 203–205
glossary 235
GMP see good manufacturing practice
"gold standards" 54–57
good manufacturing practice (GMP) 29, 30, 32

GPRD see General Practice Research Database
guidelines
  EU regulations 29, 30
  informed consent 44
  investigator responsibilities 64
  pharmacovigilance 153
  site monitoring 109
  see also International Conference on
    Harmonisation...
gypsies 3

health authorities
  adverse event reports 153
  inspection 75
  meetings 33–35
Health Canada 16
Health Insurance Portability and
  Accountability Act of 1996 (HIPAA)
  informed consent 42, 59
  Institutional Review Boards 121, 137, 144
Health Omnibus Programs Extension (HOPE)
  Act 167
hematopoietic stem cells 209
hepatitis see Willowbrook Hepatitis Study
hESCs see human embryonic stem cells
HIPAA see Health Insurance Portability and
  Accountability Act
historical control trials 97
historical perspectives
  clinical research 92
  informed consent 42
HIV testing and screening 144
Holocaust 1
HOPE Act see Health Omnibus Programs
  Extension Act
HRPP see Human Research Protection Program
human embryonic stem cells (hESCs) 209
human experience data 21
Human Genome Project 205
Human Research Protection Program
  (HRPP) 121
human rights
  Belmont Report 1, 10–11
  Declaration of Helsinki 1, 8
  Nuremberg Code 1, 3–6, 7
  Tuskegee Syphilis Experiment 1, 5–8, 9–11

IB see Investigator's Brochure
ICH see International Conference on
  Harmonisation
ICMJE see International Committee of Medical
  Journal Editors
IEC see Independent Ethics Committees
IFPMA see International Federation of
  Pharmaceutical Manufacturers &
  Associations
incentives issues 7